WHAT IS ASIA TO US?

WHAT IS ASIA TO US?

Russia's Asian Heartland Yesterday and Today

MILAN HAUNER

London and New York

First published 1990 by Unwin Hyman, Inc.

First published in paperback 1992
by Routledge
11 New Fetter Lane, London EC4P 4EE

Simultaneously published in the USA and Canada
by Routledge
a division of Routledge, Chapman and Hall, Inc.
29 West 35th Street, New York, NY 10001

© 1990 Unwin Hyman
© 1992 Routledge

All rights reserved. No part of this book may be reprinted or reproduced or utilized in any form or by any electronic, mechanical, or other means, now known or hereafter invented, including photocopying and recording, or in any information storage or retrieval system, without permission in writing from the publishers.

Library of Congress Cataloging in Publication Data

Hauner, Milan
  What is Asia to us?: Russia's Asian heartland yesterday and today
Milan Hauner.
    p.   cm.
  Includes bibliographical references.
  ISBN 0–415–08109–2
  1. Geopolitics—Soviet Union. 2. Eastern question (Far East)
3. Soviet Union—Historical Geography. 4. Soviet Far East
(R.S.F.S.R.)—Historical geography. 5. Soviet Central Asia—
Historical geography. 6. Mackinder, Halford John, Sir, 1861–1947.
I. Title
DK46.H38   1990   89–38333
947—dc20   CIP

British Library Cataloguing in Publication Data

Hauner, Milan
  What is Asia to us?: Russia's Asian heartland yesterday and today.
  1. Asiatic Soviet Union, history
I. Title
  957
  ISBN 0–415–08109–2

Typeset in 10 on 12 point Garamond by Fotographics (Bedford) Ltd
and printed in Great Britain by Billing & Sons Ltd, London and Worcester

Contents

List of Figures and Tables

Acknowledgments

Foreword by Paul M. Kennedy

1 *Introduction: What Is Asia to Us?* From Dostoevsky to Gorbachev   1

PART ONE   Asia and the Russians

2 *Russian Ideology and Asia* Asia and Us—The Russian Idea and Revolution—Long Live Free Asia—The Russian Idea Today   21

3 *Historians and Geographers* Historians and Russia's Civilizing Mission in Asia—Geographers: Russia's Vanguard in Central Asia—Colonel Venyukov—Navel of the Earth   38

4 *Easterners and Eurasianists* The Yellow Peril Threat—Yuzhakov and Fyodorov—Pan-Mongolism—Yellow Russia—Exodus to the East: Trubetskoy and Savitsky—Eurasian Rapprochement and Fusion   49

PART TWO   Russia's Central Asian Heartland

5 *Russia's Drive South* The Russian Space—Geographic Projections: What is Central Asia?—The Historic Perspective of Central Asia—

General Snesarev and the Central Asia Question—
Three Elements of Russian Strategy in the
Indo-Persian Corridor—Railroad Imperialism
in Central Asia—The Trans-Persian Railway
Dream—Dual Strategy in the Indo-Persian Corridor
—A Breakout to the Indian Ocean? 69

PART THREE   The Heartland Debate

6   *Mackinder's Concept of Heartland Russia in 1904* Land Power versus Sea Power—Who Commands the Heartland?—Importance of Railroads   135

7   *Mackinder and the Russian Quest for a New Center of Gravity* A Conspiracy of Silence?—The Elusive Center of Russian Eurasia—The Empire from Sea to Sea: Mendeleev and Semyonov Tyan-Shansky—Voeikov, Savitsky, and Lamansky—Mackinder's Heartland Russia in 1919 and 1943   147

8   *German Geopolitik, Haushofer, and the Russians* Russia and German Mediators—The Nazi Connection—A German Lawrence among the Bolsheviks—Haushofer and Mackinder's Heartland—The Indo-Pacific Space—Haushofer's Transcontinental Bloc versus Hitler's Lebensraum—Haushofer's *Liaison Fatale*   165

9   *The Heartland Revisited: Geopolitics in Soviet Perspective* Mackinder, the First Visitor—German *Geopolitik* and the new Soviet *Herzland*—the Empire's Center of Gravity Is Moving Eastward—a Heartland Navy?—Marxism and *Aziatchina*—Soviet Definition of *Geopolitika*—Demography and the New Soviet Man—Lenin, Bukharin and Geopolitics   191

Contents

10 *Geopolitics and the Soviet Eurasian Empire Today*
Environmental Determinism—still Undetermined—
the Empire's Moving Center of Gravity and the Soviet
People—Excursion I: Prokhanovshtina—an Example
of New Soviet Geopolitics or an Anachronism?—
Excursion II: the Heartland Debate After Mackinder's
Death—Why Should the Heartland Debate Be Resumed   216

11 *In Place of Conclusions What Is Asia to Gorbachev's Russia?* Where Is the Soviet Eurasian Empire
Moving under Gorbachev?—Do the Forces of
Nationalism Represent the Main Threat to the Empire's
Coherence?   244

Index   255

Figures and tables

Figures

5.1	Railroad Map of Central Asia before World War I	102
5.2	Railroad Map of Central Asia Today	111
6.1	Modifications of Mackinder's Heartland Russia of 1904, 1919 and 1943	138
6.2	Mackinder's Map of Future Railways in Eurasia (1919)	143
7.1	Mendeleev's and Semyonov's Vision of the Russian Eurasian Empire "from Sea to Sea"	154
8.1	Haushofer's Transcontinental Bloc and the Partition of Eurasia between Germany and Japan (1942)	180
10.1	Variations on the Heartland Theme	238

Table

5.1 Deployment of Soviet Armed Forces 1986   117

Acknowledgments

As I am writing these lines, extraordinary changes are taking place in the Soviet Union. I therefore dedicate this book to Soviet citizens of all nationalities, who may find this collection of three essays a stimulating contribution to the critical thinking about the recent past, the present, and the future of Soviet Eurasia. They alone should decide how their Empire should be best reconstructed for their own benefit, that of their immediate neighbors, and of humanity at large.

I am grateful to my colleagues and other specialists, Richard Hartshorne, of UW—Madison; to the late Michael Petrovich, and to Mike Harpke and Mark Bassin, all of the same university; to Ladis Kristof, of Portland State University; to Bob Canfield, of Washington University at St. Louis; to Paul Kennedy, of Yale University; and to Henry Shapiro, for many years the UPI Bureau chief in Moscow, for having read various parts of the manuscript and for offering valuable suggestions.

I wish to express my gratitude to the UW—Madison publication grant, which enabled me, with the cooperation of Onno Brouwer, head of the Cartography Lab, to prepare the maps included in this book.

A word of warm appreciation is extended to Mrs. Judith Prestigiacomo for typing the final version of the manuscript, and to Lisa Freeman and Lauren Osborne of Unwin Hyman, for supervising the editing of this book.

Last but not least, I thank my family for their extraordinary patience and for their tolerance of my eccentric preoccupation with Russian and Soviet Eurasia, the largest land mass on our planet.

Madison: June 1989   Milan Hauner

Foreword

At the end of our present century, just as at its beginning, the world is anxiously wondering about the future of the Russian Empire. By far the biggest country in territorial extent, containing massive natural resources, possessing the largest armed forces on the globe, Russia's sheer *weight* has always made it an enormously important factor in international politics. What it does—or what it chooses not to do—has serious implications for all its neighbors, from Eastern Europe to Iran, from the Black Sea to the Pacific Ocean.

Eighty or ninety years ago, the chief concern of foreign observers—and the chief hope of Russian imperialists—was the further landward expansion of the Tsarist colossus into the Near East, into Central Asia, into China, and into the Far East. Russia, along with the United States (and, possibly, Germany), was regarded as one of the world's rising Great Powers, as distinct from the relatively declining Powers of the traditional European states-system. Its swift population growth, its rapid pace of industrialization, the development of an extensive railway network, all pointed to the country's growing prospects. Just how much further Russia might rise, and how it would employ its growing power and influence, troubled statesmen from London to Tokyo. But that it *would* rise was taken for granted. A turn-of-the-century pundit, returning to this earth in (say) 1945 or 1980, might be astonished at the change of regime in Moscow; but he probably would not be surprised at Russia's expanded power position.

At the present time, by contrast, it is the possibility of an *implosion* of Russian power that concerns observers, even those harboring deep antipathies toward the Soviet Union and Russian power. Such a disintegration would very likely be attended by wide-scale unrest, ethnic and religious rivalries, and even perhaps an international crisis and hostilities.

The chief reason for the present critical condition of the Soviet Union, and for the doubts about its future position as a Great

Power, is well known. It is caused by the profound failure of the centralized communist economy to provide Soviet citizens with their material requirements and by the steady relative decline of Marxist societies as compared with the faster-growing economies of the West and, even more remarkable, of East Asia. This failure at the economic level—precisely the dimension of life in which "scientific socialism" claimed to be superior—has provoked a widespread questioning of the validity of the political system in the Soviet Union, at least as represented by the tight, centralized controls, the Communist Party's monopoly of power, and the insistence on ideological orthodoxy. Driven by this apparent failure of legitimacy of the Soviet system in the first place, the program of reforms launched by Mr. Gorbachev under the slogans of *perestroika* and *glasnost* virtually ensures that this questioning of legitimacy will continue, unless suppressed by a conservative crackdown.

With all of this focus on the crisis of the Marxist ideology and social revolution in Russia, there has been a tendency to overlook the geopolitical context in which this drama has unfolded and will continue to unfold. The great merit of Milan Hauner's *What Is Asia to Us?* is to remind the reader of the physical, geographical, and demographic problems that face *any* regime—whether Tsarist or Marxist or reformist-Liberal—that seeks to govern this vast land. As Halford Mackinder suggested in 1904, the "great geographical limits of her [*i.e.*, Russia's] existence" would always remain, despite social and political transformations.

Dr. Hauner introduces us to the geopolitical dimensions of the present crisis of Russian power in an original and highly unusual way, by analyzing the historical debate on Russia's relationship to Asia, and in particular to Eurasia. It was a debate carried on with great intensity by Russian intellectuals themselves, from Dostoevsky onward; but the best known critique in the West was that by one of the founding fathers of the subject of "geopolitics," Sir Halford Mackinder. In focusing attention on the development of a Russian-dominated "Heartland" in Eurasia, and in turn on the implications of that development for the other Great Powers (especially the maritime powers), Mackinder emphasized Russia's extraordinary position as both a European *and* an Asian, indeed, a Pacific Ocean country.

At first sight, that double position appears as a massive advantage to Russia, the beneficial legacy of centuries of landward expansion from its original Muscovite core. But it is also a massive problem, Dr. Hauner explains, and introduces an insurmountable ambivalence into Russian policymaking—as one can observe at the present time in Mr. Gorbachev's efforts to claim that Russia is an integral part of a "common European home," while announcing (in his Vladivostock speech) that it is a full member of the booming "Pacific rim." The term *Eurasia* is, of course, a testimony to that ambivalence.

To be sure, Russia is not unique in having a double position; the United States, being both an Atlantic and a Pacific power, is another good example. Why should it be such a problem for Russia?

Because, Dr. Hauner argues, of *geopolitics*. In the first place, the physical difficulties have placed severe limitations on the amount of communications between Russia and Siberia (or Soviet East Asia); in so many ways, they *are* separate countries, whereas a vast network of air, rail, and road links binds each side of the United States into a geographical integrity that is now so obvious as to be taken for granted. By extension, the precarious connections between Russia and the Far East virtually compel Soviet military planners to assume that, in the event of war, they must fight virtually separate (and self-sustained) campaigns.

But even that difficulty pales by comparison with the central one: namely, that the middle zone of the Soviet Union, the so-called Eurasian "Heartland" of Mackinder's naming, is predominantly non-Russian, with 50 million Ukrainians and 50 million in the southern, Muslim republics entertaining bitter memories of Tsarist conquest and Soviet collectivization. It is, moreover, in those areas that the population is still expanding, whereas the Russian population is now almost static and will soon be in a minority. In short, the "Heartland" represents a potential ethnodemographic time bomb, and the more that Gorbachev presses ahead with his programs of *perestroika* and *glasnost*, the more he runs the risk of an explosion. Perhaps he will achieve the dual miracle of transforming the Soviet Empire into a Russian and non-Russian "Commonwealth," *and* of keeping together a country that is both European and Asian. Whether he succeeds or fails, the region to which Dr. Hauner draws our attention—and the awful geopolitical realities of the Russo-Soviet system—are going to be of critical importance. And because of that fact *What Is Asia to Us?* merits the broadest readership and careful study.

Paul Kennedy
Yale University
New Haven, Connecticut

Preface to the Paperback Edition

I am thankful to my new publisher, Routledge, and its senior editor, Mr. Gordon Smith, for having recommended this book for a paperback edition in order to make it more accessible to the growing number of students in Eurasian affairs, and to the general public – actually long before the frenzy of renaming everything Soviet into Eurasian started.

It seems unbelievable that almost three years have passed since I wrote the acknowledgements for the hardback edition, dedicating the book to "Soviet citizens of all nationalities". I was then assuming that what I called the Soviet Eurasian Empire could be "reconstructed", in the original meaning of Gorbachev's *Perestroika*, and that it would survive into the first decade of the new century. This new geopolitical, or as I wishfully desired "geo-cultural" Soviet Eurasia, would then continue to exist for the benefit of its "Soviet" inhabitants, "their immediate neighbors and the humanity at large". In the summer of 1989 I saw three options in the offing: a sort of a commonwealth, a muddling through (slow Ottomanization à la Gorbachev), or a violent backlash leading to the establishment of a Greater Russian military dictatorship.

However, since the abortive August 1991 coup an inexorable breakup started to destroy the old edifice of the Soviet (and thus Russian) Eurasian Empire. It is a case of a triple disintegration, if not the same in intensity, then in significance like 1917, caused by the almost simultaneous collapse of the empire's political (and ideological), economic and imperial structures. In December 1991 two federalist re-constructions took place: while the first Commonwealth of three Slavic republics lasted only two weeks, its successor, the Eurasian "Commonwealth of Independent States" (CIS), which is still struggling to survive at the the time of writing, consists at the moment of eleven out of the fifteen original union republics. Essential for its survival, on the one hand, is a working relationship between Russians and Ukrainians and, on the other, the adherence of Kazakhstan, the genuine product of Soviet "Eurasian constructivism", equally divided, population-wise and space-wise, into "Russistan" and "Islamistan".

As of today, I still do consider Mackinder's profound dictum of 1904, that the Russian Eurasian Empire must be seen as an almost perfect symbiosis between natural environment and political organization, as essentially correct. I have also suggested that if the empire goes, so would the "Heartland theory in the Mackinder mold".[1] The alternative to the autocratic Eurasian empire "from sea to sea", or to the totalitarian and autarkic Soviet version, is the inevitable breakup we are witnessing today. The positive "reconstruction" – if the outside world would allow the replacement of the predominantly geo-strategic criteria with geo-cultural ones[2] – will be a twofold process characterized by: (1) the return to the world-system of geo-cultural and commercial intercourse of which Central Eurasia was a part until the thirteenth century;[3] and (2) a process of intensive and extensive regionalization of the former empire, along the theories already scrutinized by the outstanding Russian "liberal imperialists", Mendeleev, Voeikov, Semyonov Tyan-Shansky, and others.[4]

Washington, D.C., April 1992   Milan Hauner

Notes

1 See *What Is Asia to Us?*, hardback edition (1990), p. 253.
2 See for instance Immanuel Wallerstein, *Geopolitics and Geoculture. Essays on the Changing World-System* (Cambridge University Press, 1991).
3 As Janet Abu-Lughod has shown in her beautiful book *Before European Hegemony: The World System A.D. 1250–1350* (Oxford University Press, 1989), p. 35.
4 *What Is Asia to Us?*, pp. 152–9.

1

Introduction: What Is Asia to Us?

What for? What future? What is the need of the future seizure of Asia? What's our business there? This is necessary because Russia is not only in Europe, but also in Asia; because the Russian is not only a European, but also an Asiatic. Not only that: in our coming destiny, perhaps it is precisely Asia that represents our main way out. . . .

In Europe we were hangers-on and slaves, whereas to Asia we shall go as masters. In Europe we were Asiatics, whereas in Asia we, too, are Europeans. Our civilizing mission in Asia will bribe our spirit and drive us thither. It is only necessary that the movement should start. Build two railroads: begin with the one to Siberia, and then to Central Asia, and at once you will see the consequences.

(Feodor M. Dostoevsky, 1881)[1]

The East, specifically Asia and the Pacific region, is now the place where civilization is stepping up its pace. Our economy in its development is moving to Siberia and to the Far East. . . .

The Soviet Union is an Asian, as well as European country, and it wants to see that the huge Asia-Pacific region, the area where world politics will most likely focus next century, has everything it needs to improve the situation in it, and that due account is taken of the interests of all states and of a balance between them. We are against this region being somebody's domain.

(Mikhail S. Gorbachev, 1987)[2]

This book is about the place of Asia in the Russian mind and about the position that the Asian space, as the larger portion of the dual Eurasian continent, has occupied in Russian/Soviet geopolitical thinking during the last 100-odd years. Although the main concern is the preoccupation of Russian ideology with Asia, a more systematic survey of the Russian/Soviet artistic imagery of Asian themes cannot be attempted here. Nor can the scope of this volume include the various attitudes of Asian peoples themselves to Russian colonization. A survey of such attitudes would be very welcome and should constitute a natural companion to this volume.[3] Thus, in our variant of *Aziatchina* (Asiatism—an ambivalent Russian term meaning the almost unlimited capacity among Russians to identify themselves with Asia while showing their contempt for the Asian peoples and civilizations as utterly barbaric),[4] we necessarily have to confine ourselves to describing a few facets of this complex relationship, whose significance remains nevertheless crucial to our understanding of Russian and Soviet Eurasia.

The main theme is the critical assessment of the Heartland Debate, exemplified by two important interpreters of world destiny during the era when imperialist expansionism had reached both its zenith and nadir, the British geographer Sir Halford Mackinder and the German *Geopolitiker* Karl Haushofer. Today, whenever geopolitical factors that define the Soviet Eurasian power are discussed, these two names are often quoted regardless of their relevance. We should remember that Mackinder himself, when he first formulated his seminal thesis on the importance of Russia's Eurasian Heartland in 1904, remained completely ignored in Russia for many years.

Why would the Russians not want to discuss Mackinder? Here was, after all, a rational recipe for Russia's becoming the ruler of the "World Island," though subject to the behavior of the two flanking powers, Germany and Japan, located in the "marginal crescents" along the rimlands of Eurasia. The point is that the Russians did not need to be enlightened about their own Empire by some Western mentors, certainly not by Anglo-Saxons whom they suspected of evil schemes at a time of acute Anglo-Russian rivalry. They had their own fertile minds. The second point is that when Mackinder's thesis eventually found its way to Soviet Russia in the usual German receptacle, it only increased the controversy surrounding his message—before it could be appreciated and properly digested. Ironically, German *Geopolitik* became one of the most violently despised terms in the Soviet anti-imperialist vocabulary. It was as if its originator, Karl Haushofer, a lifelong advocate of Soviet-German cooperation who warmly welcomed the Nazi-Soviet Pact of 1939, was to be punished for Hitler's treacherous onslaught of the Soviet Union in 1941.

Russian authors of the Tsarist and Soviet eras shunned, for reasons of their own, discussing directly with their Western counterparts the spatial problems confronting their empire, specifically in terms that carried a certain ideological bias like geopolitics (*geopolitika*). And yet, my view, as demonstrated in the following chapters, is that both Russian and Soviet imperial thinking is implicitly geopolitical, even though the term geopolitics is carefully avoided in its vocabulary.

Our discussion, inevitably, must touch on the usage, both over- and underrated for tactical political reasons, of the imperialist and colonialist vocabularies applied to the Russian/Soviet Eurasian Empire. One problem confronting us is that most recent theoretical works on colonialism are written from the Western perspective in the wake of theories of modernization, informal empires, and under-development, which do not include the Russian/Soviet experience.[5]

Consider the obvious striking spatial likeness. Isn't there at least a superficial similarity between the Russian expansion from sea to sea along the west–east axis across Eurasia and the American experience of westward expansion from shore to shore, epitomized in the ideology of Manifest Destiny? This ideology justified further annexations west of the Mississippi in the name of "our Manifest Destiny to overspread the continent allotted by Providence for the free development of our yearly multiplying millions."[6] Many Russians, quite naturally, measured themselves, both with empathy and envy, against the fast-growing U.S. power on the American continent. Thus, Dostoevsky, reflecting on the future of the Russian Empire in Asia, felt that "to us Asia is like the then undiscovered America. With our aspiration for Asia, our spirit and forces will be regenerated." In contrast to Europe, he went on in a prophetic mood, "Asia is our future outlet, our riches are there, there is our ocean, when in Europe, because of the overcrowded condition alone, inevitable and humiliating communism is established, communism which Europe herself will loathe."[7]

Despite the fact that the Russians, among all Europeans, had developed, because of their history and geographical location, the most intimate relationship with the Asian world, this knowledge was somehow lost in the European context. The more recent manifold implications of Russian expansion in Asia have never been adequately appreciated by West Europeans, though it was an event of "formidable proportion on the highest global level."[8]

In what way did the growth of the Russian Empire, which established itself over the vast spaces of Eurasia in 400 years from the repudiation of Tatar suzerainty, differ from other colonial empires of the imperialist era? The late Hugh Seton-Watson summed it up in his usual succinct way.

> The geographical scale of the expansion is without parallel, but the methods are in no way unique. Every type of expansion and 'imperialism' known in the history of European and American states can be found in that of Russia. The Russian record is neither better nor worse than the others. Russian expansion in the Volga valley has its parallel in the Spanish *reconquista*, the absorption of the Ukraine in the French absorption of Burgundy and Lorraine, the colonisation of Siberia in the colonisation of North America, the subjection of the Caucasus in the English subjection of the Scottish Highlands, the annexation of Central Asia in the creation of the British and French empires, Russian imperialism in the Far East in the aggressions of other European imperial powers against China. Indeed the Russo-Japanese War shares with the Anglo-Boer War the distinction of more nearly approaching the Marxist model of an imperialist war undertaken for economic motives than any other examples in history.
>
> The Russian record is as imperialist as that of any other great nation. Nevertheless Russian writers, from the Slavophiles of the mid-nineteenth century to the post-war Soviet historians, have frequently maintained that Russians are a people in some way incapable of aggression, and that the non-Russian peoples in some way 'voluntarily united with' Russia. There is also a widespread belief, especially strong among some Asian and African nationalists, that because Russian conquests were all over land, not over sea, they were somehow 'less imperialistic' than those of the European Atlantic nations.[9]

It is no accident that Seton-Watson begins and ends his summary with references to geography. He refers to the all-too-common visual delusion in our minds whenever we look at a colored map of Eurasia and contemplate with awe the impressive compactness of the Russian/Soviet Eurasian territory. Unlike the British or French overseas empires, there are no conspicuous natural barriers or large divisions of blue water. The second element that tightened the territorial cohesion of Russian Eurasia along its west–east axis of expansion was the absence of organized state power east of the Urals, backed by a sizable population that would oppose Russian expansionism. The fur-hunting Cossack bands roaming Siberia faced few difficulties in subduing or exterminating the local tribes. By controlling, without foreign interference, the inner communications consisting of rivers and later railways, Russia was able to settle in these vast and almost empty territories thousands of her own Slav settlers, predominantly Russian, who soon outnumbered the sparse Turco-Mongol populations. Only along the north–south axis of expansion, in the Caucasus and in Turkestan, was Russian expansionism confronted with a different geographic, demographic, and political situation. But even here the principle of possessing the monopoly of access, without interruption, and of annexing a contiguous territory had been preserved. What lay outside the defense perimeter of this largest land fortress on earth (Russian Alaska, for example) had to be abandoned sooner or later.

If 80 years ago at least a dozen countries could be listed as empires, today the only true remaining imperial conglomerate, which survived the successive shock waves of two world wars and the appeal of decolonization, is the Soviet Union, or more cogently, the Soviet Eurasian Empire. Some ex-colonial old hands with practical experience in the field have argued that, regardless of the geopolitical provisions for the territorial continuity from the Russian to the Soviet Empire, the decisive fact for the preservation of the Empire was that among all imperialist powers the Russians alone never lost their nerve.[10] Do the Soviets appear to run their inherited imperial possessions successfully where the others failed?

The answer to this question is both historical and contemporary. It is historical because it must explain the success of the Bolsheviks who, in the chaos of the civil war following the disintegration of the Russian Empire after 1917, emerged as the only internal contender for power sufficiently ruthless to impose authority. They did not control the borderlands, but rather the administrative and geographic centers of the Russian metropolis, which also served as the communication hubs for the rest of the Empire. Lenin proved to be a much more skillful tactician than his rivals because he knew when to cede the ground temporarily; he was also the only significant leader who had accepted in principle the right of self-determination for the non-Russian subjects.¹¹ Even Mackinder, who arrived in South Russia at the beginning of 1920, could see that the prospect for a multinational, anti-Bolshevik alliance of governments along Russia's southwest borderlands, stretching from Polish nationalists to Georgian Mensheviks, looked very unpromising.¹²

Before the contemporary dimension can be examined, the question of continuity between the Tsarist Empire and the Soviet Union must be addressed. Recently, Dietrich Geyer tried to answer the question of continuity and discontinuity between the two models from the perspective of modern inperialism theory.¹³ First, Geyer has difficulty classifying pre-1914 Russian imperialism as modern because of the ambivalent function the Tsarist Empire exercised. It was clearly an imperialist power as well as a semicolonial country dependent on foreign investments, which because of its economic backwardness, it was incapable of creating. The exceptions were in northern Persia and briefly in Manchuria, its own spheres of economic influence. Second, Geyer finds that the concept of modern imperialism fits the Soviet Union after 1917 even less than it fits the Tsarist Empire, but for different reasons. By virtue of its creation, the Soviet Union represents the antithesis rather than a special form of imperialism. Whatever the Soviet power structures, economy, and society are, Geyer argues quite sensibly, "they are not 'capitalist.' "¹⁴ Only after discussing these two qualified denials from the perspective of the modern imperialism theory, which evolves around the model of indirect rule through the creation of informal empires, is Geyer willing to admit that there is indeed a continuity problem between the two types of empires that cannot be ignored. Thus, if we move only a quarter of a century beyond 1917 and look at Russian and Soviet history from the vantage point of World War II (the Great Patriotic War from the Russian/Soviet perspective), the continuity is so striking that it cannot be contested.

According to Geyer, this continuity is characterized by three factors. The first and most important factor stems from the geopolitical reality of the present empire's size and shape, which covers almost the identical territory as did its tsarist predecessor. In my opinion, this physical continuity—regardless of the social system and political regime in power—determines the empire's obsession with security and stimulates its temptation to improve it by direct annexation of neighboring territories into its multinational *Lebensraum* (for example, new territories annexed as a result of the Ribbentrop-Molotov Pact of 1939–41). Indirect forms of rule were applied by the Soviet Union initially only in Outer Mongolia, where a Soviet protectorate was established in 1921. Its primary function was not economic but strategic—namely, to form a buffer against Japan's overland expansion in northern China. Only after World War II did Moscow seize the unique opportunity to expand by establishing an informal empire on an unprecedented scale, first in Eastern Europe and later in Asia where it backfired (Northern Iran, Eastern Turkestan (Sinkiang), China, and most recently Afghanistan).

Related to this is the second factor, based on the relatively rapid resumption of Russia's traditional great power status within the international system. This is best illustrated by Stalin's maneuvering and gambling between two hostile imperialist coalitions during the early stages of World War II. The third factor, in spite of the dramatic upheavals inside the Soviet Union and the appearance of new elites, is exemplified by the continuity of nationalist and imperialist attitudes. These may have "a Soviet flavor, but are undoubtedly of Russian origin."[15]

Within this theme of continuity juxtaposing the two Eurasian empires the specific role of geopolitical and ideological components must be discussed. These two elements appear to be the most characteristic for determining the typology of the Russian version of imperialism. While concentrating on this peculiar Russian form of the *Drang nach Osten (Dvizhenie* or *Stremlenie na Vostok)* in the quest of a new heartland, we find these two factors closely intertwined in Asia. Moreover, they are imbued with special relevance today. If we take Secretary Gorbachev's *perestroika* seriously—and I think we should—the largest multinational empire is standing on the threshold of a series of radical structural changes that are bound to have wide repercussions in its Eurasian borderlands, among its immediate and distant neighbors, and on its global hegemonial aspirations. In many respects, the Soviet Eurasian Empire of the 1980s finds itself at a crossroads between several, often opposing, forces.

On the most basic level of major economic forces, the Soviet Union is witnessing a growing contrast. Its traditional industrial centers of manufacturing comprise also the bulk of its (European) population in the cis-Ural regions (between 70 to 75 percent in both cases); on the other hand, nearly 90 percent of its energy and mineral resources is found in the trans-Ural territories. But the wasteful expansion of the extractive industries east of the Urals is only one factor characterizing the steady eastward shift of the Empire's center of gravity.

The demographic and social forces of Asian nations, those living within or without the contemporary boundaries of the Soviet Eurasian Empire, constitute another powerful factor complicating Russia's agelong eastern drive toward integration and assimilation with Asian territories, which today comprise three-quarters of the Empire. Although the climatic and physical obstacles of Siberia, as well as the great distances between the European metropolis and the far-flung Pacific region, can be conquered to a considerable degree by technology, capital, and forced labor, the ethnic, cultural, and racial diversities require much more subtle human efforts.[16] This dichotomy, represented at one pole by the autarkic vision of an assimilated, self-contained Russian/Soviet Eurasian Empire and at the other by the perennial obstacles of physical and human geography, is the major reason Soviet Eurasia has not yet been, and perhaps never will be, effectively integrated into one empire from sea to sea (at least not to the same extent as the United States).

In one area, however, the Soviet leadership can claim a semblance of successful integration and correlation—the military-security sphere. Soviet Eurasia is in a singular strategic position because it touches on three great geopolitical realms: the Atlantic (West European and U.S.), the Pacific (East Asian), and potentially the South Asian (covering the Indian Ocean area and part of the Middle East).[17] The potential European theater of war (in Russian military jargon known as *GTVD*, meaning Major Theater of Military Activities), comprising about half of the Soviet military machine and manpower, has been traditionally the main one since the end of World War II. However, during the last two decades, two more major military theaters have emerged, both in the Asian hinterland of the Empire—the Far Eastern *GTVD* (since 1978) and the Southern *GTVD* (since 1984).[18] Thus, in spite of the fact that past national economic policy decisions from Moscow usually were influenced by the priorities of the European metropolis, they often could be overridden by two principal security concerns connected with the Asian hinterland: (1) strategic requirements dictated by the Sino-Soviet antagonism (prior to 1945 by the Japanese threat), coupled with the Soviet great power ambitions in the Pacific and Indian Ocean realms; (2) concerns about holding together the ethnosocial cohesion of the multinational Empire, especially along its soft underbelly, the Central Asia belt, occupied by the fast growing Muslim population, having the highest birth rates within the Soviet Union.

Visualize for a moment our world of international politics and conflicts suddenly frozen for the next several decades or so. Even allowing the elementary biological forces to work on their own, without the continuous interference of political imponderables, the Soviet Union around the year 2080 will not be what it is today. Its Muslim subjects, with their high birthrates, will outnumber by a wide margin not only the Great Russians (who have ceased, in any case, to form the majority of the USSR's population and may now not exceed 48.5 percent), but also the entire European stock of the USSR.[19] This perspective alone should stimulate our curiosity in resuming the Heartland Debate, precisely when the present leader of the Soviet Empire has indicated that his country may have reached the critical junction in its domestic evolution and must decide whether to change its course before the end of this century.

How is the Soviet Union going to cope with its Asian domains and cross-border relationships under this challenge? Has she not already, to use the analogy of Paul Kennedy's *Rise and Fall of the Great Powers*, overstretched herself; has she not assumed too many overextended commitments?[20] Does the contemporary Soviet Empire already belong in the category of the languishing empires of the past, with Habsburg Spain, Bourbon France, Ottoman Turkey, or Edwardian England? Has it already entered the cycle of self-paralyzing imperial overstretch? And if so, are the cracks in the imperial edifice more visible west or east of the Urals?

Nowhere is the dichotomy between the ambitious legacy of the Russian colonial mission in Asia and the present Soviet geostrategic position more pronounced than in the Asia-Pacific region, where, according to Gorbachev, "civilization is stepping up its pace."[21] However, it is precisely here, east of Lake Baykal, that the present Soviet imperial presence appears most anachronistic and out of pace with the dynamic development of this pivotal region. The economy has been vibrant and trade competition fierce during the last two decades, and the modest but conspicuous economic success in communist China's modernization program has probably created a serious ideological challenge to Moscow. (Indeed, I argue that China's visible success with economic liberalization, backed up not by Soviet economic advisers but by the technological know-how of East Asia and the West, must have constituted one of the chief motives for Gorbachev's decision to start with *perestroika*.)

How did the Soviet Empire respond prior to Gorbachev? By first doubling and then tripling its armed forces in the region, by expanding its Pacific Fleet to make it the largest and most offensive of its four separate fleets, by establishing the Far Eastern *GTVD*, and by instituting a whole series of military measures threatening the security of China and Japan. Indeed, the contrast between this hypermilitarization and the steady decline, both in absolute and relative terms, of the civilian sector in the Soviet Far East (which has virtually not participated in the burgeoning economies of the East Asia-Pacific region) prompted one leading expert on the economic geography of Soviet Asia to use the term *parasitic* to characterize the relationship between this region and the metropolis.[22]

Having thus briefly described, from a spatial, geopolitical perspective, one of the most apparent paradoxes of the present Soviet Eurasian Empire, we are still left with the perennial dilemma of where this multifarious imperial conglomerate belongs. To Europe? To Asia? Or should it be considered a realm of its own, like the Indian subcontinent?

Gorbachev, I am obliged to warn readers of his *Perestroika* book, is merely stretching farther the age-old mystification with the Empire's geo-historical identification. Thus, while talking to West European readers, Gorbachev shows his anger with those who "are trying to exclude the Soviet Union from Europe" and makes a passionate plea, nay, an emotional demand for a "pan-European policy" in the name of "Europe—our common house." Is Gorbachev's Soviet Union perhaps claiming the European heritage because the communist ideology originated in Western Europe? Not at all. The term *communism* has been carefully avoided in the *Perestroika* book. Surprisingly but very effectively, Gorbachev has been using two old-new arguments in favor of the European linkage, arguments that are fundamentally prerevolutionary and that were used by the Russian *Zapadniki* (Westerners) throughout the nineteenth century: (1) We Russians are Europeans because we are Christians; together with other Christian subjects of our Empire we regard ourselves as the lawful inheritors of the great European civilization (at this point, one ought to ask, What about the Tatars, the Caucasian nations, the Uzbeks, and all the other Asian peoples inhabiting the Soviet Union? Which "heritage," which "great civilization," should they claim?); (2) We have saved Europe from the Nazi tyranny, and it was our people, more than 20 million of them, who "laid the greatest sacrifices at the altar of the liberation struggle against Hitler's fascism."[23] (Until the defeat of Hitler, the analogical justification was the "First Great Patriotic War" the Russian people fought against Napoleon.)

Even the geographic boundaries of "our common European house" are clearly outlined in Gorbachev's emotional sermon. With a transparent anti-American purpose (they belong to a different civilization, cannot appreciate the European heritage, and above all, created NATO, through which "Europe once again found itself harnessed to a chariot of war, this time one loaded with nuclear explosive),"[24] Gorbachev has cleverly adopted General de Gaulle's vision.

> Europe, 'from the Atlantic to the Urals,' is a cultural-historical entity united by the common heritage of the Renaissance and the Enlightenment, of the great philosophical and social teachings of the nineteenth and twentieth centuries. . . . Generally, in Europe the new, salutary outlook knows much more fertile soil than in any other region where the two social systems come into contact.[25]

If this is true, how does Gorbachev reconcile himself with the fact that three-quarters of the Soviet Union's territory and almost 80 million of its subjects are in Asia? In his memorable Vladivostok speech of July 1986, Gorbachev defined the Soviet Union merely as being "also an Asian country."[26] The following year, in his *Perestroika* book, while still focusing almost exclusively on the "Asia-Pacific Knot," he upgraded the Asian dimension in his equation to reach the same degree of importance as hitherto enjoyed by the European component: "The Soviet Union is an Asian, as well as European country."[27] But he did not embroider the subject of historical links; his chapter on Asia is very pragmatic, concerned primarily with economics, with nuclear and conventional demilitarization, and with offering improved relations to Asian nations.

To ascertain how many common houses apart from Europe, the Soviet Union really has, it might be useful to listen carefully to what the peripatetic Soviet leader says about every outpost of the Empire's frontier. In July 1986, Gorbachev was waxing lyrical in Vladivostok about the Pacific frontier—our common house; a few months later, he was in India stating something similar about the Indo-Soviet friendship with regard to the Indian Ocean region; almost a year later, in October 1987, Gorbachev went to Murmansk, where he appealed to the Scandinavians and Canadians, mentioning the Arctic—our common house. The problem seems to be, as Martin Walker pungently captured it in his article on the importance of geography in Russian history, that "the Soviet Union is so damned big that it has too many common homes for the comfort of its many neighbors."[28]

It is not Russia, which can claim her historical attachment to Europe, that is at issue here, but the Soviet Eurasian Empire as a whole, the largest surviving conglomerate from the era of imperialist expansion. If the Kremlin's power were limited to the boundaries of the old Grand Duchy of Muscovy, or at most to the quadrangle stretching from the Baltic to the Black Sea, and from Poland up to the Volga rather than to the Urals,[29] then one might perhaps accept the claim that she was a European nation. By the same token, we could no more object to Russia inviting herself to the much relished seat at today's Council of Europe, than could Lord Castlereagh or Talleyrand at the Congress of Vienna in 1815, or certainly Metternich, who said on many occasions that Asia began at the gates of Vienna.

It is obvious that neither Dostoevsky nor Gorbachev has provided a definitive answer to what is Russia's common house. Perhaps a better clarification might be achieved by narrowing our inquiry to the notion of national interest before we tackle the notion of the *Russian Idea*. What, then, is, or rather was, the Russian national interest in relation to Asia? Is the Soviet national interest different? Winston Churchill, in the often-quoted radio broadcast of 1 October 1939, tried to interpret the Soviet invasion of Poland in the wake of the Nazi attack. He contemplated the USSR much the same way as he did the Russia of the tsars, "as a riddle wrapped in mystery inside an enigma." Searching for a key that could explain Russia's future actions, he felt "that key is Russian national interest."[30]

The problem really starts with the attempt to give the Russian/ Soviet national interest a certain logical pattern and hierarchy. What are its priorities, both geopolitical and ideological? What does Russia seek in Asia? Why did the Russians colonize it in the first place, and why do they still cling to the vast and empty stretches of inhospitable Asian territory? Are they interested in the riches of Siberia (furs in the old days, now fuels, minerals, and energy resources)? Are they still seeking a warm-water outlet to alleviate their major geostrategic handicap? Do they see themselves still as a nation with a mission to perform in Asia, to assimilate different cultures and races under the cloak of a russified Soviet ideology? It is obvious that the assets of this vast colonial enterprise in Asia are just as problematic as are its liabilities.

Did Mikhail Gorbachev indicate the Russian/Soviet national interest vis-à-vis Asia when he spoke in Vladivostok on 28 July 1986? This city is the terminus of the 9,000 km Trans-Siberian Railway holding the Eurasian Empire together. Its name (Ruler of the East) must still ring in the ears of the Chinese as one of the most offensive vestiges of the European colonization of Asia. Gorbachev opened his speech with a eulogy on the theme of the unbreakable unity between the outermost province of the Empire and the motherland (*rodina*),

> always linked in our minds with the immense expanses of the Land of the Soviets, from the Baltic and the Black Sea to the Pacific Ocean. It is linked with the valor, industry and steadfastness of the people who settled and defended this land.[31]

Such an approach by the present leader of the Soviet Union is highly reminiscent, as the reader will soon discover, of the prerevolutionary geopolitical vision of the Russian Eurasian Empire spanning "from sea to sea" (*ot morya do morya*). As if requesting the highest theocratic authority of Russian Marxism to legitimize the permanent Soviet presence in the Far East, Gorbachev noted that Lenin had called "with special warmth the town of Vladivostok 'our very own' town (*nashenskiy*) . . . and praised the exploits of our fellow countrymen, of those trailblazers who laid the road to the Pacific Ocean."[32] Furthermore, the secretary general explicitly praised the exploits of the Russian naval officer G. N. Nevelskoy (1814–76), one of the explorers of the Amur region and a founder of the city of Nikolaevsk on the Pacific shore. As an educated Russian, Gorbachev must have recalled the famous quote with which Emperor Nicholas I, whose name the town still bears, indignantly rejected the request of his foreign minister to return Nikolaevsk to the Chinese. "No," replied the Tsar, "where once the Russian flag has been raised it must never be lowered."[33]

The fictional determination to hold the Far East, come what may, became a reality with the decision to build the great Trans-Siberian Railway (1891–1904). The Russian rulers in the Far East thus reached the point of no return. Vladivostok has not changed its provocative name during the entire Soviet era, whereas one would look in vain through the former colonial territories of the Western powers to find another locality bearing such an offensive imperialistic name. There is little reason to expect that the present Soviet rulers of the Far East would hold their red flag in any less esteem than their tsarist predecessors held theirs. Western analysts, commenting on Gorbachev's Vladivostok speech, have completely overlooked this deeply emotional reassurance the representative of the motherland brought to the faraway Russian settlers on the Pacific shore.

It is astonishing how much of the Russian colonial presence in Asia is taken for granted by the outside world. Is it because we have grown accustomed to contemplating Eurasia as one huge continent, without any natural disruptions, such as wide stretches of sea water, and with Russian settlers firmly entrenched all along the Trans-Siberian Railway? A surrealistic analogy would be the present British Prime Minister using the introductory passage of Gorbachev's Vladivostok speech on a tour of South Africa and addressing the white settlers on the theme of how to defend this land of ours.

Thus, one could tentatively conclude that this peculiar correlation between geography and ideology has determined and guided Russia's national interest toward the East, to the Pacific shore as well as to the Pamir plateau, thereby creating the longest and widest land corridor of territorial expansion in the history of colonialism. This statement is subjected to continuous scrutiny in the following chapters as we trace the important stages in the Heartland Debate, trying to understand how important Asia was and still is to the Russians.

Notes

1 From Dostoevsky's article, "Goek-Tepe. Chto takoe Aziya dlya nas?," written in the aftermath of General Skobelev's massacre of the Turkmens in 1881. See F. M. Dostoevsky, *Polnoe sobranie sochineniy* (St. Petersburg, 1896), vol. 21:513–23, and *The Diary of a Writer*, translated and annotated by Boris Brasol (New York: Charles Scribner, 1949), vol. 2:1043–52.

2 Mikhail S. Gorbachev, *Perestroika: New Thinking for Our Country and the World* (New York: Harper & Row, 1987), 180.

3 A contemporary update of Emanuel Sarkisyanz's *Geschichte der orientalischen Völker Russlands bis 1917* (Munich: R. Oldenbourg Verlag, 1961) would be most welcome. Zeki Validi Togan's *Bügünki Türkili (Türkistan) ve Yakin Tarihi* (Turkestan Today and Its Recent History) (Istanbul, 1947), still awaits its translation into a Western language. Numerous monographs by Baymirza Hayit are available only in German, such as: *Turkestan und der Orient* (Düsseldorf, 1960); *Sowjetrussische Orientpolitik am Beispiel Turkestans* (Cologne-Berlin, 1962); *Turkestan im Herzen Eurasiens* (Cologne, 1980).

The widely acclaimed *Orientalism* by Edward W. Said (New York: Pantheon Books, 1978) is completely unsatisfactory from our point of view because it is limited both geographically (to the Eastern Mediterranean and Maghreb) and nationally (to English and French sources and influences). The outstanding contributions the Germans made in this field are dealt with very superficially, and the achievements of Russian Orientalism (*Vostokovedenie*) are completely ignored by Said.

As an exception, the work of Vasiliy V. Barthold (1869–1930) should be mentioned here. B. Nikitine, the French translator of Barthold's *Istoriya izucheniya Vostoka v Evrope i Rossii*, expressed the opinion that the great Russian Orientalist had presented the Russian historiography "as seen from the Orient rather than from the Occident, in contrast to what was done before him" (V. V. Barthold, *La Découverte de l'Asie. Histoire de l'Orientalisme en Europe et en Russie* [Paris: Payot, 1947], 12). Throughout his work Barthold was careful to avoid "Eurocentrism," because he always considered European history a passing phenomenon. In a letter to P. N. Savitsky, a prominent geographer of the Eurasianist Movement, Barthold argued that Russian attitudes vis-à-vis the East, Russian geographical science, and indeed the whole Oriental science, although heavily influenced by West European scholars, followed their own special path and, as a scientific discipline, should be regarded as separate from Western Europe (ibid., 10–11).

4 Although it could be argued that the East is organically absorbed in Russian history and that it largely determined its course (as during the Mongol invasion), it is equally true that the Russian elites contemplated the world of Islam more or less like the ancient Greeks viewed the East, that is, with contemptuous eyes. Hence *Aziatchina*, used for barbarity, is usually closely associated with the notion of Oriental despotism of Muscovy, which in turn had derived its roots from the Mongol dominance.

5 For example, Wolfgang J. Mommsen, *Theories of Imperialism* (New York: Random House, 1980); Tony Smith, *The Pattern of Imperialism* (Cambridge University Press, 1981).

6 Attributed to journalist John L. O'Sullivan (1845). See Frederick Merk, *Manifest Destiny and Mission in American History: A Reinterpretation* (New York: Vintage Book, 1963).
7 See references in note 1.
8 Heinz Gollwitzer, *Die Gelbe Gefahr. Geschichte eines Schlagworts. Studien zum imperialistischen Denken* (Gottingen: Vendenhoeck & Ruprecht, 1962), 94.
9 Hugh Seton-Watson, *The New Imperialism* (London: Bodley Head, 1961), 22–23.
10 Geoffrey Wheeler, *The Modern History of Soviet Central Asia* (London: Weidenfeld & Nicholson, 1964); Olaf Caroe, *Soviet Empire. The Turks of Central Asia and Stalinism* (New York: St. Martin's Press, 1967), xi.
11 Lenin's unambiguous statements acknowledging the right of self-determination for the non-Russian subjects predate the outbreak of World War I. These statements are contained in his various articles, including the critical "On the National Pride of the Great Russians" (1914) and the long unpublished essay, "On the Right of Nations to Self-determination" (1914), as well as the texts of the two declarations following the November 1917 coup in Petrograd ("Declaration of Rights of the Peoples of Russia," "To All Toiling Muslims of Russia and the East"). See the volume *Lenin o druzhbe s narodami Vostoka* (Moscow: Gosizdat polit. literatury 1961).
12 Report by Sir Halford Mackinder on the situation in Southern Russia, *Documents on British Foreign Policy 1919–39*, 1st Series/iii (London: HMSO, 1949), 768–87.
13 Dietrich Geyer, "Modern Imperialism? The Tsarist and the Soviet Examples." In *Imperialism and After. Continuities and Discontinuities*, ed. W. J. Mommsen and J. Osterhammel (London: Allen & Unwin, 1986), 49–62.
14 Ibid., 51.
15 Ibid., 53.
16 Leslie Dienes, "Central Asia and the Soviet 'Midland': Regional Position and Economic Integration." In *Afghanistan and the Soviet Union: Collision and Transformation*, ed. Milan Hauner and Robert Canfield (Boulder: Westview, 1989), 61–100. See also Leslie Dienes's excellent monograph, *Soviet Asia: Economic Development and National Policy Choices* (Boulder: Westview, 1987).
17 Saul B. Cohen distinguishes between "Geopolitical Regions" and "Geostrategic Realms," the latter being a somewhat "broader ideological and military strategic organizational framework." See his *Geography and Politics in a World Divided* (OUP, 1963).
18 John Erickson, "The Soviet Strategic Emplacement in Asia," *Asian Affairs* XII/2 (February 1981), 5–18; Michael MccGwire, *Military Objectives in Soviet Foreign Policy* (Washington: The Brookings Institution, 1987); idem, "Update: Soviet Military Objectives," *World Policy Journal* (Fall 1987), 723–31.
19 Mikhail S. Bernstam, "The Demography of Soviet Ethnic Groups in World Perspective." In *The Last Empire: Nationality and the Soviet Future*, ed. Robert Conquest (Stanford: Hoover Institution Press, 1986), 320.
20 Paul Kennedy, *The Rise and Fall of the Great Powers* (New York: Random House, 1987), 488–514.

Introduction 17

21 Gorbachev, *Perestroika* (1987).
22 Leslie Dienes, "Economic and Strategic Position of the Soviet Far East," *Soviet Economy* 1/2 (1985),146–76; idem, "Current Military Deployment and Strategic Prospects under Gorbachev." In *The Soviet Far East: Development and Prospect*, ed. A. Rodgers (London: Croom Helm, 1988), 29–47. The population dichotomy within a radius of 2,500 km from Vladivostok could not be more staggering; according to Dienes, around 12 million Soviet citizens face 1 billion Asians, that is two-thirds of China's inhabitants and the populations of Taiwan, the two Koreas, and Japan.
23 Gorbachev, *Perestroika* (1987), 191.
24 Ibid., 193.
25 Ibid., 198.
26 For the Russian text of Gorbachev's Vladivostok speech of 28 July 1986, see *Problemy Dal'nego Vostoka* 60 (1986), 3–21; English version in the *FBIS* (Foreign Broadcast Information Service) *Daily Report: Soviet Union*, 29 July 1986, section R 1–20.
27 Exactly 1 year after his Vladivostok speech, Gorbachev was interviewed by the editor of the Indonesian daily *Merdeka* on several aspects of his new Asia-Pacific strategy (see Gorbachev, *Perestroika*, 181). See also Richard N. Haas, "The 'Europeanization' of Moscow's Asia Policy," *SAIS Review* 7/2 (Summer–Fall 1987),127–41.
28 Martin Walker reporting from Moscow for *The Guardian:* "The Challenges for Gorbachev on the Soviet Frontiers." Reprinted in *The Manchester Guardian Weekly* of 14 February 1988.
29 Although in Russian literature and folklore the Volga is portrayed as the great Russian river, it is equally legitimate to argue that right up to the end of the nineteenth century the Volga, or as it was known under its Tatar name, the *Idel*, remained, in population, a Tatar (i.e. Turkish) river (cf. Seton-Watson 1961, 12).
30 Winston S. Churchill, *The Second World War* (London: Cassell, 1948), 1:353.
31 See note 26.
32 See note 26. Gorbachev made no such geopolitical pronouncement concerning the significance of Central Asia to Moscow during a stopover in Tashkent en route to India in November 1986. Instead, he condemned corruption and Islamic revivalism (*Time*, January 12, 1987). On the other hand, while in New Delhi, he lavished geopolitical appellations on "Great India" and was particularly careful to include references to India as the predominant power of the Indian Ocean region in his general security program (something he neglected to emphasize several months earlier in Vladivostok where he had seemingly replicated "the American policy approach of ignoring Asia beyond the Irrawady" (see Thomas R. Thornton, "Gorbachev's Courtship of India," *The Round Table* 304 [1987], 460).
33 Violet Conolly, *Beyond the Urals. Economic Developments in Soviet Asia* (London and New York: Oxford University Press, 1967), 11–12.

Part I

Asia and the Russians

2

Russian Ideology and Asia

Asia and Us

Because of the unique impact of history and geography, which blended the European and Asian portions of the Russian Empire, the Russians have long claimed a close and intimate relationship with Asia. Not so long ago, before being pushed out by the Cossacks and land-hungry Russian peasants, the banks of the Volga, the Kuban, and the Ural rivers were inhabited by peoples originating from Asia. These nomads penetrated Russia's European steppe much farther west than today's settlements of Asiatic population in the USSR would indicate.

This is the not the place to argue where Europe ends and Asia starts. That definition is a matter of pure convenience for the onlooker. We must, however, attend to the peculiar Russian claim of a special relationship with Asia and its peoples or races (*plemena*). We must also investigate their self-confident belief that they understand Asia and its inhabitants better than do any other European people. The basis of this strange claim is a combination of collective suffering and territorial aggrandizement. In other words, it was the special sacrifice of the Russian people that saved Europe from the Asiatic invaders; and their capacity to endure the Mongol occupation, which Nicholas Riasanovsky rightly calls "the most traumatic historical experience of the Russian people,"[1] entitled the Russian people and government to special considerations for territorial expansion on the grounds of security. Here the attitudes toward Asia, the contrast between eastward, southward, and westward expansion, must be fully evaluated. How did the several generations of Russians envisage the future confines of the Russian Empire? And, how did the Soviet heirs to the tsarist legacy behave in similar circumstances?

Russia under Peter the Great, although largely engaged against Sweden and Poland in securing access to the Baltic and Black seas, consolidated control of Siberia and thrust out into the Caucasus, Central Asia, and the Far East. However, despite Peter's serious attempt to promote the knowledge of Asian studies, Petrine Russia tried to interpret the Orient in terms of Western Europe.[2] Consequently, the inhabitants of Asia came to be seen as inefficient and backward people, and the Western-educated Russians eventually found themselves in the mainstream of the European ideology of imperialism, stressing on occasion the unique Russian capacity to combine European cultural superiority with special empathy for the Asiatic way of life.

Throughout the nineteenth century, many Russian intellectuals wrote and preached of their fascination with the Orient. Many of them believed sincerely that Russia was destined to study the cultures of the East and, ultimately, to rule over it. Count Sergei Uvarov (1786–1855), the enlightened minister of education (1833–49), believed, for instance, that because "the Orient has been unanimously recognized as the cradle of all civilization of the universe . . . it makes it impossible for us to deny that Asia is the central point from which all the rays of the light scattered over the globe emanate."[3] In 1810, Uvarov conceived the idea of an Asian Academy, which, however, did not materialize. Others, like Alexei S. Khomyakov (1804–60), despite his loyalty to Russian Orthodoxy and opposition to the Ottoman rule over Christians and fellow Slavs, valued Islam higher than Catholicism. Khomyakov studied Sanskrit, and though familiar with the Western culture, he opposed its cult of individualism by stressing cooperation and togetherness (*sobornost*). As one of the founders of the Slavophile Movement, Khomyakov saw the Slavs as the outstanding representatives of the Aryo-Iranian race.[4] The mystic Slavophile poet Fyodor I. Tyutchev (1803–73) preached a future great Orthodox Slav empire, with Rome having an Orthodox pope subordinated to the Russian Tsar residing in Constantinople.[5] Even to the ultraconservative Slavophile Konstantin Leontev (1831–91), the wishful image of the future Russian Empire in Asia differed from a Western imperialist stereotype. Tibetan and Hindu traditions were more inspiring to him than was Western Christianity. Like Khomyakov, Leontev had a strong racial vision (for example, see his *Racial Politics as a Weapon of World Revolution*, 1888) and equally strong hopes that the Turanian element would shape the Russian Slavic culture into something spiritually more elevated and distinct from Europe.[6]

As far as the Russian revolutionaries were concerned, they first despised Asia, just as Marx did, while justifying European colonial expansion as the inevitable vehicle of progress that would transform the whole globe into a socialist world order.[7] But soon the process of *embourgeoisement* of the European working class disappointed the Russians. Alexander Herzen (1812–70), Russia's most prophetic exile revolutionary, forecast an anti-Western rising in the East in revenge for the colonial exploitation. It was in resistance to Westernization and what Herzen called "Petrograndism" that the Russian peasant communes would rise. It was among the Russian muzhiks that the original meaning of democracy had been apparently preserved; "Petrograndism" introduced only social revolution through forced labor, and this might be repeated under communism as well.[8]

The most original former Russian revolutionary, in many respects a direct predecessor of universal historians like Oswald Spengler and Arnold Toynbee, was the Pan-Slavist ideologue Nikolai Y. Danilevsky (1822–85). After recanting his revolutionary views like Dostoevsky, he developed in *Russia and Europe* (1869) a breathtaking spatial vision of a future Russian-dominated Pan-Slav Union stretching from the Adriatic to the Pacific, with Tsar-Grad (Constantinople) as its natural seat. Danilevsky never accepted the fashionable view that Europe had been historically involved in a perennial struggle with Asia. Arguing from the perspective of his cyclical typology of civilizations, the geographical and cultural division between Asia and Europe did not make sense to him; he argued instead that major Eurasian races (Aryan, Semite, Turanian, etc.) and religions (Judaism, Christianity, Islam) originated in Asia. In a mirror image of Pan-Germanism, Danilevsky saw a deep cleavage between Western Europe, represented by the current dominant Romano-Germanic type of civilization, and the Greko-Slav civilization. The war between the two was inevitable and was to culminate in the establishment of a Pan-Slav Union, seen as the crowning achievement of the past efforts of Philip of Macedon, Alexander the Great, and Emperor Constantine. The so-called Eastern Question, according to Danilevsky, would find a logical solution in Russia's succeeding Byzantium and Ottoman Turkey as the historical heir of Constantinople—the ontological center of the world.[9]

Thus, notwithstanding Danilevsky's extreme view, we can observe the following dualism in the Russian attitude toward Asia: while Westernized Russians claimed to be the avant-garde of European colonization of the East, the populist approach rejected Petrine Russia as embodied in the St. Petersburg State. Emanuel Sarkisyanz, for instance, is convinced that no racial distance separated the Russian Orthodox peasants from indigenous Asians. Paradoxically, this was due not only to the 300-year-long Mongol yoke, but also to the geopolitical reality of the gradual and continental character of the Russian penetration and colonization. As a result of this process, the emerging Russian Eurasian Empire preserved the geographical unity of the dual continent and did not create a spatial gap between the natives and the Russian settlers, as existed between the West European powers and their overseas colonies.[10] By 1881, when the conquest of Turkestan by the Russian army was almost completed, it was Dostoevsky who pointed toward Central Asia as the future New Russia, which "will arise and in due time regenerate and resurrect the old one."[11] This unexpected involvement of Russia's major writer represented a serious challenge to the traditional obsession of the Russian public, supported by the press and the Pan-Slavists, with the fate of their coreligionists in the Balkans under the Ottoman rule and with the dream of seizing Constantinople. What Dostoevsky was proposing represented nothing less than a redirection of Russia's traditional imperial dream, associated with the resolution of the Eastern Question, away from the Balkans, away from the deceitful European powers that robbed Russia of her fruits of victory after the last Balkan War, toward a new civilizing mission in "our Asiatic Russia."

The Russian Idea and Revolution

Even contemporary images of Asia applied by Russian intelligentsia contain little of the obligatory Marxist-Leninist dosage of ideology.

This is largely due to the pervasive legacy of Great Russian nationalism in combination with the Orthodox Christian tradition, the one which provides the powerful link of continuity with both the Greek and Byzantine civilization. This tradition does not rest solely on the vision of Moscow as the Third Rome, but also includes the conquest of the East by Alexander the Great. The coexistence between Marxism-Leninism and what Dostoevsky and Berdyaev called the *Russian Idea* created a very peculiar symbiosis that inevitably led to the deformation of the original Russian Idea.[12] Yet, not only is the role of this specifically Russian ideology important for understanding how Russia became a great Asian power, but it also remains, in its various contemporary mutations, a key factor for predicting the future of Soviet Asia.

Several scholars have tried to explain the extraordinary power of the Russian idea to survive all the radical tribulations since World War I. Tibor Szamuely, whose own life was so closely linked with international communism, believed that in Leninism the Russian autocratic tradition reasserted itself after a brief period of revolutionary aberration. The spiritual bond holding this tradition together was the Russian idea, with its inner mystery of century-long suffering for the Orthodox faith, "the conviction that Russia alone had been entrusted with the divine mission of resuscitating the rest of the world by sharing with it the revelation that had been granted to her alone."[13] This is, of course, pure Dostoevsky. Moreover, the Russian nation alone was entrusted with the notion of a "God-bearing people" (*narod bogonosets*), as the Monk Philotheus prophesied in 1510 to his Tsar.

> Know then, a pious Tsar, that all the Orthodox Christian realms have converged in thy single empire. Thou art the only Tsar of the Christians in all the universe. . . . Observe and hear, o Tsar, that all Christian empires have converged in this single one, that two Romes have fallen, but the third stands, and no fourth can ever be.[14]

Lenin himself was convinced that class loyalties would eventually replace the national and ethnic ones after the victorious proletarian revolution. He did recognize almost immediately the importance of nationalism as a weapon for undermining the cohesion of the Tsarist Empire; consequently, he defended the right of national self-determination up to its logical consequence, that is territorial secession of the non-Russian nationalities clustered along the borders of the Empire. But as soon as he switched his role from an exiled revolutionary, writing inflammatory articles in relative safety, to the chief government executioner in charge of millions of non-Russians, he had to reconsider his rhetorical stand. The question now was How far and how much? Under duress Lenin had made several far-reaching concessions to nationalist separatists in order to preserve Soviet power at the center for the time being. The most humiliating had to be that at Brest-Litovsk under the dictate of the victorious German imperialists and their allies. After the German surrender in November 1918, Lenin could instantly reverse his policy. The time had come for the Bolsheviks to reclaim the territories that had been given away (Finland, the Baltics, Poland, the Ukraine, the Caucasus), together with between 50 to 60 million ex-Tsarist subjects, according to the Peace Treaty signed at Brest-Litovsk in March the same year. For Lenin it was no longer a question of defending unconditionally the right to national self-determination, but rather arguing in favor of the "more progressive" proletarian solidarity, in which the elder Russian brother dictated the terms from the perspective of the universal class war.[15] Despite the fact that Lenin continued to hate Great Russian chauvinism,[16] he would now sanction, albeit grudgingly, the reconquest of the rebellious borderlands of the Tsarist Empire by the cosmopolitan, internationalist Red Army, consisting during the early period mostly of ex-prisoners of war. He would support national emancipation movements only as long as they served the cause of communist revolution.

"Long Live Free Asia!"[17]

How did Lenin's attitude toward Asia develop? Contrary to what one might suspect, the Bolshevik leader did not want to imitate the German strategy of subversion with which he was intimately familiar (having been assigned in it the role of an important pawn in 1917).[18] Lenin actually became an advocate of Euro-Asian solidarity between the Western working class and the exploited toilers of the Orient shortly after the Revolution of 1905.[19] In 1908, he went on record stating that "the class-conscious European worker now has comrades in Asia, and their number will grow by leaps and bounds."[20] Lenin defended his thesis in sharp and often vicious polemics with West European comrades, particularly the German social democrats.

Long before the Bolshevik seizure of power in Petrograd, Lenin's anticolonial policy, part of his revolutionary strategy of undermining the war effort of the great powers, included on its list of demands the renunciation of all colonies, territorial conquests, and imperialist treaties concerning the future partition of spheres of influence. He did not hestitate to apply his demands to the Great Russian nation in the first place, insisting that Great Russians would have to abandon Poland, the Baltic provinces, the Ukraine, and Finland and withdraw their troops from Galicia, as well as from Armenia and Persia.[21]

The recurrent theme that kept rekindling Lenin's faith after 1905 was the vision of successive anticolonial revolutions in Asia, which seemed to be confirmed by the events in Turkey, Persia, and China. He kept repeating that Russia's Bolshevik Revolution was bound to lead to a universal anticolonial uprising of 1 billion Asians against Western imperialism. When the Bolshevik drive westward collapsed at the gates of Warsaw, and several communist takeovers failed to materialize in Europe, the advocates of anticolonial revolutions, including a number of brilliant activists of Asian extraction, succeeded in winning over Lenin for their own schemes. They wanted to divert the main thrust of the Bolshevik Revolution from Europe toward the East.

After the Second Komintern Congress and the Congress of the Eastern Peoples in Baku, held in July and September 1920, respectively, the revolutionary strategy of the Bolsheviks switched to the pursuit of anticolonial subversions and uprisings in Asia. The reconquest of Turkestan and of Trans-Caucasia by the Red Army seemed to have predestined Central Asia as the most convenient base for cross-border subversive activities. These activities were directed at Turkey, Persia, and British India (via Afghanistan), which became the main target of Bolshevik propaganda to enhance world revolution by striking at the most vulnerable spot in the edifice of British colonialism.[22] Although this Bolshevik Eastern strategy had to be abandoned in Central Asia after less than three years, it was pursued to some extent in East Asia. As for Lenin, in spite of being overwhelmed by the urgent tasks of the internal reconstruction of Russia and having to shelve for a while the ambitious program of world revolution, he never lost his faith. "In the last analysis, the outcome of the struggle will be determined by the fact that Russia, India, China, etc., account for the overwhelming majority of the population of the globe... so that in this respect there cannot be the slightest doubt what the final outcome of the world struggle will be." "In this sense," Lenin concluded, "the complete victory of socialism is fully and absolutely assured."[23]

Emanuel Sarkisyanz, drawing on Berdyaev, seems to have captured the ambiguity of Russian Bolshevism quite accurately when he reminds us that its specific Leninist contribution, namely, the incorporation of Asia into the European scheme of the class war, was never part of Marxism as such. The Bolshevik appeal to the "toilers of the Orient to overthrow the robbers and enslavers," launched shortly after the October Revolution,[24] can be seen as the recrudescence of the Russian Idea. With its quintessential notion of suffering, the key element of Russian messianism was absorbed into the Western Marxist notion of world proletarian revolution. Furthermore, the Komintern, the supreme directorate that was supposed to guide this world revolution and set the Orient ablaze, was given the alternative title of Third Intenational, which sounded like a metamorphosis of the Third Rome, the traditional Orthodox image of Holy Russia.[25]

The Russian Idea Today

It would be a serious error of judgment to assume that the Russian Idea was completely extinct after 1917 as a result of the communist challenge. World War II, the Great Patriotic War as the Russians refer to it, was a glaring testimony of how it triumphed over international Marxism, which was circumscribed in any case by Stalin's order to dissolve the Komintern in 1942. Moreover, the majority of Soviet Central Asian soldiers taken prisoner joined the enemy—a fact still hidden from the Soviet public today.[26] The Great Patriotic War is also a good example of a merger between territorial aggrandizement and the collective suffering of the Soviet family of nations led by the elder Russian brother.

Another striking example is the Sino-Soviet border clash along the Ussuri River in 1969, which most Russians understood in racial terms. Here, the spectre of a new Genghis Khan, contained in the

"Yellow Peril" warnings of Vladimir Solovyov, but which were revoked in Evtushenko's anti-Chinese poem published in *Pravda*, seemed to carry more weight than the dead repository of Lenin's appeals to international proletarian solidarity. The Soviet occupation of Afghanistan resulted in similar popular reactions based on racial prejudice, whereas official propaganda tried in vain to emphasize the Marxist idea of industrial progress to be achieved through international help in a backward country to fight the mounting tide of Islamic obscurantism.[27]

During the mid-1960s, the so-called Russian Idea emerged again amid a broad spectrum of Russian nationalist undercurrents in both the censored Soviet media (for example, the youth journal *Molodaya Gvardiya*) and the *samizdat* (for example, the now suspended *Veche*).[28] A number of external and internal causes lay at the roots of this phenomenon. The most acute appeared to be the serious rupture in Sino-Soviet relations, which raised the spectre of racial war just as Leontev and Solovyov had predicted. This was coupled with the growing awareness on the part of the Great Russians and other Slavs that a fundamental, probably irreversible, demographic shift was taking place inside the present Soviet Eurasian Empire; a rapidly growing Muslim population was experiencing a birth rate three to four times higher than that of the European inhabitants.[29] Certainly another factor must have been the frustration among the Russian intelligentsia with the failure of Russification, the principal means of achieving, through increased militarization, industrialization, and urbanization, the Leninist dream of assimilation—the gradual merger of the Empire's nationalities into one, Russian-speaking Soviet people (*Sovetski Narod*). How long are the Great Russians going to exercise control over the USSR federation and beyond (for example, over an informal empire like the Warsaw Pact), exploiting the holding company principle[30] in which some 135 million Great Russians in 1983 dominated some 385 millions spread over much of the Eurasian Continent?[31] This is a question that can be answered today by reliable demographic forecasts.[32]

Under Nikita Khrushchev, in a gesture of premature optimism, a three-stage formula of "flowering-rapprochement-merger" (*rastsvet-sblizhenie-sliyanie*) was adopted in 1961. The Brezhnev-Kosygin leadership tried to modify this policy during the 1970s into the less excessive *obshchnost* (community), with the Russian

Republic (RSFSR) as the bulwark and brotherly helper of all the other republics of the federation. All Soviet peoples were supposed to cluster together on ideological grounds, but without suggesting a cultural, let alone biological (racial), homogenization.[33] However, faced with the steady cultural pressures on the part of the minorities, Yuri Andropov, Brezhnev's successor, had to admit (on the occasion of the sixtieth anniversary of the founding of the USSR [1922]) that "national differences will continue much longer than class differences."[34] He thereby definitively reversed the Leninist dream of ethnic fusion.

Today a convulsive return to the Stalinist policy of Great Russian chauvinism seems even less likely than it was under Gorbachev's predecessors. However, the Russification policy that continues faces increasing problems due to the radical demographic shift and to the growing cultural self-awareness in the union republics, especially those in the Baltic area, the Caucasus, and Central Asia. Gorbachev seems to have subordinated the ethnic problem to the overall drive for economic *perestroika;* in his book he speaks in favor of the rapprochement theory under Russian guidance.[35] He may yet have to reconsider his priorities in the face of the Armenian and Azerbaijani riots (February 1988). It is only a question of time before ethnic disturbances will hit Central Asia.

Soviet ethnographers, led by Yuryi V. Bromlei, have been busy in recent years adapting their theories of Ethnos (*etnos*) to the new reality.[36] The strongest dissenting, but also disquieting, voice is that of Lev N. Gumilyov, who published a series of articles between 1965 and 1973 in natural science journals (which perhaps explains why they escaped the attention of censorship). He started to publicize his esoteric "bio-geographical conception of ethnic history," which has some relevance to our discussion on the fate of the Russian Idea today. Gumilyov challenges the official interpretation. "Ethnos," according to his use of this term, is not a historical or social phenomenon but a biological one, which should be further differentiated according to the level of "innate drive" (*passionarnost*). This quality alone divides the "Ethnos" into "Superethnos" and "Subethnos" and has nothing to do with whether the nation is less or more socialist. This drive is outside the "biochemical" environment, in which Gumilyov examines the "ethnogenesis." Gumilyov's peculiar theory bears a striking similarity to the racial doctrines of National Socialism. He diffuses ideas prescribing racial segregation and eugenic laws prohibiting interethnic (exogamous) marriages, especially between the Slavic-Orthodox and Turkic-Muslim "superethnoses," on the grounds that they lead to cultural, political, and genetic deformations.[37] Is Gumilyov proposing that the USSR should adopt the policy of apartheid, following the anachronistic and internationally condemned example of the Republic of South Africa? Despite the fact that Gumilyov has been officially criticized in strong terms, he continues to advance his pervasive ideas at the Leningrad University and elsewhere.[38] Russian nationalist dissidents, usually quick to react to any "Yellow Peril" type of warning, became involved in deeply emotional discussions on the pages of *Veche*, pondering over the dramatic decline of Russian fertility rates and the controversial theme of interethnic marriages.[39]

Considering the authoritarian system of media control in the USSR, one remains baffled by Gumilyov's escape through the net and by the sudden eruption of traditional nationalism—from the full-blown Great Russian chauvinism, with its inevitable racial and anti-Semite overtones, to the rich palette of Christian opinions. But was it so sudden? In fact, the origins of *National Bolshevism*, a term for one of the main currents, go back to the early postrevolutionary years. It was coined in 1921 by Nikolai V. Ustryalov (1891–1938), a talented journalist who migrated from Moscow after the Revolution to the largest Russian colonial town outside the Empire's boundaries, Kharbin in Manchuria. An active supporter of the expansionist Tsarist imperialism during World War I, Ustryalov later became a supporter of the October Revolution. In numerous articles, he attacked the internationalist strategy of the Bolsheviks, which he desired to supplant with resurrected nationalism. He was neutral to the Orthodox religion, moderately anti-Semitic, and in favor of the Russian Empire's being ruled by an efficient dictatorship. Gradually, National Bolshevism, under Ustryalov's instigation, developed into a quasi-fascist ideology, stressing the cult of the strong man (*krepkyi chelovek*), of youth and heroic vitalism, and of industrial and military might, but combined, paradoxically (like Italian Fascism and German National Socialism), with strong ecological and preservationist sentiments.[40] Whereas Ustryalov disagreed after 1917 with Russian expansionism, Isaiah Altshuler-Lezhnev (1891–1955), a National Bolshevik who lived inside the Soviet Union, advocated the export of revolution abroad, according to his model of "Turkestan socialism" (in contrast to the classic Marxist "Basel socialism"). Lezhnev's expansionism was also messianic, as he argued that "Russian imperialism (from ocean to ocean), Russian messianism (*Ex Oriente lux*), Russian Bolshevism (on the world scale) are all magnitudes of the same dimension."[41] All this has made National Bolshevism an ideal ideology that, although lacking at present a mass following, could one day become attractive to the officer caste in the Red Army.[42]

Another tendency, more recent than National Bolshevism, is a trend combining Russian nationalism with the Orthodox religious tradition, which is basically anti-Soviet. Supporters have received a variety of names: *Vozrozhdentsy*,[43] Pseudo-Slavophiles,[44] and the less flattering Ultras.[45] This undercurrent includes a much wider variety of personalities, including Alexander Solzhenitsyn,[46] who became Russia's most famous contemporary writer even before his exile, mathematician Igor Shafarevich,[47] and one of the *Veche* editors, Vladimir Osipov.[48] One might also include such mild dissidents as the established "village" (*derevenshchiki*) authors Valentin Rasputin and Vasiliy Belov, or even the immensely popular nationalist painter Ilya Glazunov.[49]

In view of the main focus of this study, we must note one controversial area in which the *Vozrozhdentsy*, representing today the Russian Idea, seem to differ considerably. This is the multinational character of the Soviet Eurasian Empire. Most of them wish to dismantle the Empire in one way or another, but they differ as to how to reach an accommodation with the minority nationalities within the future Eurasian federation. Most Russian nationalists seem to agree, however, that all nations within the present Soviet federation should enjoy full cultural and religious freedom and that past Stalinist crimes should be corrected, at least by allowing the Crimean Tatars and Meshketian Turks to return to their homelands and ethnic Germans, Jews, and Poles to emigrate abroad. How many would support the evacuation of Russian migrants from the borderlands remains a question. On the controversial issue of the future boundaries of the Russian federation, that is, whether the Baltic, Caucasian, and Central Asian Republics should be offered the choice of secession, there is even less agreement.[50]

The Chinese scare, in the form of both demographic pressure and war, believed to be unavoidable, led Solzhenitsyn in the fall of 1973 to compose two famous essays: *Repentance and Self-Limitation*[51] and *Letter to the Soviet Leaders*.[52] He calls on the Russian people to repent the crimes of the Bolsheviks, epitomized in the millions of Gulag victims. In a grandiose gesture of self-limitation, the great writer suggested, Russia should not only withdraw and demobilize her armed forces, retaining only limited troops for "genuinely defensive purposes," but also retreat from external expansion in principle and concentrate her energies on developing the Eurasian North-East, the enormous but empty permafrost space along the Arctic coast. In a style reminiscent of Dostoevsky's essay on Asia, and revoking the cult of soil and of the Russian peasant colonizing the empty spaces of Asia (as Sergei Yuzhakov and Nikolai Fyodorov were advocating at the turn of the century),[53] Solzhenitsyn exhorts his fellow Russians to resume the peaceful expansion of the great Novgorod Republic, which was squashed by the conquest of Muscovy.

> Our Ocean is the Arctic, not the Indian Ocean... not the Mediterranean nor Africa... we have no business there! These boundless expanses, senselessly left stagnant and icily barren for four centuries, await our hands, our sacrifices, our zeal and our love. But it may be that we have only two or three decades left for this work: otherwise the imminent world population explosion will take these expanses away from us.[54]

In 1980, when Russia celebrated the 600th anniversary of her victory over the Tatars at the Battle of Kulikovo, several authors (incidentally, Lev Gumilyov among them) resumed the Europe-Asia controversy, resuscitating the media discussion on the virtues of the Russian Idea. Fedor Nesterov, a mediocre writer employed at the Lumumba University in Moscow, which had been training cadres for revolutionary movements in the Third World, published a book with an extreme, anti-Western message. He basically repeats the old messianic appeals of the Slavophiles: Russia is separated from the West by an abyss; the special qualities in the Russian national character have been acquired through centuries of fighting external enemies; hence, the idea of complete submission of individuals to the State. Nesterov argues in the true spirit of the Slavophiles when he states that Russian autocracy had been usurped by German adventurers. Russian expansion, Nesterov says, was fundamentally different from European colonization because the Russians never treated other peoples as inferior races but always as equal.[55] The most pro-Asian message, from a Russian standpoint, was formulated the following year by Vadim Kozhinov, an extreme Russian nationalist. When he dismissed the bonds between Russian Orthodoxy and European Christianity and promoted the idea of a Russo-Asian alliance directed against the West, Kozhinov encountered several outraged critics who argued the opposite case.[56]

The brief review of the relationship between Asia and Russian ideology has revealed several trends that survive today. The following two chapters are confined historically to shorter periods but direct our attention to four important ideological groups for whom the relationship between Russia and Asia was fundamental.

Notes

1. Nicholas V. Riasanovsky, "Asia through Russian Eyes." In *Russia and Asia*, ed. Wayne S. Vucinich (Stanford: Hoover, 1972), 5. See also George Vernandsky, *The Mongols and Russia* (New Haven: Yale, 1953).
2. Ibid. See also Richard N. Frye's contribution on "Oriental Studies in Russia" in Vucinich, *Russia and Asia* (1972), 34–36.
3. Nicholas V. Riasanovsky, "Russia and Asia: Two Nineteenth-Century Russian Views," *California Slavic Studies* 1 (1960), 170–81; Riasanovsky, *Asia through Russian Eyes* (1972), 11–13.
4. Ibid. Emmanuel Sarkisyanz, "Russian Conquest in Central Asia: Transformation and Acculturation." In Vucinich, *Russia and Asia* (1972), 248–88.
5. F. I. Tyutchev, *Sochineniya* (St. Petersburg: Trenke & Fyusno, 1886), 141; Kirill V. Pigarev, *F. I. Tyutchev i ego vremya* (Moscow: Sovremennik, 1978), 137–38.
6. K. N. Leontev, "Plemennaya politika kak orudie vsemirnoi revolyutsii." In *Vostok, Rossiya i slovyanstvo*, collected essays from 1885–89, published in *Sobranie sochineniy* (Moscow: V. Sablin, 1912), 6:145–93.
7. For Marx's views on China, India, and Russia in connection with the "Asiatic mode of production," see: "Karl Marx über China und Indien," *Unter Dem Banner des Marxismus*, vol. 1 (1927), 379–83; Karl A. Wittfogel, *Oriental Despotism* (New York: Vintage Book, 1981), xxi–Liv, 5, 372–89; V. N. Nikiforov, *Vostok i Vsemirnaya Istoriya* (Moscow: Nauka, 1975).
8. Emanuel Sarkisyanz, *Russland und der Messianismus des Orients* (Tübingen: J. C. B. Mohr, 1955), 154–67.
9. N. Y. Danilevsky, *Rossiya i Evropa* (St. Petersburg: Panteleevykh, 1869).
10. Sarkisyanz, "Russian Conquest in Central Asia" (1972), 248–88; Owen Lattimore, *Studies in Frontier History 1928–1958* (London: OUP, 1962).

11 See note 1, chapter 1. Dostoevsky, *The Diary of a Writer* (1949), 2:1043–1052.
12 Nicolas Berdyaev, *The Russian Idea* (New York: Macmillan, 1948); idem., *Les sources et le sens du communisme russe* (Paris: Gallimard, 1963), 309.
13 Tibor Szamuely, *The Russian Tradition* (London: Secker & Warburg, 1974), 69.
14 Ibid. Cited after P. N. Milyukov, *Ocherki po istorii russkoi kultury* (St. Petersburg: Panteleevykh, 1909), 2:23.
15 Alain Besançon, citing Lenin and Stalin, in "L'Empire russe at la domination soviétique," *Le Concept d'Empire*, ed. Maurice Duverger et al. (Paris: P.U.F., 1980), 370.
16 *Lenin o druzhbe s narodani Vostoka* (1961), 113–16, 334–37.
17 Lenin's greeting to the "Indian Revolutionary Association," published in *Pravda*, May 20, 1930; see *ibid.*, 290.
18 Fritz Fischer, *Germany's Aims in the First World War* (New York: Norton, 1967), 120–54.
19 *Lenin* (1961), 22–26.
20 Ibid., 29.
21 Ibid., 245–47.
22 See details in chapter 5. For a recent lively description, see Peter Hopkirk, *Setting the East Ablaze* (London: John Murray, 1984).
23 "Better Fewer but Better," published in *Pravda*, March 4, 1923; see *Lenin*, (1961), 338–40.
24 Ibid., 261–63. Appeal to "All Toiling Muslims of Russia and the East" of December 3, 1917, signed by Ulyanov-Lenin and Dzhugashvili-Stalin.
25 Sarkisyanz, *Russland und der Messianismus* (1955), 200–203. The more prosaic explanation is that the Third or Communist International (Komintern: 1919–43) was founded in Moscow as successor to the Second International (1889), which itself replaced the First International (1864), the one that Karl Marx helped to establish. For a comprehensive treatment, see Mikhail Agursky, *The Third Rome: National Bolshevism in the USSR* (Boulder: Westview, 1987).
26 In spite of the fact that the non-Russian Soviet nationalities were treated as mercenaries or cannon fodder by the Germans, an estimated force of between 300,000 and 400,000 volunteered for the German armed forces during World War II. They came primarily from various Central Asian and Caucasian nationalities, from the Crimean and Volga Tatars, and Kalmyks. As soon as the Red Army advanced, Stalin's punishment was mass deportation of the Volga Germans, Crimean Tatars, Kalmyks, and several north Caucasian nationalities, altogether some 1.5 million persons, including old people, women, and children. For figures, see Alex Alexiev, *Soviet Nationalities in German Wartime Strategy, 1941–1945*, The Rand Corporation, Note R–2772–NA (Santa Monica: August 1982).
27 Many examples of the so-called Yellow Peril mentality survive in the USSR today: Andrei Amalrik, *Prosushchestvuet-li Sovetskiy Soyuz do 1984 goda?* (Amsterdam: The Herzen Foundation, 1969); Dev Murarka, "The Russian Intervention of Afghanistan: A Moscow Analysis," *The Round Table* 282 (April 1981), 122–139; Vladimir Rybakov, *The Burden* (London: Hutchinson, 1984); Gordon Brook-Shepherd, "Captured Red Army Letters Tell the Story of the Russians at War," *The Sunday Telegraph*, June 9, 1985, and June 16, 1985; Martin Walker in *The Manchester Guardian Weekly* of July 7, 1985;

Arthur Bonner in *The New York Times* of November 1, 1985; Vassily Aksyonov in *The New York Times Magazine* of May 3, 1987. The classic treatment of the Yellow Peril in today's USSR is, of course, Harrison E. Salisbury's *The Coming War between Russia & China* (London: Pan Books, 1969), 28–38. See also his dissenting introduction to Victor Louis, *The Coming Decline of the Chinese Empire* (New York: Times Books, 1979). For a comprehensive review of the Russian-Muslim relationship in Central Asia, see S. Enders Wimbush, "The Soviet-Muslim Borderlands," in Conquest, *The Last Empire* (1986), 218–34.

28 Interview between V. N. Osipov, editor of *Veche* (Assembly) and two American correspondents, Stephen Browning and Dean Mills, April 25, 1972, RFE-RL, *Arkhiv Samizdata*, no. 1599:11–18.

29 Alexander Yanov, *The Russian New Right* (Berkeley: Institute of International Studies, 1978), 10–11.

30 Term adopted in the perceptive study by J. Krejčí and V. Velimský, *Ethnic and Political Nations in Europe* (London: Croom Helm, 1981), 112–14. Both authors argue that by dominating the Russian/Soviet Federated Socialist Republic (RSFSR), the largest "parent" holding company of the empire, the Great-Russians controlled all the "daughter" companies within the USSR and the Soviet bloc.

31 Zbigniew Brzezinski, "Tragic Dilemmas of Soviet World Power: The Limits of a New-Type Empire," *Encounter* 61/4 (December 1983), 10.

32 Mikhail Bernstam predicts that there will be a mere 107 million Great-Russians by the year 2050, whereas Soviet Muslims will number 141 million, if the present fertility rates persist. See Bernstam in Conquest, *The Last Empire* (1986), 322–3.

33 John B. Dunlop, *The Faces of Contemporary Russian Nationalism* (Princeton, N.J.: Princeton University Press, 1983), 136.

34 Frederick C. Barghoorn, "Russian Nationalism and Soviet Politics: Official and Unofficial Perspectives," in Conquest (1986), 32; Teresa Rakowska-Harmstone, "Minority Nationalism Today: An Overview," ibid., 237.

35 Gorbachev, *Perestroika* (1987), 118–22.

36 Yu.V. Bromlei, *Etnos i etnografiya* (Moscow: Nauka, 1973); idem, *Soviet Ethnology and Anthropology Today* (The Hague: Mouton, 1974); idem and K. V. Chistov, "Velikiy Oktyabr' i Sovetskaya etnografiya," *Sovetskaya Etnografiya* 5 (1987), 3–18. For a recent analysis, see Peter Skalnik, "Towards an understanding of Soviet etnos theory," *South African Journal of Ethnology* 9/4 (1986), 157–66.

37 See the summary critique of Gumilyov in V.I. Kozlov, "O biologogeo-graficheskoi kontseptsii etnicheskoi istorii," *Voprosy istorii* 12 (December 1974), 73–85; and its abbreviated version in *The Current Digest of the Soviet Press* 27/20 (June 11, 1975), 1–5.

38 *Literaturnaya Gazeta* (Moscow) of May 28, 1986.

39 Dunlop, *Faces of Contemporary Russian Nationalism* (1983), 141–45.

40 Agursky, *The Third Rome* (1987), 184–87. See also Agursky, *Ideologiya Natsional-Bolshevizma* (Paris: YMCA Press, 1980); Nikolai V. Ustryalov, *Pod znakom revolyutsii* (Kharbin, 1927).

41 Agursky, *The Third Rome* (1987), 283–87, 313–15.

42 See Sergei Semanov's patriotic book *Serdtse rodiny* (The Heart of Motherland, 1977), with a strong cult of military leaders and in which the Russian idea is contrasted with the Western-inspired Jewish-Masonic conspiracy against it. John B. Dunlop, *The New Russian Nationalism* (New York: Praeger, 1985), 90. For speculations on future military dictatorship in the USSR by the end of the century, see views of leading Western sovietologists: Michel Tatu in *Newsweek* (November 22, 1982), 42, and Jerry Hough in *Problems of Communism* (September-October 1982), 27.
43 Dunlop, *Faces of Contemporary Russian Nationalism* (1983), 242; idem, *New Russian Nationalism* (1985), 88.
44 Barghoorn in Conquest, *The Last Empire* (1986), 34, 39.
45 Yanov, *Russian New Right* (1978), 113, 127.
46 See *From under the Rubble*, ed. A. I. Solzhenitsyn (London: Fontana, 1976).
47 Ibid. for three essays by Igor Shafarevich.
48 See note 28. Dunlop, *Faces of Contemporary Russian Nationalism* (1983).
49 On Ilya Glazunov as the protagonist of the Russian idea and his popularity among the Russians, see Vladislav Krasnov, "Russian National Feeling: An Informal Poll," in Conquest (1986), 109–30.
50 See Dunlop, *Faces of Contemporary Russian Nationalism* (1983), 164, who nevertheless believes that a majority of Russian nationalists was then in favor of the secession of non-Russian republics.
51 Solzhenitsyn, *From under the Rubble* (1976), 105–43.
52 Included in A. Solzhenitsyn, *East and West* (New York: Harper & Row, 1980), 75–142.
53 See chapter 4, Yuzhakov and Fyodorov, pp. 52 ff.
54 Solzhenitsyn, *From under the Rubble* (1976), 141–42.
55 Fedor Nesterov, *Svyaz' Vremyon* (Moscow: Molodaya Gvardiya, 1980).
56 M. Agursky, "The Prospects of National Bolshevism," in Conquest (1986), 103–105.

3

Historians and Geographers

Historians and Russia's Civilizing Mission in Asia

In tracing one of the most important ideological roots of Russia's drive to the East (*Stremlenie na Vostok*) into the steppes and mountains of Asia, one must single out the popular, patriotic Russian historiography, which consistently presented Russian territorial expansion as the unfolding of Manifest Destiny.

Mikhail P. Pogodin (1800–75), a prominent history professor at the Moscow University, became a passionate Pan-Slavist, preaching the superiority of the Russian Aryan race (the tribe of Japheth) predestined to rule over Eurasia. His racial imperialism was stronger than his Russian patriotism. He applauded the British victory over the Sepoy Mutiny in India—despite widespread anti-British feelings among the Russian population following the Crimean War. Pogodin's views on the benefits of imperialism were inflexible. He remained convinced that it was "impossible to educate Africa and Asia, except by fitting out an army from all of Europe and sending it on a crusade against them. Let Europeans . . . establish a European order of things there. . . . The happiness of mankind depends on it."[1] Although Pogodin was less concerned with Asia than with Europe, he said enough about the former to reveal one powerful undercurrent of Russian imperialistic ideology. Although his country lay defeated and isolated after the Crimean War, Pogodin urged his countrymen to divert the expansionist drive eastward.

Leaving Europe alone, in expectation of more favorable circumstances we must turn our entire attention to Asia, which we have almost entirely left out of our considerations although it is precisely Asia that is predestined primarily for us. And it is also Asia that our enemies . . . not with good intentions, want to hurl us! What would the English have done with our territorial and other connections in Asia! . . . Let the European peoples live as they best know how . . . whereas to us belongs, in addition, half of Asia, China, Japan, Tibet, Bukhara, Khiva, Kokand, Persia, if we want to, and perhaps must, extend our possessions to spread the European element in Asia, so that Japheth may rise above his brothers.[2]

Sergei M. Solovyov (1820–79), the eminent historian and author of a 29-volume history of Russia and of numerous textbooks used in schools and universities,[3] emphasized three basic traits of Russia's territorial expansion: (1) geography, as the principal determinant of Russia's historical expansion and her march into Asia; (2) the role of natural frontiers, which in Solovyov's interpretation had made Russia into a state characterized by an "organic formation" and which, therefore, must expand in the absence of mountian barriers right across the entire Eurasian steppe;[4] and (3) Russia's colonization of the east as an important part of disseminating European civilization among the Asiatic barbarians, thereby facilitating the eventual assimilation by the Great Russian people.[5]

To the leading historian, Vasiliy O. Klyuchevsky (1841–1911), the history of Russia was the history of a country in a process of colonization and assimilation. To Klyuchevsky colonization was the common denominator, the central theme of his understanding of national history, and the dominant axiom in Russia's fulfillment of the civilizing mission across the steppes of Eurasia, along the Volga, in the Caucasus, and in Turkestan. Natural geographic frontiers were less important to him than the ever-advancing ethnographic boundary formed by the presence of the Cossacks and Russian settlers.[6] The formation of the Great Russian nation, in Klyuchevsky's views, was the outcome of amalgamation with other races (*plemena*) through military conquest and colonization, completed with Russification.

The great liberal historian and politician, Pavel N. Milyukov (1859–1943) likewise saw the process of Russian colonizaton as a merger of diverse ethnographic groups, at all possible stages of

Russification, into one Great Russian nation, which was to become eventually a single political and cultural community.[7]

Such was the legacy of leading Russian historians of the imperialist era. Whether conservative or liberal, they helped build the consensus not only for ceaseless expansion, but also for the aggressive policy of Russification in the western borderlands after the 1880s. Yet, the prevalent ideology with regard to racial coexistence favored assimilation—not segregation. Non-Russians, provided they became Orthodox Christians, were not considered inferior. Vis-à-vis their Muslim subjects, Russian administrators did not apply a uniform policy. Among Tatars and Kazakhs, broadly speaking, the policy of slow assimilation was pursued, whereas in Turkestan strict noninterference into native religious and legal matters prevailed.[8] In Central Asia the Russians made a conscious effort to appear as bearers of a superior Western civilization because they knew the world viewed them as direct challengers to the British colonial venture on the Indian subcontinent.

According to the leading Bolshevik historian and Lenin's friend, Mikhail N. Pokrovsky (1868–1932), the Russian Empire had been built exclusively on aggression and boundless expansion; he could not detect a single case of "voluntary annexation," not even in the case of Georgia. Although himself a Great Russian, Pokrovsky referred to "Russia's civilizing mission" with scorn and contempt. In his work he subordinated all historical factors to the supreme criterion of class struggle. He rejected the idea, later cultivated by the anti-Pokrovsky school of Soviet historians, that Tsarist colonialism had brought progress to the peoples of the Caucasus and Central Asia and that these non-Russian peoples had preferred the Russians to other conquerers (for example, the Turks, Persians, and British).[9]

In 1929 the historian V. Karpych, drawing a parallel between Russia's colonizing mission and Marx's positive appreciation of British imperialism in India, disagreed with Pokrovsky's main thesis that Tsarist colonial policy in Central Asia had been anything other than an unmitigated tragedy. Karpych's arguments appeared to be, at the time, the first and modest harbingers of later Soviet contentions leading to the "progress and lesser evil" thesis. Stalinist historians of the anti-Pokrovsky school argued the theory that Tsarist annexations of the borderlands resulted in social and economic progress, which the Soviet regime could further develop.[10] Karpych's views were refuted in 1934 by another historian of Central Asia, E. Shteinberg, who adhered to the Pokrovsky thesis. He obviously knew how to quote the founding fathers with greater skill.

> Marx, as well as Engels, always underlines the characteristics of Russian colonial expansion as a movement which was reactionary, Asiatic, and semi-medieval.... Therefore one cannot equate British policy in India, a policy which was carried out by a young capitalistic, manufacturing state, and Russian aggression in Central Asia, coming from a barbaric, half-Asiatic, feudal, gendarme empire.[11]

Geographers: Russia's Vanguard in Central Asia

Another strong intellectual impulse for the expansion into Asia came from the Russian Geographical society, founded in St. Petersburg in 1845. Its talented members, spearheaded by a group of enterprising military geographers, played the Great Game of Central Asia with their British counterparts.[12] An interesting phenomenon in Russia's geographical exploration and military conquest of Asia was the extraordinarily large number of Germans, most of them of Baltic origin, who inspired and led a great many of these ventures. Their influence on the military and administrative sides of the Russian eastward expansion is well known. Some of the recognized experts and internationally renowned scholars active in the Society must be mentioned here: Karl Baer, P. Helmerson, R. Maak, P. Köppen, G. I. Radde, L. E. Schwartz, W. Struve, F. P. Wrangel, and, of course, the society's founding vice-president, Admiral F. F. Lütke.[13] Although the German presence was resented from the beginning by a promising group of young Russians (future explorers and scholars V. V. Grigorev, N. N. Muravyov, G. I. Nevelskoy, P. P. Semyonov), their influence was to remain predominant throughout the entire period.

The cross-fertilization of Russian experience and tradition with German scholarship and exploration was indeed extraordinary, particularly far away from the Baltic, Eastern Europe, and the Balkans, where the German *Drang nach Osten* clashed with Russian interests moving in the opposite direction. But east of the

Urals, in remote Asia, the German *Drang* went for the most part hand in hand with Russia's *Stremlenie na Vostok*. Although Kaiser Wilhelm II advocated a Teutonic alliance against the Slavs in Eastern Europe, he was in the habit of writing enthusiastic letters to his "dearest Nicky," in which he encouraged his imperial cousin to proceed with the colonial expansion in Central Asia and the Far East.

> I should certainly do everything in my power, to keep Europe quiet and to protect Russia's back, so that no one could interfere with your action directed to the Far East. For here lies obviously Russia's great future task, to turn her attention toward the Asiatic Continent and to protect Europe against the attacks of the yellow race.[14]

The geographers shared with the historians the notion of Russia's messianic mission in the East. The orientalist, V. V. Grigorev, asked rhetorically in 1840, "Who is closer to Asia than us? . . . Which of the European races preserved in itself more of the Asiatic element than the Slavs, who were the last to leave their primeval homeland?" He argued that it must have been Providence that preserved the Asian population untouched by foreign influence so that the task of colonizing them in a virgin state would befall the Russians.[15] One of the most prominent members of the Society and its second vice-president (1873–1914), Pyotr P. Semyonov (1827–1914), thought likewise. Having studied in Berlin under the great geographer, Karl Ritter, whose *Erdkunde Asiens* he later helped to translate into Russian, Semyonov soon became known for his own explorations in Asia (the Tsar gave him the title *Tyan-Shansky* in commemoration of the mountain range in Central Asia). In 1855 Semyonov published in the Society's journal the following programmatic words on Russia's *Mission Civilisatrice* in Asia:

> Selected by God as an intermediary between the West and the East, having received Christianity in the capital of an Eastern Empire [i.e., Constantinople], having spent its adolescence as a European hostage in captivity of Asiatic tribes, and having been cast by a will of genius [i.e., Peter the Great] into the midst of European development, she has identical similarities to both Europe and Asia, and belongs equally to both parts of the world.[16]

Colonel Venyukov

Some 20 years later, when Russian troops had already swallowed up western Turkestan, Semyonov's younger colleague, the Military geographer and noted explorer, Colonel Mikhail I. Venyukov (1832–1901), published "The Progress of Russia in Central Asia." This significant article is a remarkably sophisticated and eloquent argument justifying Russian colonization of Central Asia on cultural, religious, economic, political, and racial grounds; indeed, one might even describe it as a Russian version of the Manifest Destiny in Asia. The racial argument, in Venyukov's language called "ethnological," was elaborated on to score an advantage against the British in India. Venyukov spoke, namely, of the legitimate Russian claim demanding the "return of the Slavs to the neighborhood of their prehistoric home . . . and the cradle of the Aryan or Indo-European race . . . at the sources of the Indus and Oxus," whence "our ancestors" had been displaced by the Turko-Mongol invaders. Moreover, despite the profound cultural differences between the Russians and Central Asian Muslims, Venyukov believed in a kind of racial merger. Mixed marriages between the two peoples would preserve the best qualities of the Aryan and Turanian races through selective breeding, what we would call today social eugenics. Quoting the example of the Terek Cossacks, who had long been marrying the daughters of Caucasian mountaineers, Venyukov felt confident that the Russian type of colonization was superior to that of the British in India.

> We are not Englishmen who in India do their utmost to avoid mingling with the natives, and who moreover, sooner or later, may pay for it by the loss of that country, where they have no ties of race. Our strength on the contrary lies in the fact that up to the present time we have assimilated subject races, mingling affably with them. It is desirable that this historical result should not be forgotten also in the future, especially on our arrival at the sources of the Oxus, where we must create an entirely Russian border country as the sole guarantee of the stability of our position in Turkestan.[17]

Navel of the Earth

What caused the redirection of Russian expansion toward Central Asia? The causal chain was probably forged during the Crimean War (1853–56). The lost war and Russia's subsequent political failures in Europe helped delay her aggressive designs against the Ottoman Empire. The suppression of the Polish uprising of 1863, which further alienated Russia from the West, coincided with the final conquest of the Caucasus. After the surrender of the legendary Imam Shamil, the 200,000-strong Army of the Caucasus, pushed by its ambitious officer corps, became available for another civilizing mission just across the Caspian Sea.[18] In the absence of an overriding economic motivation (in 1880 Russian imports from Asia as a whole still accounted for a mere 5 percent and exports for 3 percent),[19] such unquantifiable impulses as the spirit of *reconquista* among the Russian military, anxious to defeat the descendants of the Great Tatar horde, played an important role.[20]

The restoration of Russia's national prestige became the number one priority. Under the new Tsar Alexander II (1855–81), Russia was to undergo a series of internal reforms and redirect her foreign policy toward Asia, primarily Central Asia. The architect of this Asia first policy was the able Prince A. M. Gorchakov, the new foreign minister (1856–83). In his first memorandum to the Tsar in 1856, he argued that Russia should turn away from Europe and expand in the future her national interest in Asia, even at the price of directly confronting her major rival, the British Empire.[21]

In the approaches to Central Asia, military considerations proved decisive. The Russian military were taking full advantage of the ill-defined "moving frontiers" (*podvizhnye granitsy*), insufficiently covered by the Cossacks in the steppes of Central Asia.[22] Here new opportunities presented themselves to adventurous proconsuls who tried to exploit their fortunes by steadily pushing the undefined frontiers ahead, often in defiance of instructions from St. Petersburg. This then created the classic environment for the pursuit of the Great Game on the fringes of the Empire in Central Asia.

Like the British advancing from their Indian stronghold in the northwest direction, the Russians became entangled, as Prince Gorchakov put it in his often-quoted circular note of November 1864, in the same dilemma of being drawn "from annexation to annexation . . . and of not knowing where to stop."[23] Gorchakov cleverly insisted that Russia, in the interests of further trade and introducing law and order among wild tribes in Central Asia, was doing nothing but following the example of the United States in America, Great Britain in India, and France in Africa. It is surprising that he did not use a much more effective argument in favor of Russian imperialism, namely, that its territorial expansion proceeded in regions contiguous to the homeland. Russia did not have to cross the seas to conquer distant islands and continents that could not possibly threaten the European metropolis. Following the military frontiersmen came thousands of Russian and Ukrainian landless peasants. Freed from serfdom after 1861, they pushed their settlements deeper and deeper into the interior of Siberia and Central Asia. It was Prince Gorchakov and his British counterpart, Lord Clarendon, who together created the legend of military insubordination, blaming adventurous army officers, Russian and British alike, for ignoring instructions from their respective governments and for enjoying the Great Game too much.[24]

However, the overriding factor stimulating Russia's expansion southward was the desire to challenge the British Empire along the Asian rimland, for purposes of strategic diversion and subversion and for the sake of prestige. Russia wished to appear as an equal rival in the fulfillment of a "Civilized Christian Mission" in areas considered more underdeveloped than Russia proper. This is turn boosted the egos of the conquerors and helped them to forget the backwardness of Mother Russia.[25]

A strong element of fatalism pervaded this race to the southern tier, whose definitive border line was never specified. Was it the Oxus, the Pamir range called the roof of the world, the Hindu Kush, the Indus, or the distant attraction of the Persian Gulf, which had already been mentioned in the apocryphal testament of Peter the Great? In rapid succession the great cities of Turkestan, Chimkent, Tashkent, Khojend, and Samarkand were taken. "General Chernyaev took Tashkent," noted the interior minister, Count P. A. Valuev, in his diary of July 1865, "nobody knows why and for what purpose . . . there is something erotic (*nechto eroticheskoe*) in all our activities at the distant periphery of the Empire."[26]

The southeast drive to the imaginary center of Eurasia indeed seems to have possessed an almost mystical attraction for the

Russians, as seen in the case of Venyukov. There was a widespread belief that somewhere between the great civilizations of China and India, in the midst of the highest mountains in the world where few Europeans had ventured after Marco Polo, there lay an ancient center of Aryan cosmography, "a mountain of blazing appearance, the central core of the universe and navel of the Earth . . . an Asian Olympus of cosmic proportions."[27] It was also widely believed that from the slopes of this mysterious mountain, called Kailas, the four mighty rivers of Central Asia sprang, "believed to have rocked the cradle of our race," as Lord Curzon wrote in 1898.[28] Whoever controlled the sources of these waters could one day become the caretaker of the shrines belonging to the "first Adam" on our planet, the originator of the Aryan race. It was, therefore, not just a coincidence that the Russian Emperor, already credited with the successorship to the Second Rome (that is, deriving from Constantinople, the capital of Byzantium) and the guardianship of Christ's tomb (that is, "the second Adam") in the Holy Sepulchre Church in Jerusalem, added to his many titles that of the ruler of Pamir (*Pamirsky*).[29]

The Russians and the British were not the only ones attracted by this powerful magnet in the center of Eurasia. Centuries ago, the great Alexander of Macedonia was allured, and more recently, Napoleon. It required a romantic German mind, one also rigorously trained by the modern *Wissenschaft* (as in the case of Sven Hedin), to wander to these far-off places toward which the Nietzschean and Wagnerian *Übermensch* interminably traveled.[30]

Notes

1 Riasanovsky, "Russia and Asia" (1960), 181, and "Asia through Russian Eyes" (1972), 14–16.
2 M. P. Pogodin, "O russkoi politike na budushchee vremya," *Istoriko-politicheskie pis'ma i zapiski v prodolzhenii Krymskoi voiny, 1853–56* (Moscow, 1874), 242–43.
3 S. M. Solovyov, *Istoriya Rossiis drevneishikh vremën*, 29 vols. (Moscow, 1851–79); second edition, 15 vols. (Moscow: Izdatel'stvo sotsialno-ekonomicheskoi literatury 1959–66).
4 S. M. Solovyov, "O vliyanii prirody russkoi gosudarstvennoi oblasti na istoriyu," *Otechestvennye zapiski* 69/ii (1859), 229–44.
5 Summed up by Seymour Becker in "The Muslim East in Nineteenth-Century Russian Popular Historiography," *Central Asian Survey* 5/3–4 (1986), 25–47.

6 Ibid.; V. O. Klyuchevsky, *Kurs russkoi istorii* (Moscow, 1956), I:31–32.
7 P. N. Milyukov, *Ocherki po istorii russkoi kultury* (St. Petersburg, 1896), I:54–55.
8 Richard A. Pierce, *Russia in Central Asia 1867–1917* (Berkeley: University of California Press, 1960), 203–20; Martha Brill Olcott, *The Kazakhs* (Stanford: Hoover, 1987).
9 M. N. Pokrovsky, *Diplomatiya i voiny tsarskoi Rossii v XIX stoletii* (Moscow: Krasnaya nov', 1923). The fate of the Pokrovsky school in the USSR is discussed in *Rewriting Russian History*, ed. Cyril E. Black (New York: A. A. Knopf, 1956); Lowell Tillett, *The Great Friendship: Soviet Historians on the Non-Russian Nationalities* (Chapel Hill: University of North Carolina Press, 1969).
10 Tillett, *The Great Friendship* (1969), 360–61.
11 Ibid.; E. Shteinberg, *Ocherki istorii Turkmenii* (Moscow-Leningrad, 1934), 47–59.
12 For the origins of the Great Game in Central Asia, see M. Hauner, "The Last Great Game," *The Middle East Journal* 38/1 (Winter 1984), 72–84.
13 Mark Bassin, "The Russian Geographical Society and the Great Siberian Expedition 1855–1863," *Annals of the Association of American Geographers* 73/2 (1983), 242. For more details on the overwhelming German influence on Oriental studies in Russia, see R. Frye, "Oriental Studies in Russia" (1972), 30–51.
14 Gollwitzer, *Die Gelbe Gefahr* (1962), 212.
15 V. V. Grigorev, *Ob otnoshenii Rossii k Vostoku* (Odessa, 1840); cited in Bassin, "The Russian Geographical Society" (1983), 243.
16 P. P. Semyonov, *Vestnik Imperatorskogo Russkogo Geograficheskago Obshchestva* 15 (1855), 254; cited in Bassin, "The Russian Geographical Society" (1983), 244.
17 M. I. Venyukov, "Postupatel'noe dvizhenie Rossii v Srednei Azii," *Sbornik gosudarstvennykh znaniy* 3 (1877), St. Petersburg; see also India Office Records: L/P&S/18/C 17 (hereinafter abbreviated as 'IOR').
18 Sir Louis Mallet, "Historical Summary of the Central Asian Question," April 30, 1874, IOR: L/P&S/18/C 9.
19 Dietrich Geyer, *Der russische Imperialismus* (Göttingen: Vandenhoeck & Ruprecht, 1977), 77. For the standard Soviet interpretation that, in all instances, subordinates military conquest to economic motivation, see N. A. Khalfin, *Prisoedinenie Srednei Azii k Rossii* (Moscow: Nauka, 1965).
20 Michael Rywkin, *Moscow's Muslim Challenge: Soviet Central Asia* (Armonk: Sharpe, 1982), 18.
21 G. V. Chicherin, "Rossiya i aziatskie narody," *Vestnik NKID*, no. 2, August 13, 1919. Reprinted in idem *Stati i rechi* (Moscow: Izdatel'stvo Sotsialno-ekonomicheskoi literatury, 1961), 86–98.
22 On the Russian parallel to Frederick J. Turner's Frontier Theory, see the following: Carsten Goehrke, "Geographische Grundlagen der russischen Geschichte," *Jahrbücher für Geschichte Osteuropas* 18 (1970), 161–204; Goehrke, "Die geographischen Gegebenheiten Russlands in ihrem historischen Beziehungsgeflecht," in *Handbuch der Geschichte Russlands* 1/I, ed. Manfred Hellmann (Stuttgart: A. Hiersemann Vlg, 1981), 9–72; R. J. Kerner, *The Urge to the Sea: The Course of Russian History* (Berkeley:

University of California Press, 1942); B. H. Sumner, *A Short History of Russia* (New York: Harcourt, Brace & World, 1943); Hans Raupach, "Atlantische und eurasische Wirtschaft," *Politische Bildung* 45 (1954), 183–97; Raupach, "Space, Time and the Choice of a Centralized System," *Jahrbuch der Wirtschaft Osteuropas* 2 (1971), 123–36; J. L. Wieczynski, "Toward a Frontier Theory of Early Russian History," *Russian Review* 33 (1974), 284–95, and *The Russian Frontier. The Impact of Borderlands Upon the Course of Early Russian History* (Charlottesville: University of Virginia Press, 1976).

23 W. Kerr Fraser-Tytler, *Afghanistan* (New York: Oxford University Press, 1953), 319–23; Hans Rogger, *Russia in the Age of Modernisation and Revolution 1881–1917* (London: Longman, 1983), 164–65.

24 Firuz Kazemzadeh, *Russia and Britain in Persia, 1864–1914. A Study in Imperialism* (New Haven: Yale University Press, 1968), 15.

25 Geyer, *Der russische Imperialismus* (1977), 80–81.

26 P. A. Zaionchkovskyi (ed.), *Dnevnik P. A. Valueva, 1865–1876*, vol. 2 (Moscow, 1961), 60–61, entry July 20, 1865.

27 Charles Allen, *A Mountain in Tibet. The Search for Mount Kailas and the Sources of the Great Rivers of India* (London: Futura, 1983), 11–13, 192–93.

28 G. N. Curzon, *The Pamir and the Source of the Oxus* (London: Royal Geographical Society, 1898), 1.

29 Sarkisyanz, *Russland und der Messianismus* (1955), 105, 211. See also chapter 4 on Yuzhakov and Fyodorov.

30 Robert Strausz-Hupé, *Geopolitics. The Struggle for Space and Power* (New York: Putnam, 1942), 155. See chapter 8 for more on Sven Hedin.

4

Easterners and Eurasianists

The "Yellow Peril" Threat

For Dostoevsky, Asia was exemplified by Muslim Central Asia rather than by Buddhist East Asia, because he regarded the Christian struggle against Islam and the opposition to the British world hegemony as Russia's legitimate aspirations. However, an extremist branch of frustrated Slavophiles appeared on the scene during the 1880s and turned their attention more exclusively to East Asia. Called the *Vostochniki* ("Easterners"), they preached that Russia's holy mission could no longer be accomplished in the regions of the traditional Pan-Slavist ideology, that is, in predominantly the Balkans and Eastern Europe, but rather in the opposite direction, in faraway Inner and East Asia.

In their ranks figured such prominent personalities as professors Fyodor F. Martens (1845–1909) and Vasiliy P. Vasilev (1818–1900); Martens was Russia's foremost authority in international law, Vasilev a leading sinologist at St. Petersburg University. Martens, in his two propaganda pamphlets (*Russia and China; Russia and England in Central Asia*), justified the Russian conquest of Central Asian and Chinese territories by arguing that "international rights cannot be taken into account when dealing with semibarbarous peoples."[1]

As an influential international promoter of Prince Gorchakov's Asia first policy, Martens tried his best to defuse the growing Anglo-Russian antagonism by stating unambiguously that the two empires should actually cooperate in Central Asia, where they were the only representatives of European civilization. Russia was not trying to defeat the British in India, Martens wrote, because such a dubious victory with the assistance of native troops would be extremely counterproductive to Russia. It would almost certainly revolutionize not only India but also Asia. It was not in Russia's national interest to stir up the smoldering flames of yet another anti-British rebellion in India, such as the Great Mutiny put down in 1858. The establishment of independent Asian states, argued Martens, would cause only immense embarrassments in St. Petersburg, which preferred "the existence of a civilized and Christian government in Calcutta."[2]

By the same token, Martens eloquently wrote in his second propaganda pamphlet that China must not be allowed to succeed over Russia. Such an event would only inflame more hatred against all European powers and lead to a forceful expulsion of all "foreign devils" from China.[3] As for Professor Vasilev, he preached publicly that Russia was advancing in the East, in contrast to all other European colonial powers, in order to liberate oppressed peoples from the "tyranny of internecine strife and impotency."[4] In his article "China's Progress," Vasilev painted the specter of another Mongol invasion. He warned that if China were to control the rich islands of the Pacific, "she could become simultaneously a threat to Russia, America, India and Western Europe . . . and ultimately destroy the whole world, which will then be populated exclusively by the Chinese."[5]

A somewhat softer and seemingly more benevolent attitude toward non-Aryans was demonstrated by the most noted explorer of Russia's Asiatic frontiers, General Nikolai M. Przewalski (1839–88). He tried to assure the Russian public that the inhabitants of Mongolia and Sinkiang were eager to become subjects of the White Tsar, to whose name they allegedly attributed the same mystic powers as that of the Dalai Lama.[6] Even the leading Russian anarchist of the nineteenth century, Mikhail A. Bakunin (1814–76), felt compelled to make rather bizarre contributions to the unfolding "Yellow Peril" debate. After escaping from Siberian exile via Japan and the United States to England in 1861, he presented his vision in a pamphlet called *La théologie politique de Mazzini et l'Internationale*. Bakunin's vision of the future global conflict was basically a racial, bipolar image of the world divided into a white

Caucasian group of some 350 million threatened with destruction by a bloc of some 850 million Asians. Bakunin had already predicted the demise of the large colonial empires of Great Britain and Russia. He regarded Russian control of the Amur region and of Siberia as fictitious, because there could never be enough European settlers to offset the vast Chinese potential in cross-border immigration. Russian possessions in Asia, he predicted, would not last more than another 50 years.[7]

Bakunin saw as the solution a world proletarian solidarity that would, regardless of racial differences, unite the have-nots on the basis of class struggle. Another Russian of a completely different professional background saw the solution against the "Threat from the East" as a kind of colonial solidarity between the Christian powers of the West, notably Russia and Great Britain, opposing the non-Christian forces of Asia. This man was General Aleksei N. Kuropatkin (1848–1925). He participated in the conquest of Central Asia as one of General Skobelev's adjutants, served as Russia's minister of war (1898–1904), shared in the responsibility for the defeat of Russian troops by the Japanese in 1905 as commander-in-chief in the Far East, and terminated his career as the last governor general of Turkestan (1916–17). His views, however, that the thin Russian settlements in Asia could not survive the oncoming waves of the yellow race were substantially the same as those of the anarchist Bakunin.[8]

The views of Martens, Vasilev, and the like represented one extreme of the "Russian Idea" vis-à-vis Asia, an attitude that could only be identified with racial imperialism of which the most conspicuous manifestation was the fear of the "Yellow Peril" (Zhëltaya Ugroza). Advocates of this dark perspective instinctively opposed the idea of assimilation between the Russian-Aryan race and the yellow and Turanian races of Asia. The assimilation view, on the other hand, was favored by liberal imperialists like Colonel Venyukov. The scope of both public and official Russian attitudes toward the "Yellow Peril" is much more complex than a one-dimensional, black and white image of two contrasting views. One would also have to include, among many other varied sources, Tolstoy's "Letter to the Chinese"[9] or the opinions of the remarkable self-made pacifist and theoretician of war, Johann S. Blokh (1836–1902).[10]

Like that of other European colonial powers, Russian imperialist thinking, in its preoccupation with the "Yellow Peril," could not escape the influence of a certain biological and economic determinism, such as propounded in neo-Malthusian and neo-Darwinian theories. Such theories warned of the rising imbalance between overpopulation (growing in geometrical progression) and the means of subsistence (increasing in arithmetical progression).[11] In Russia's case, however, the fear of overpopulation was usually not applied to her own subjects (on the contrary, as we see, the Russian demographic explosion as confirmed by the 1897 census, gave her an undisputed lead among all great powers and another stimulus to the liberal imperialist camp[12]), but to the Chinese "coolies" who were seen as migrating irresistably in all directions.[13] The thin layer of Russian farmers and tradesmen in the Cossack settlements along the Amur and Ussuri borderlands could not withstand the influx of resourceful Chinese and Koreans without the protection of the racially discriminatory Tsarist ordinance of 1882, which barred non-Russians from acquiring land in Siberia.[14]

Yuzhakov and Fyodorov

As Britain and Russia came close to war over Afghanistan, Sergei N. Yuzhakov (1849–1910) in his *Anglo-Russian Conflict* offered the historical-philosophical interpretation of the two contrasting expansionist drives in Asia. Peasant Russia came to rescue other Asiatic agricultural countries from nomadic Asia, from Turan ("Ahriman's Asia"). Russian colonialism, based on military-peasant settlements, developed, therefore, in sharp contrast to usury inspired, British trade colonialism, which was based on reckless exploitation of Asian resources without putting anything back into the soil. Writing on behalf of the *narodniki*, Yuzhakov suggested that Russia, through the influx of her peasantry, could be the renovator of Asia. She could protect the Asian nationalities of Siberia and spread the message of agrarian socialism among the peasant communes of India and China in order to rally them against Western capitalist exploitation.[15]

The dualism between the civilization based on the cultivation of soil and that of the nomadic steppe formed the dynamic principle of history in the philosophy of Nikolai F. Fyodorov (1828–1903), regarded by many as the most formidable and original Russian thinker of the nineteenth century.[16] He believed that the Russian peasant communes possessed unique virtues that could save the world from decadence; that agriculture, as opposed to trade and usury, was endowed with the resurrectional quality that transformed the dead ancestral dust into live plants and animals. In Fyodorov's vision, the agrarian civilizations of Russia and Asia (that is, Iran, India, and China) were waging a defensive struggle against the nomadic powers of the steppe allied with the sea powers. He visualized the struggle between China and England as one prolonged conflict between the "cult of ancestors" and the "cult of gold." As for Russia, she must align herself with one or the other. She could join the West in strangling "the oldest empire in the world," or she could abstain from such wicked association and work for the "eternal peace between the white and yellow tsars." Fyodorov's advice was that Russia should separate herself from the "European and American bandits" and side with the underdogs of Asia; she should, for instance, assist the Indian peasants to regain possession of the soil.[17]

Fyodorov's preoccupation with the Indian question was not mere caprice. In 1899 he visited a friend in Ashkhabad, the capital of Russian Transcaspia, and traveled in Turkestan as far as the Pamirs. In Ashkhabad Fyodorov agreed to publish two installments in the local journal presenting his reflections about the Anglo-Russian rivalry and its solution. The anonymous article (the utopian philosopher Fyodorov refused to publish it under his name or to accept an honorarium) carried an unusual title: "About the Conversion of Destructive Weapons into Weapons of Salvation."[18] Russia, Fyodorov assures his readers, does not want to rule over India; she is merely seeking justice for the sake of the destitute Indian peasant and in "defense of all exploited peoples." The most effective "non-destructive weapon" Russia can use to force industrial Britain to relinquish her rule over the peasant India, Fyodorov suggests, is the extension of a railroad to the gates of India.

Eventually, Fyodorov stood in awe before the Pamirs, the "roof of the world," which played such an important symbolic role in his cosmology. The vicinity of the Pamirs could only enhance the universal influence of India, for Fyodorov recognized two focal centers of civilization: one was Constantinople, the living metropolis where the Greko-Slav world met the Christian West, and the other the Pamirs, the ancestral necropolis of the Aryan race and the cradle of Indo-European languages. His utopian vision led him to believe that one day this sacred summit would witness a reconciliation between Russia and Great Britain.[19]

Fyodorov's utopian reflections on the cosmic importance of the world "center of expiation"[20] had only a very limited circulation inside Russia because he published so little during his lifetime. They were known to a few close friends, like V. A. Kozhevnikov and N. P. Peterson, and to their mutual acquaintances, including Dostoevsky, Tolstoy, and Solovyov, who acknowledged their intellectual indebtedness to Fyodorov. There was, however, a major shift in Russia's imperialist policy, which Fyodorov did not seem to notice during the last two decades of the nineteenth century—a little diversion here and there in Central Asia against the British notwithstanding. Russia's Asian policy was focusing on the Far East, where it was only a question of time before she would clash with Japan's own expansionism directed against China and Korea. The anticipation of this approaching clash was to stain the whole Asian debate among various groups of Russian intelligentsia and allow "Yellow Peril" advocates to prevail over the moderates.

Pan-Mongolism

Perhaps no one appeared more obsessed by the specter of Russia defending Europe against the oncoming hordes of Asiatic invaders than the remarkable religious philosopher and mystic, Vladimir S. Solovyov (1853–1900), son of the great historian S. M. Solovyov. Vladimir Solovyov's explicitly racist variations on the theme of "Yellow Peril," such as his famous poem *Panmongolism* (1894) or his last essay *The Antichrist* (1900), which depicted a new Mongol invasion of Europe under Japanese leadership in the course of the twentieth century, commanded large audiences in and out of Russia.[21] Solovyov believed, as did many of his contemporaries who used the "Yellow Peril" threat, that what he classified as "inferior" races were condemned either to submission by "superior" ones or to "disappearance." Only the anarchists, like Peter Kropotkin, dared to challenge Solovyov's views directly.[22] The Bolsheviks did so, but from a rather simplistic platform, when they drew parallels between the official "Yellow Peril" propaganda and anti-Semitism.[23]

Solovyov's pervasive preaching was strongly reflected in the writings of Russia's leading group of poets, the Symbolists, including Andrei Belyi[24] and Alexander Blok, Solovyov's former disciple. Blok's famous poem *The Scythians*, written on the eve of the Brest-Litovsk Peace, is consciously prefaced with Solovyov's opening stanza from *Pan-mongolism:* "Panmongolism! Though the name is fierce, yet it caresses my ear." Blok's poem gave name to an entire literary movement (*Skify*).[25] Distorted by Russia's tragic fate, Blok reverses his master's message and advocates a Russo-Scythian alliance against arrogant Europe; his warning is an undisguised *aziatchina:*

> You're millions, we are hosts—and hosts—and hosts!
> Engage with us and prove our seed!
> We're Scythians and Asians too, from coasts
> That breed squint eyes, bespeaking greed!
>
> Russia is a Sphinx! Triumphant, though in pain,
> She bathes her limbs in blood's dark stream.
> Her gaze on you—gaze and gaze again
> With hate and love in single beam![26]

Even as late as 1923, after Bolshevik Russia won the Civil War, another gifted Russian poet, Sergei Esenin, wrote from Germany making no pretense to conceal his deep contempt for Europe:

> Let us be Asians, let us stink, let us scratch our buttocks shamelessly in sight of everyone. Even so, we don't have such a putrid smell as they have inside. No revolution is possible here. Everything is at a standstill, a dead end. Only an invasion of barbarians like us can save and reshape them. The march on Europe is necessary.[27]

Neither the Russian public nor the Tsarist government embraced the aggressive ideology of the *Vostochniki*. Instead they continued to link the future of Russia with the traditional outlets of an imperialist doctrine centered on Europe, which favored Tsarist expansion in the direction of the Balkans and the Turkish Straits. Moreover, the risky Asian venture was criticized in the press as a transparent trap conceived by the German lobby, always influential in St. Petersburg and credited with inventing Russia's Asian mission as a giant diversion to facilitate Germany's own *Drang nach Osten* in Eastern Europe and later along the entire Berlin-Baghdad axis.[28]

"Yellow Russia"

The bizarre and ambivalent "Yellow Russia" movement (*Zheltorossiya*), the most peculiar and extreme variant of the *Vostochniki*, was best exemplified in the writings and entrepreneurial activities of Prince Esper Ukhtomsky (1861–1921). The owner of several newspapers, he was a close collaborator of Russia's leading statesman, Sergei Yu. Witte, in promoting the Trans-Siberian Railway, and tutor to the future emperor, crown prince Nicholas. Ukhtomsky developed a megalomaniacal vision based on a questionable theory about the alleged organic affinity of Russia with China, and even with India.[29] He was able to sing the praises of Chinese civilization, but his underlying leitmotiv was unmistakably the "Yellow Peril" threat hovering silently in the background. What the historian Andrew Malozemoff called the ideological quintessence of the *Vostochniki* is captured in Ukhtomsky's credo.

> Asia—we have always belonged to it. We have lived its life and felt its interests. Through us the Orient has gradually arrived at consciousness of itself, at a superior life. . . . We have nothing to conquer. All these peoples of various races felt themselves drawn to us, by blood, by tradition, and by ideas. We simply approach them more intimately. This great and mysterious Orient is ready to become ours.[30]

Thus, on the surface, one could say that the optimistic version of Russia's *Mission Civilisatrice* toward the East, one based on racial and cultural assimilation, or at least cooperation and tolerance, and which Venyukov heralded in the 1870s with regard to Central Asia, was to be applied to East Asia. Witte, himself, was a proponent of the view that the Russian Empire, set between Europe and the Buddhist, Indian, and Islamic worlds, was a world to itself. What made Russia different from the West, according to Witte's 1893 memorandum to the Tsar, was her unique national spirit. This spirit, apart from other elements providing her with the necessary cohesion (for example, geographical position, Orthodox Christianity, and autocracy) created "a strong kernel, closely united yet free from nationalistic exclusiveness, possessed of a vast capacity for friendly companionship and cooperation with the most diverse races and peoples."[31]

The same year, Witte submitted another memorandum to the Tsar endorsing a highly subversive and questionable scheme designed by Petr A. Badmaev, a Buriat quack doctor who converted to Orthodox Christianity with the Emperor Alexander III acting as his godfather. This bizarre plan was based on the systematic penetration by Russian-trained Buriats (as commercial agents), of China's backyard, the western borderlands stretching from Sinkiang to Mongolia and Manchuria, including Tibet as well. Incidentally, the plan was tried out between 1895 and 1897, but it misfired completely. The Russian axis of advance was to be a new railroad to Lanchow in the Kansu province. However, the main covert activity was to be the promotion of an anti-Han general rebellion among the Mongolians, Tibetans, and Chinese Muslims. Had the Badmaev scheme succeeded, along with the completion of Witte's major Trans-Siberian Railway plan, then Witte would have been justified in concluding that "Russia from the shores of the Pacific Ocean and the peaks of the Himalayas will dominate not only Asiatic but also European affairs."[32] Although Witte wanted the outside world to believe his assertions that Russia could achieve her mission in Asia through "peaceful and cultural means," the ultimate object of Russia's expanionist course in Asia by means of railroad building and commercial ventures, both heavily if not exclusively subsidized by the state, was, after all, colonial domination.[33]

For a while, Russian imperialism toward Asia rode the crest of a wave of optimism accompanying the progress of the construction of the great Trans-Siberian Railway. Ukhtomsky was a chief promoter of the railway, as well as of the systematic Russian economic penetration into China through Manchuria. His chief public relations officer dealing with Western Europe, Hermann Brunnhofer (1841–1916), adopted an almost lyrical language to depict the bright future of Eurasia. Linked from the Baltic and the Black Seas to the Pacific Ocean through this phenomenal railway, which would mutually benefit commercial and cultural exchange, all races were going to live in perfect harmony under the Tsar's scepter. Unlike the British in India, Brunnhofer argued, the Russian soldier and peasant had no complex of racial superiority vis-à-vis the Asians.

> Slavic and Turanian blood will soon mix together, new border people of half European and half Asian stock will grow up and form a connective bond through which the Slavs will make the higher forms of life of the Christian-European culture acceptable to the still enclosed heart of Inner Asia.[34]

The refrain sounds familiar; the inspiration could almost have come from Venyukov or even from the earlier Pan-Slav poet Tyutchev, who in one of his bizarre poems, "The Russian Geography" (1848), dreamed of the future Russian Eurasian Empire as stretching "from the Nile to the Neva, from the Elbe to China, from the Volga to the Euphrates, from the Ganges to the Danube."[35] Writing at the time of the Sino-Japanese War (1894–95), however, Brunnhofer's counterimperialist concept of "Yellow Russia" had a clear political purpose. Besides offering the lofty vision of a potential Sino-Russian symbiosis, he tried to warn the Western public against Japan's expansionist ambitions. Japan would create a kind of a Pan-Asiatic zone of influence under the banner of Buddhist solidarity, first limited to Japan, Korea, and China and then gradually extended with the occupation of Taiwan to Southeast Asia. In one of his articles, Brunnhofer predicted with remarkable foresight the future Greater East Asia Co-Prosperity Sphere that was to come into existence some 50 years later.[36] Brunnhofer's warnings fall, nevertheless, into the category of the "Yellow Peril" specter, which we find in Solovyov or even much earlier in Leontev. Despite his optimistic portrait of a future "Yellow Russia," he, too, worried occasionally about the prospect of industrialized Chinese masses pushing irresistably westward under Japanese leadership. The only power capable of forestalling this potential Buddhist tide, Brunnhofer insisted, was the universal Russian Eurasian Empire.

A rather grotesque revival of the Buddhist theme could be witnessed during the Russian Civil War. The "Mad Baron" von Ungern-Sternberg, an ex-Tsarist general, reacted to the Russian Revolution by turning to Buddhism to protest what he saw as a bankruptcy of Western civilization. In 1921 his combined Cossack-Mongolian-Chinese forces seized Urga, the capital of Outer Mongolia (today's Ulan Bator), where he proclaimed himself the new Genghis Khan. A few months thereafter, this eccentric symbol of *Aziatchina* and *Zheltorossiya*, combined in one person, was defeated and executed by the Bolsheviks.[37]

In spite of all this wishful thinking on the theme of future racial fusion for the sake of a more homogeneous Eurasia, under benevolent Russian guidance, of course, it is important to realize that this ideology was never allowed in Tsarist Russia to dominate the decision-making process in St. Petersburg, however narrowly it was defined at the time. In the end it was *Realpolitik* that prevailed—the Badmaev episode notwithstanding—when several balancing factors, ideology perhaps included, had been played against each other. By contrast, one might argue that Bolshevik Russia conducted her Asian policy during the Civil War, and for a brief period thereafter, more as a function of ideology. The idea of assimilation between the Slav-Aryans and Turanians could enjoy a certain support among the more liberal section of the Russian intelligentsia only as long as the Russian birth rates remained among the highest in the world, as was the case throughout the Tsarist period (for example, the census of 1897).[38] This, in turn, encouraged the officially sponsored colonization of Russian Asia by peasants of European stock, predominantly Slavs.

The opening of Central Asia and the Far East for the benefit of Russian colonization would have been slower and less complete had it not been for the outstanding contribution of scientists, experts, and explorers. They left the Soviet state a firmly established tradition of high standards of scholarship and scientific enquiry, especially in Oriental studies and geography. The existence of this tradition, often overlooked in the West, is useful to be reminded of, particularly today when a great deal of speculation surrounds the present Soviet role in Asia.[39]

Even the outstanding Russian Orientalist, Vasiliy V. Barthold (1869–1930), who managed to stay aloof from official propaganda during the Tsarist as well as the Bolshevik era, basically agreed with what he regarded as a historical necessity to create world empires approximating those of Alexander the Great, the Mongols, or the Arabs, or even the present Russian Empire in Central Asia. He sincerely believed that, in the long run, it was the larger framework that provided better conditions for cultural rapprochement between peoples of different racial origin, in spite of the ravages of war that went with the creation of such empires.⁴⁰

Exodus to the East: Trubetskoy and Savitsky

Despite the setbacks caused by the Russo-Japanese War and World War I, Russia's quest for a special relationship with Asia continued among her intelligentsia with even greater intensity during the years of the Revolution and Civil War, and immediately thereafter. This is best exemplified by the Eurasianist Movement, which gathered together Russia's most brilliant minds in exile during the 1920s. Despite their frequent disagreements, they were convinced that only by adopting a specific Eurasianist *Weltanschauung* could the uniqueness of Russia's contribution to civilization, based on the Greco-Byzantine heritage as well as on the Mongol conquest, be preserved. In their first manifesto, *Exodus to the East* (1921), the two outstanding linguists, Prince Nikolay S. Trubetskoy and Roman O. Jakobson, advocated a Eurasian association of languages and cultures (the so-called *Sprachbund* theory) by consciously overstating the influence of the Turanian element.⁴¹

Whereas the Bolsheviks and Marxism were viewed as the worst consequence of Western culture, the Revolution itself was seen by Eurasianists as the great and necessary catalyst, for it destroyed the old world and aroused the Russian masses together with the peoples of the Orient. Thus, Trubetskoy's *Europe and Mankind* (1920) reads like a combination of Danilevsky and the Second Komintern Congress appeal. It is a definite indictment of Western imperialism, in which the exclusively Eurocentric approach to Asia is rejected. Russia's humiliation in the wake of war and revolution, Trubetskoy argued, could provide a unique opportunity for a radical transformation of attitudes toward non-Russian peoples: "A colonial country herself, Russia could lead other colonial countries, in particular her 'Asiatic sisters,' in a decisive struggle against the Romano-Germanic colonizers."⁴²

One of the most original thinkers among the Eurasianists was geographer Petr N. Savitsky (1895–1968). His concept of Eurasia was that of an authentic geographical and cultural entity with an added potential for territorial expansion (*mestorazvitie* or "topogenesis"). When Savitsky refers to Russia's southward and eastward expansion since the sixteenth century, he tries to explain it as a defensive measure within the concept of "Forward Frontier," which of course is analogous with the British policy in India. Moreover, Savitsky argues that the entire Russian expansion must be seen as a continuous natural process of organic development. In his description this looks almost like an ecological process, with no political motivation behind it, let alone power politics of imperialist rivalry linked with the Central Asian and Far Eastern questions. Consequently, as Savitsky would argue, Russian Eurasia is a geopolitical unit in itself (*geopoliticheskoe edinstvo*), brought about by a cultural process of "genuine mutation" (*geneticheskaya mutatsiya*), not by conquest and destruction.[43] This interpretation does not seem to be very different, as we see, from Friedrich Ratzel's concept of a dynamic *Lebensraum*, which Karl Haushofer adopted in the 1920s.

Eurasian Rapprochement and Fusion

What is even more intriguing is the remarkable similarity between the Eurasianist vocabulary and Soviet terminology of the Khrushchev era on the topic of cultural and ethnic fusion, supervised with loving care by the elder Russian brother. In the writings of Savitsky, and especially in those of historian Georg V. Vernadsky, one frequently encounters terms like *sliyanie* and *peremeshivanie* to describe cultural merger and mixing, which allegedly took place during the process of territorial expansion, culminating in the estabishment of the "Great Russian culture" (*Velikorusskaya kul'tura*). Vernadsky's remark, for example, that "under external diversity inner unity is hidden," reminds one of the current Soviet slogan "unity in diversity" (*edinstvo v mnogoobrazii*).

Such inclusion (*vklyuchenie*) of non-Russian groups into the multinational Eurasian empire offered enormous economic and cultural advantages and led to participation in "universal life," Vernadsky argued in a manner not very different from the standard Soviet viewpoint. However, Vernadsky also insisted that this unity must be "ecumenical," without compulsion, for "the Russian State is a Eurasian state and all separate nationalities of Eurasia must feel and recognize that it is *their* state" (emphasis by Vernadsky). Furthermore, even if the "Russian people constitute the main force of the Eurasian state, and the Russian language the fundamental layer of Eurasian culture," it must not be enforced and regimented on other people. The strength of this Eurasian entity lies in its "free cultural creativity."[44] Despite these lofty ideas expressed by the Eurasianists in exile, who carried no political responsibility and little influence inside the new Soviet Eurasian empire, other Slavic nationalities, especially the most numerous ones after the Russians (for example, Ukrainians and Poles), deeply distrusted the aims of the Eurasianists and turned against them.[45] Unfortunately, nothing is known of the reaction of Asian intellectuals, especially those living under Soviet rule, to the teachings of the Eurasianists; but it could be safely assumed that they saw in it nothing but a more sophisticated justification of Russian imperialism.

The Eurasian Movement thus contributed unwittingly to the creation of the utopian Soviet man—that artificial *homunculus* of Soviet propagandists, a creature of no certain racial or ethnic origin, but speaking and feeling, of course, Russian. The contemporary Soviet trinity model consisting of the three stages *rastsvet-sblizhenie-sliyanie* ("flowering-rapprochement-fusion"), which reached its advanced stage during the Khrushchev era,[46] is strikingly reminiscent of the Eurasianist vision of the 1920s. It also reflects the accumulated historical experience of Russian intelligentsia in addressing the ethnic and racial questions raised by Russian intellectuals during the nineteenth century.

As Hélène Carrère d'Encausse has shown, the whole Soviet concept of formulating and legalizing the relationship between the Russians and non-Russians had undergone many peripeties.[47] In contrast to Lenin's utopian vision of states and nations withering away and being replaced by a new univeral community of proletarian class solidarity, the more brutal and inward looking Joseph Stalin gradually transformed the idea of cultural federation into one of centralized Russian control over the nominally autonomous member nations of the Soviet Union. This reality turned Soviet theorizing on such issues into a rather hollow enterprise, for what Stalin did has yet to be undone. Nevertheless, the main themes of the Eurasianist Movement remain relevant, regardless of whether they are discussed loudly or merely whispered inside the Soviet Union today. The long-term survival of the multinational Soviet Eurasian land fortress, still being guided almost exclusively by the wiser "elder Russian brother," will depend largely upon solving those issues.

Notes

1 Andrew Malozemoff, *Russian Far Eastern Policy 1881–1904* (Berkeley: University of California Press, 1958), 42.
2 F. F. von Martens, *Russland und England in Zentralasien* (St. Petersburg, 1880); Heinz Gollwitzer, *Geschichte des weltpolitischen Denkens* (Göttingen: Vandenhoeck & Ruprecht, 1982), I:52–70, 133–36.
3 F. F. von Martens, *Le Conflict entre la Russie et la Chine* (Bruxelles, 1880).
4 Gollwitzer, *Die Gelbe Gefahr* (1962), 93–103; W. P. Wassiliew, *Die Erschliessung Chinas* (Leipzig, 1909).
5 Wassiliew, *Die Erschliessung Chinas* (1909), 49.
6 N. M. Prejevalsky (Przewalski), *From Kulja, across the Tian Shan to Lob-Nor* (London: Sampson Low, 1879). Reprint (New York: Greenwood Press, 1969).
7 M. A. Bakunin, *La théologie politique de Mazzini et l'Internationale* (Neufchâtel, 1871), 102, 110.
8 A. N. Kuropatkin, *Memoiren* (Berlin, 1909), 71, 74.
9 Gollwitzer, *Die Gelbe Gefahr* (1962), 14, 23–24, 111.
10 J. S. Bloch, "Les Illusions de la Conquete Chinoise," *Revue des Revues* (August 15, 1900).
11 Gollwitzer, *Die Gelbe Gefahr* (1962), 14.
12 See section on D. I. Mendeleev in chapter 7.
13 Herold J. Wiens, *China's March toward the Tropics* (Hamden, Conn.: Shoe String Press, 1954).
14 Gollwitzer, *Die Gelbe Gefahr* (1962), 24.
15 S. N. Yuzhakov, *Anglo-russkaya rasprya* (St. Petersburg, 1885); Sarkisyanz, *Russland und der Messianismus* (1955), 208–09.
16 N. F. Fyodorov, *Filosofiya obshchego dela*, vols. 1–2 (Vernyi, 1906, and Moscow, 1913); quoted here from Fyodorov, *Sochineniya* (Moscow: Mysl', 1982). On Fyodorov's influence on Dostoevsky, Tolstoy, Solovyov, Berdyaev, Bulgakov, and others, see: Stephen Lukashevich, *N. F. Fedorov—A Study in Russian Eupsychian and Utopian Thought* (Newark: University of Delaware Press, 1977), 13–34.
17 Fyodorov, *Sochineniya* (1982), 343; Sarkisyanz, *Russland und der Messianismus* (1955), 210–11; N. A. Setnitskyi, *Russkie mysliteli o Kitae* (Kharbin, 1926).
18 Vladimir L'vov, *Zagadochnyi starik* (Leningrad: Sovietskiy pisatel, 1977), 129–35; Fyodorov, *Sochineniya* (1982), 335–36.
19 Fyodorov, *Sochineniya* (1982), 216, 340, 382, 669.
20 Ibid., 300.
21 V. S. Solovyov, *Tri rozgovora* (St. Petersburg: Trud, 1904); T. G. Masaryk, *The Spirit of Russia* (London: Allen & Unwin, 1919 and 1968), II:225–86; Gollwitzer, *Die Gelbe Gefahr* (1962), 114–20.

22　Malozemoff, *Russian Far Eastern Policy* (1958), 43.
23　V. I. Lenin on the war in China in *Iskra* of December 1, 1900; Gollwitzer, *Die Gelbe Gefahr* (1962), 113.
24　A. Belyi, *Petersburg* (London: Penguin, 1983), 65.
25　Sarkisyanz, *Russland und der Messianismus* (1955), 200, 216–18.
26　Translation based on Sir Cecil Kisch, *Alexander Blok, Prophet of Revolution* (London: Weidenfeld & Nicholson, 1960), 152–54.
27　S. Esenin, *Sobranie sochineniy* (Moscow, 1970), 5:107, quoted in Agursky, *The Third Rome* (1987), 278.
28　Gollwitzer, *Die Gelbe Gefahr* (1962), 42, 98–99.
29　Sarkisyanz, *Russland und der Messianismus* (1955), 218–22.
30　Malozemoff, *Russian Far Eastern Policy* (1958), 43–44.
31　B. H. Sumner, "Russia and Europe," *Oxford Slavonic Papers* (1951), II:1–16. In *Readings in Russian Civilization*, ed. Thomas Riha (Chicago: University of Chicago Press, 1964), II:473.
32　Malozemoff, *Russian Far Eastern Policy* (1958), 48–9; Sarkisyanz, *Russland und der Messianismus* (1955), 378–91.
33　Gollwitzer, *Geschichte* (1982), I:138–40.
34　Hermann Brunnhofer, *Russlands Hand über Asien. Historisch-geographische Essays zur Entwick lungsgeschichte des russichen Reichsdenkens* (St. Petersburg, 1897), preface. Brunnhofer, of Swiss nationality, advocated Russian expansion in Central Asia and in the Far East in a series of articles first published in the German-language newspapers, *St. Petersburger Zeitung* and *St. Petersburger Herold*. Brunnhofer tried to substantiate Russia's expansionism in Asia with his own study of Aryan mythology. He produced, among other works, an ambitious three-volume work, *Urgeschichte der Arier in Vorder-und Centralasien: Historisch-geographische Untersuchungen über den ältesten Schauplatz des Rigvedas und Avestas* (Leipzig, 1893). Brunnhofer also translated Prince Ukhtomsky's lavish official account of the crown prince Nicholas's trip to the Far East: *Orientreise seiner Kaiserlicher Hoheheit des Grossfürsten Thronfolgers*, 2 vols. (Leipzig: Brockhaus, 1894 and 1898).
35　Tyutchev, *Sochineniya* (1886), 141.
36　"Ein ostasiatischer Dreibund und die buddhistische Weltpropaganda." In Brunnhofer, *Russland Hand über Asien* (1897), 24–29, first published in *St. Petersburger Zeitung* in 1894.
37　Louis Fisher, *The Soviets in World Affairs* (Princeton: Princeton University Press, 1951), II:534–37; Sir Fitzroy Maclean, *To the Back of Beyond* (London: Cape, 1974), 119–21.
38　See also chapter 7.
39　Conolly, *Beyond the Urals* (London: Oxford University Press, 1967), 374–75.
40　*Akademik Barthold-Sochineniya* (Moscow: Izdatel'stvo vostochnoi literatury, 1963), II/1:13, 164–66, 345–50.
41　*Iskhod k Vostoku. Predchuvstviya i svercheniya. Utverzhdenie Evraziitsev* (Sofia, 1921), with articles by G. V. Florovsky, Roman O. Jakobson, P. P. Savchinsky, P. N. Savitsky, and N. S. Trubetskoy. Basic literature on the Eurasianists: D. S. Mirsky, "The Eurasian Movement," *The Slavonic and East European Review* 6 (1927), 311–20; Otto Böss, *Die Lehre der Eurasier* (Wiesbaden: Harrassowitz, 1961); H. A. Stammler, "Europe-Russland-Asien."

Der 'eurasische' Deutungsversuch der russischen Geschichte," *Osteuropa* 12 (1962), 521–28; Georges Nivat, "Du Panmongolisme au mouvement eurasien," *Cahiers du monde Russe et Soviétique* 7/3 (1966), 460–78; Nicholas V. Riasanovsky, "The Emergence of Eurasians," *California Slavic Studies* 4 (1967), 39–72.

42 N. S. Trubetskoy, *Evropa i chelovechestvo* (Sofia, 1920); Mirsky, "The Eurasian Movement" (1927), 312–13; Riasanovsky, "Emergence of Eurasians" (1967), 56; Leonid Luks, "Die Ideologie der Eurasier im zeitgeschichtlichen Zusammenhang," *Jahrbücher für Geschichte Osteuropas* 34 (1986), 374–95.

43 P. N. Savitsky, "Geopoliticheskie zametki po russkoi istorii." In G. V. Vernadsky, *Nachertanie russkoi istorii* (Prague, 1927), 234–60. See also by Savitsky: *Geograficheskie osobennosti Rossii*, 2 vols. (Prague, 1927); *Rossiya, osobyi geograficheskiy mir* (Paris, 1927). Charles Halperin, "Russia and the Steppe: George Vernadsky and Eurasianism," *Forschungen zur osteuropäischen Gechichte* 36 (1985), 55–194, and *Slavic Studies* 41 (1982), 477–93.

44 Vernadsky, *Nachertanie* (1927), 230–31, 259–60; Halperin, "Russia and the Steppe" (1985), 99–104.

45 Riasanovsky, "Emergence of Eurasians" (1967), 70.

46 See chapter 2.

47 H. Carrère d'Encausse, *Decline of an Empire: The Soviet Socialist Republics in Revolt* (New York: Harper, 1981), 13–46.

Part II

Russia's Central Asian Heartland

5

Russia's Drive South

The Russian Space

The insoluble problem of racial fusion in the vast multi-ethnic conglomerate, which we have referred to as the Russian (or Soviet) Eurasian Empire, has been further exacerbated in geographic terms by the enormous spatial imbalances that bear directly on the Empire's overall geostrategic position.

In a metaphoric abbreviation, the history of the Russian Empire has sometimes been reduced to the "tragic obsession with space (*prostor*)," or "tragic gift of space."[1] According to this imagery the Russians, both as defenders and aggressors, were continuously challenged by the vast distances of Eurasia, until the centripetal power of Muscovy succeeded in absorbing and consolidating the entire portion of the northern hemisphere stretching between the Atlantic and Pacific Oceans north of the 50th parallel. There is an amazing semblance to the expansion of the United States westward and south of the 50th parallel, which established over a much shorter time and space a kind of empire "from sea to sea." Since then, both the Russians and the Soviets have prided themselves that their enormous land fortress could accommodate 2.3 Americas, 40 Frances, or 93 Great Britains.[2] Between 1600 and 1900 the Russian Empire added altogether 17 million square kilometers of new territories (on average 57,000 sq. km added every year, that is, territories of the size of Pennsylvania or Cuba every other year).[3] Judging by these results one could easily conclude that geography has indeed exerted "a pervasive influence on Russian and Soviet perceptions of Asia."[4]

The geographic factor thus appears to be "of the utmost importance" in the history of the Russian people[5]—especially in light of the spatial hyperextension underlying Russia's imperialist policy. Two geographic features have made the Russian case special. First, the uniformity of the geographic relief, with its monotonous landscape, enabled a centralized political authority to maintain and expand control along the great riverways in the north-south direction. This control facilitated the passage of goods, settlers, and troops.[6] According to the distinguished Russian historian, Klyuchevsky, the expansion of Muscovy must be understood as the rise of a centripetal power that gained control of four riverheads in Central Russia and, in turn, controlled access to four seas: the Baltic, the White Sea, the Black Sea, and the Caspian.[7]

Second, because of the climatic extremes in the northern half of Eurasia, Russian eastward penetration could follow only a narrow wedge across the southern tip of Siberia, itself the largest wilderness in the world. This west-east corridor, where settlers from European Russia soon outnumbered the sparse indigenous population of Turco-Mongolian origin, has since the 1890s become identical with the steel tracks of the Trans-Siberian Railway, without which the Europeanization of Russian Asia would have been impossible. North of this corridor the climate was too cold for agricultural activities; south of it farming was difficult without irrigation.

However, the deeper Russia expanded into Asia, the more problematic its geostrategic options became. The acquisition of the Amur borderland aggravated the inevitable antagonism between the Russians and the yellow peril, personified by Japan and China. Another zone of potential conflict developed in the 1860s along the southern tier in Central Asia as a result of the Russian conquest of Turkestan. This conflict became part of the Central Asian Question, the major bone of contention in the Anglo-Russian rivalry. Because of its inadequate communications and the enormous distances involved, the Russian state could not allocate the same resources to both places simultaneously in the event of a military emergency. Until the late 1880s the government could not decide which zone should be given overriding priority: the Far East or Central Asia. This dilemma remained even after the completion of the two important strategic railways in Asia around

1905, that is, the Trans-Siberian and the Orenburg-Tashkent lines, which radically improved Russia's military emplacement there and her flexibility due to better and faster internal communications.

The decision to build the great Trans-Siberian Railway (1891–1904) must be understood as Russia's irrevocable determination to hold onto her Far Eastern possession. This already had been emphasized in 1860 by the foundation of Vladivostok (Ruler of the East), the main Russian stronghold on the Pacific shore. The vital importance of the west-east axis, identical with the strategic corridor created by the new transcontinental railway, was critically tested during the Russo-Japanese war (1904–05). The military defeat taught Russian strategists a bitter lesson: they have been haunted since then by the trauma of a two-front war imposed simultaneously at the opposite extremities of Eurasia. In addition, Central Asia, situated halfway between Russia's European glacis and the Pacific coastline, could easily become a third theater of war. Moreover, there was the specter of a fourth front developing inside the Empire in case of domestic ethnic and social upheavals, whose outcome was the least predictable as the events of 1905 and 1917 had demonstrated. The Soviet Eurasian Empire inherited this geostrategic trauma from its Tsarist predecessor. There may have been revolutions and civil wars before one system overpowered the other, but the trauma has remained. The missile and nuclear dimension of contemporary warfare has not made the Soviet preoccupation with the vulnerability of the west-east axis across Eurasia less acute.

Geographic Projections: What Is Central Asia?

To understand more fully the Russian strategic emplacement in Central Asia, we must first clarify the substantial differences between the traditions of Western and Russian cartographic projections. For the last 400 years, the Western view has been conditioned by the prevailing type of cylindrical maps derived from the sixteenth-century Mercator projection of the earth (after the Dutch geographer, Gerardus Mercator, 1512–94). Such maps produce considerable distortion in the higher latitudes above the equator, that is, those along which the Russian Eurasian Empire had expanded. However, the Russians, while contemplating

Central Asia, are looking "down" from the north. Therefore, an azimuthal (polar) projection, based on the northern hemispheres, makes better sense. A similar one was used by Richard Edes Harrison in his *Fortunes Atlas* during World War II.[8]

A more recent distortion occurred during World War II. The delineation of Central Asia, South Asia, and the Middle East was deliberately confused for reasons of temporary military convenience. The British set up the Middle East Command, with headquarters in Cairo, Egypt, lumping together not only all countries of the Maghreb and of Arabia proper, but also Iran, the Persian Gulf, Turkey, Greece, and Cyprus in the north, as well as Sudan and East Africa in the south. Moreover, the Mideast Command overlapped clumsily with the already established defense perimeter of the India Command, which claimed responsibility over the entire vast area stretching from Hong Kong to Egypt, including the whole of the Indian Ocean. Ironically, the U.S. Rapid Deployment Force today claims roughly the same strategic perimeter as the British Mideast Command did during World War II (under the designation of Southwest Asia), except that Israel, Lebanon, Syria, and Turkey are not explicitly included because of Washington's political expedience.

For their part, the Russians have long considered Central Asia (*Srednyaya Aziya*) part of the Middle East (*Sredniy Vostok*), the middle piece between the Near East (*Blizhniy Vostok*), stretching from the Maghreb to the head of the Persian Gulf, and the Far East (*Dal'niy Vostok*), the regions facing the Pacific Ocean. Hence, *Sredniy Vostok* would begin at the great divide between the Caucasus and the Persian Gulf, which not only separated geographically the Black and the Mediterranean Seas from the Caspian Sea and the Indian Ocean, but also served as the great historic divide between the former Ottoman realm and those of Iran and India. Looking southward and eastward from the Kremlin's observation platform, this triple division of the Orient made perfect sense, and in my view, it still does.[9]

Less clear is the answer to the questions of how far east or south *Sredniy Vostok* or *Srednyaya Aziya* stretched, and particularly how much of the Indian subcontinent, which the British claimed for themselves, would Russian geographers consider an organic part of the above. Whereas Mongolia was usually considered the easternmost frontier of Russian Central Asia with no sharp demarcation line, there was no hesitation in visualizing all of Turkestan (and all its components, that is, Persian, "Russian," Afghan, and Chinese) as the natural sphere of Russian territorial claims. In parallel to *Srednyaya Aziya*, which literally means "Middle Asia," Russian geographers began to apply the Russian equivalent of the German and French term for Central, that is *Tsentral'naya Aziya*, first applied in the path-breaking work of the great explorer and scientist, Alexander von Humboldt, who visited Central Asia in 1829. In a somewhat narrower sense, it meant all Central Asian territories without access to the sea, which consequently fell under Russia's Eurasian heartland. Only in the use of the geoethnical term *Vnutrenyaya Aziya* ("Inner Asia"), which is outside the sphere of geopolitics and which is applied to the strip delineated by Turkestan and Mongolia between the 40th and 50th northern latitudes and slightly beyond, do we find close correspondence with the western designation Inner Asia.[10]

In terms of physical geography, Central Asia can be described as "the island part of Asia, farthest removed from the world oceans, in the midst of the greatest land mass on earth."[11] Russian geographers of the imperialist era tended to view Central Asia as part of the dual Eurasian continent. If a larger view is taken of what might be called Greater Central Asia, that is, a cultural area distinct from both the Middle East and South Asia, notwithstanding a certain overlapping due to entrenched political borders, then we are confronted with a much larger region stretching along the southerly latitude all the way from Mongolia to the Caspian Sea and eastern Turkey.[12] Strongly reminiscent of Timur's short-lived empire (1360–1405), its heartland remains Turkestan divided into three parts: the ancient Sogdiana (*Transoxiana* in Latin, *Ma-waran Nahr* in Arabic), to which Khorezm and Khorasan can be linked; *Yeti Su* or Semirechie; and Eastern Turkestan (Sinkiang) or Kashgaria. This central Asian region is characterized by several centuries of continuity in Islamic cultural ethnic patterns and affinities of the Irano-Turkic and Mongol peoples that spread from Inner Asia to the Mediterranean and from Siberia to the Indian Ocean. The Russian element, first as adventurous Cossack fur hunters and later as agricultural settlers, began to expand eastward into Siberia behind the Ural barrier from the sixteenth century onward. Two centuries later the Russian invasion and migration were diverted southward to penetrate the Kirghiz steppe and Turkestan: the *Dar-ul-Islam* was being progressively contaminated by the *Dar ul-Harb* ("world of war").

The Historic Perspective of Central Asia

Essentially, there have always been three basic options in Russia's expansion with regard to Asia; each option confronted the invader with a different set of geopolitical problems. The oldest route was the northeastern one along the Arctic coast, which had been pioneered by the historic Republic of Novgorod until its defeat and absorption by the Duchy of Muscovy. Its lonely advocate today is the famous author Alexander Solzhenitsyn.[13] The other two routes were also difficult but nevertheless more suitable for moving settlers and troops. Once the Cossacks crossed the Idel-Volga river and the Ural mountains, they could follow the older "Siberian route" via the Irtysh and Lake Baykal, along the Amur, and farther toward the Pacific Coast; or they could turn south and follow the shorter "Orenburg route" in the direction of Lake Aral, the Amu and Syr Daryas, and into the heart of Turkestan.[14]

British and Russian authors during the era of imperialism, in order to legitimize the claims of their governments on Central Asia from the historic perspective, indulged themselves in frequent references to former empires that had once existed on the centerstage of the Eurasian heartland and that in most cases, had been linked with the invasion of the Indian subcontinent. They were keen to draw lessons from the military campaigns of Alexander the Great, Genghis Khan, Timur, and Babur, and with the last attempt of Nadir Shah of Persia to create a self-contained Central Asian empire during the first third of the eighteenth century. Within four millennia, these authors established, about 20 major invasions had been undertaken against India. Because there were no other access routes, all the invasions were launched across the pivotal territory located at the focal point of Central Asia between the historic *Turan*, *Iran*, and *Hind* (known since the eighteenth century as Afghanistan).[15]

Not until the emergence of the Central Asian question, which characterized the Anglo-Russian rivalry over the approaches to the Indo-Persian corridor and became better known under its romanticized name of the Great Game, did the Russian definition of Central Asia purposefully coincide with the British view. Thus, the remarkable Russian military geographer and Orientalist, General Andrei E. Snesarev, defined Central Asia in his seminal work, *India as the Main Factor in the Central Asian Question*, as consisting of the following territories: "our" Turkestan, Khiva, Bukhara, India (northern), Kashgaria, the Pamirs, Tibet, Afghanistan, Baluchistan, and eastern Persia.[16] It is obvious that Snesarev's definition included the logical extension of Russian ambition to gain access to the Persian Gulf, because this alternative offered the optimal solution to Russia's geopolitical predicament in having been denied access to warm sea waters from the southern rimland of her Eurasian Empire. However, any discussion concerning the "main factor" would necessarily have involved Afghanistan, which alone has no significance whatever. She has acquired her notorious strategic significance over the millennia, argues Snesarev in quoting a sixteenth-century Indian historian, Abu Fazl-i-Allami, "because she constituted the gateway to India."[17]

Prior to the era of the Great Game, Russia and Britain had first clashed over India during the Napoleonic wars. This period in European, and, indeed, world history was characterized by the emergence of the first modern superpower with universal aspirations. Napoleon's most embittered rival was Great Britain, which tried to build up her colonial empire overseas but alone could not challenge France on land. To defeat England, Napoleon found himself unable to cross the mere 20 miles of water between Calais and Dover. Attracted by the mysterious Orient in general, and by Egypt in particular, due to his early acquaintance with abbé de Raynal's history of European colonial expansion in India and America (1770), Napoleon abandoned any direct threat to the British Isles. He turned instead to the indirect menace of an overland invasion all the way from Europe to the emerging British overseas empire in India, thus facing the analogous geopolitical predicament that would befall Adolf Hitler some 150 years later.[18]

For 10 years (1798–1808) Napoleon refused to give up the idea of defeating Britain in India. His early alternative, in pursuing the path of Alexander the Great, was his Egyptian Campaign, which took Napoleon no farther than Syria. Two years later Napoleon put forward an even more ambitious plan of a direct invasion of

India, based on a joint Franco-Russian military campaign (35,000 French troops, 25,000 regular Russian troops, and 10,000 Cossacks). From Astrabad at the southern tip of the Caspian Sea, the invading allied troops were to reach the Indus river via Herat and Kandahar at the fantastic rate of 45 days, which can only be explained by the European ignorance of Central Asian topography.

Although the French contingent had not begun its march toward India, Emperor Paul I of Russia ordered General Orlov, in January 1801, to advance with his Don Cossacks in the direction of India. Shortly thereafter, however, Paul's assassination terminated the first Russian march on India, which Snesarev characterized as "a picture of incredible strategic and political donquiotism" belonging to the "sphere of psychopathy."[19] Failure to persuade Paul's son, Tsar Alexander I, to participate in the Indian scheme led Napoleon, in 1807, to try out his last Indian project, which consisted of first penetrating Persia by means of a French military mission under General Gardanne and then calling on Russia's assistance. The British, however, counteracted successfully the following year by sending into Afghanistan and Persia their own mission with military advisers under Mountstuart Elphinstone, one of their most able administrators in India, who succeeded in averting the potential threat.[20]

The interesting legacy of Napoleon's failure lies not only in his being first to frighten the British before the Russians threatened to invade India, but also in the striking similarity between this joint European overland invasion of India and the strategic alternative developed in Hitler's Germany during 1939–40. Had General Snesarev lived for another several years, he most certainly would have been amazed by the resemblance between these two schemes.

General Snesarev and the Central Asian Question

The place of Andrei Evgenievich Snesarev (1865–1937) in Russian Oriental scholarship and strategic thinking appears even today quite unique, despite the fact that his name is hardly ever mentioned by Western authors. We mention him primarily for two reasons. Snesarev represents the finest symbiosis between an Oriental scholar and a military strategist. He spoke fourteen languages and served mostly in Turkestan, traveling widely from there throughout

Central Asia. In 1899 he spent seven months in India as a member of a Russian military mission under Lt. Colonel A. A. Polevtsov; at Simla he was introduced to Lord Curzon with whom he discussed the Central Asian Question.[21] After various staff and teaching appointments, he advanced to the rank of Lt. General and commanded an army corps in World War I.

The second reason for mentioning Snesarev is that he exemplifies in a unique way the continuity of Russian geopolitical tradition with regard to Central Asia from the Tsarist into the Soviet period. As indicated, this continuity was based on the powerful perception that India should constitute the focus not only of the Central Asian Question, but also of the whole Anglo-Russian rivalry. All other regions and states surrounding British India in a semicircle were regarded by Snesarev as natural strategic buffers. He was convinced that as long as India constituted the most important possession of the British Empire, which was the case during his lifetime regardless of whether the Russian Empire was ruled by the Tsars or the Bolsheviks, this strategic approach was fully justified. Consequently, Snesarev would argue, India must become of primary importance to Russian Eurasia as well; Russia must reject the British lead and behave more aggressively in Central Asia. "We, the Russians, must dictate the British our will," he lectured the influential audience in St. Petersburg. "Not far from us, beyond the snow-covered mountain chain of the Hindu Kush, lies India, the backbone of the British Empire and perhaps the political key to the whole world."[22]

Snesarev also believed that it was Russia's historic mission to reach the warm waters of the Indian Ocean by continuously probing the defenses the British were forwarding in northern and western India. In his earlier military-geographic analysis of the *North Indian Theater*, he contemplated the future playground of military activities from an imaginary observation post on the top of the Pamir plateau, the roof of the world. Poised to follow in the footsteps of the earlier conquerors of India, whose deeds he had studied assiduously to the smallest militarily relevant detail, Snesarev bitterly complained that Russia should have occupied the strategically important Wakhan Corridor and prevented the British from seizing Chitral.[23] Had it not been for the aggressive British diplomacy and its policy of annexation in north-western India, the Russian march down to the warm waters of the Indian Ocean would have been smooth. "At first we were advancing in Central Asia with a speed and energy suited to a great power," he argued. "From the moment the British put themselves in our path, however ... we got stuck hopelessly along the Amu Darya, stopping a few hundred versts [1 *versta* = 1,0668 km] from the ocean."[24]

Such was Snesarev's belief in Russia's historic mission in Central Asia that he did not consider that the Bolshevik Revolution constituted a fundamental change in Russia's geopolitical position. Under Moscow's new Eastern strategy, the Bolsheviks recognized that they must switch communist subversion and penetration from the abortive experience in Western Europe to the more fertile ground in colonial Asia, specifically in British India via Persia and Afghanistan. Already in the autumn of 1919 Snesarev was recalled by Leon Trotsky from his commanding post on the Western Front against Poland to become director of the General Staff Academy in Moscow. He resumed his courses on the military geography of Central Asia, during which he exhorted future Soviet generals and diplomats: "If you want to destroy capitalist tyranny over the world—beat the British in India!"[25]

Naturally, Snesarev's blueprint for a military invasion of India by the revolutionary Red Army was an updated compendium of the old Tsarist plans. British India was to be reached in a series of quick marches along three main avenues of attack: the western route via Kushka, Herat, and Kandahar to Quetta; the central route from Amu Darya across the Hindu Kush and Kabul to Peshawar; and the eastern route commencing from the Pamirs via Chitral and Gilgit to Peshawar. Even the longest route, from Kushka to Quetta via Kandahar, was supposed to take no more than 43 legs, not counting days of rest. Snesarev calculated his daily rates for marching infantry supported by cavalry and horse-drawn artillery. The infantry columns would actually be moving more slowly than the swift horsemen in the days of Genghis Khan or Timur, who had also tried to conquer India along Snesarev's central route.[26] Although the Red Army had never attacked India—notwithstanding a limited cross-border raid into Afghanistan in May 1929 in support of King Amanullah, who was facing a widespread tribal uprising[27] —the British administration of India continued to consider the communist infiltration as the main external threat.[28] The Indian General Staff definitely viewed Soviet Russia, virtually until June 1941, as the greatest menace to its Indian defense perimeter.[29]

Three Elements of Russian Strategy in the Indo-Persian Corridor

Rather than dwell on the excitements of the Great Game, which will never lack admiring chroniclers, it might be more rewarding to look into the genuinely substantial aspects of the Russian military strategy in Central Asia. Three elements have characterized Russian and Soviet military strategy vis-à-vis the Indo-Persian corridor in the hundred years since the conquest of Turkestan: diversion, subversion, and the drive to the warm waters of the Indian Ocean.

Diversion

The essence of strategic diversion in Central Asia (as exemplified in the first plans conceived during the Crimean War[30] by Russian military leaders, General A. O. Duhamel, the future Admiral Nikolai Chikhachëv, and General Stepan Khrulev,[31] and later supplemented by those of Generals Mikhail Skobelev and Alexei Kuropatkin) was to foster fear in the British that a Russian invasion of India was imminent.[32] This strategy would relieve British pressure in other theaters of war where Russia was active, such as the Balkans, the Turkish Straits, the Caucasus, and the Far East. Although devoid of serious logistical appreciation and topographical knowledge of the terrain, like the previous plans of Paul I and Napoleon, these early schemes are good examples of how strategic diversion could become an instrument of political vengeance for a lost war. Duhamel's plan, for instance, surmised that a Russian army, marching with a steady pace of 25 versts a day, could cover the distance from Astrabad to Herat in 33 days, Herat to Kabul via Kandahar in 43, and Kabul to Peshawar in 14. Despite the enmity between the Persians and Afghans, characterized by the dispute over Herat, the Russians speculated that the former could be won by a mixture of "threats and intimidation, presents and pensions," combined with territorial concessions at the expense of the Ottomans, allied at the time with Britain. The Afghans, on the other hand, were to be won by the prospect of an overall Muslim uprising in India. They would be encouraged to cooperate with the Sikhs, who were still outraged by the recent British annexation of the Punjab (1849) following the disintegration of the great Sikh kingdom after the death of Ranjit Singh in 1839.[33]

Even before General von Kaufman's conquest of Turkestan, the Russians suspected the British of hatching a diabolic scheme to create an anti-Russian confederacy consisting of the three Uzbeg Khanates (Bukhara, Khiva, and Kokand), supported on one side by Yakub Beg of Kashgaria and on the other by the Persians and Afghans. The British, of course, suspected the Russians of similar scheming by trying to incorporate these states into their forward defense of Turkestan against India. Exponents of the Forward School argued that to forestall successfully a Russian advance against India, the British must build up a strong position at Kandahar, supported via Quetta, enabling them to exercise control both over Kabul to the east and Herat to the west. The foremost exponent, and one of the leading Russophobes of his day was the remarkable Sir Henry Rawlinson. Soldier, diplomat, politician, explorer, archeologist, and scholar, he became notorious because of his insistence on the British occupation of Herat, widely regarded as the gateway to India.

Before the coming of railways the British "Forward Strategy," exercised in the name of defending India, focused on one particular threat, namely, Persia's becoming the vehicle for the expansion of Russian influence into Afghanistan and thence to India. It was precisely in this context that Herat emerged as a vital strategic location in the defense of India, a position Herat was to retain for many years. At that time all serious military writers agreed that the route from the Oxus across the Hindu Kush to Kabul was impracticable for an invading force (the Salang Pass tunnel was not completed until the 1960s) and that the only likely route was through Herat.[34] The ex-Tsarist General Snesarev, when lecturing to the future Soviet general staff officers and diplomats, liked to repeat an old saying to which he attributed the same mixture of geographic determinism and Oriental mystique as his British counterparts: "He who rules Herat, commands Kabul, and he who rules Kabul, commands India."[35]

In Rawlinson's parable Russia was advancing toward India like an army investing a fortress. She had already laid the first parallel, "a mere line of observation," along the Orenburg-Irtysh fortified line, and was ready to take up the next one, a "line of demonstration," from the Krasnovodsk Bay to the Oxus river and farther to the Pamir plateau. Some day she planned to seize the third parallel, running from Astrabad to Herat and on to Kabul and Kandahar, if she survived "revolution in Europe and catastrophe in Asia." "Established in full strength at Herat," Rawlinson went on, "and her communications secured in one direction with Astrabad through Meshed, in another with Khiva through Merv, and in a third with Tashkent and Bukhara through Maimana and the passage of the Oxus . . . her position would indeed be formidable . . . and all the forces of Asia would be inadequate to expel her."[36] Although it would take more than 100 years for the arguable fulfillment of Rawlinson's prophecy, his powerful image of Russia, an immense land fortress herself, pushing ahead her parallel lines against the distant Indian fortress, fascinated even Russian geographers, Snesarev included.[37]

The next stage of diversionary actions took place during the Russo-Turkish War of 1877–78, when the Congress of Berlin met to thwart Russian designs on the Bosphorus. The Russians had already reached the gates of Constantinople and were reluctant to give up the precious prize. To divert British attention, a major military demonstration was staged in Central Asia, involving 20,000 troops dispatched in three columns onto the Afghan and Pamir border. Simultaneously, a diplomatic mission under General Stoletov was sent to Kabul to sign a secret agreement with the Amir of Afghanistan. Furthermore, in response to the arrival of a British squadron in the Sea of Marmara, the Russians considered sending a military expedition into Tibet and their cruisers from Vladivostok into the Indian Ocean to test British reaction.[38] The situation could not be closer to Rawlinson's vision of Russia crossing the "line of demonstration" and preparing to occupy the fateful third parallel.

At that point the flamboyant General M. D. Skobelev put forward a plan for a rapid advance against India with 15,000 men from Russian Turkestan. Skobelev's plan consisted of three stages: (1) instituting a political agreement with the Amir of Afghanistan, combined with an occupation of Kabul by Russian troops; (2) subverting all "disaffected elements in Hindustan"; and (3) "hurling masses of Asiatic cavalry upon India as a vanguard under the banner of blood and rapine, thereby reviving the times of Timur."[39]

This was more than the British could digest, and the sum of Russian diversionary activities led to their second invasion of Afghanistan (1878–82), which forced the Russians to abandon their short-lived Afghan alliance. Despite the continuing tension between the Russians and the British, highlighted by the Panjdeh Incident of 1885 and by further clashes in the Pamirs, both sides finally agreed in 1895 on the demarcation of Afghanistan's boundaries. But Great Britain was to control the latter's external relations until 1919.

From about 1885 on, however, Russia's Asian strategy was undergoing an important shift from Central Asia to the Far East, which escaped the notice of most contemporary military writers. This shift can be documented by the steady flow of reinforcements to the Amur and Ussuri frontier, even before the completion of the Trans-Siberian Railway. Here, east of Lake Baykal, her military strength between 1892 and 1903 increased from 23 to 89 battalions, from 13 to 35 squadrons, and from 8 to 25 batteries; in western Asia, which consisted mainly of the Turkestan Military District, the increase was insignificant. At the same time, following the acquisition of Port Arthur, Russia's Pacific Fleet with its modern battleships soon became the most powerful component of her naval forces. Even after her lost war with Japan, Russia continued to maintain a formidable military strength in the Far East.[40]

Following the disaster of 1905, one can observe that the trauma of the two-front war, to be fought simultaneously at both of the Empire's extremities, some 15,000 km apart and connected for most of the distance by the then inefficient and vulnerable Trans-Siberian Railway, was to become a principal geopolitical factor that the Soviet Eurasian strategy inherited. Without bearing in mind this fundamental strategic factor, one cannot, for instance, understand Stalin's balancing policy between East and West, right up to Hitler's attack, or the underlying motives that led to the enormous Soviet military and naval build-up in the Far East since the 1960s.

There is a striking parallel between the recent vast military build-up in the Soviet Far East and the one undertaken under Stalin in the late 1930s. If today the Far Eastern Theater of Military Operations (TVD) is deploying between one-quarter and one-third of Soviet military manpower and material,[41] in 1940 the Special Far Eastern Army was proportionally even more important. It contained at least 600,000 men in 34 rifle, 8 cavalry divisions, and 8 mechanized brigades (compared with 55, 9, and 20 in the West, respectively). Convinced that the Japanese would not attack in the East, by December 1941 half of the Far Eastern contingent had already been dispatched westward to save Moscow from the German onslaught.[42]

Barely four years later, as the defeat of Hitler's Germany became a foregone conclusion, the *Stavka* managed to swing the pendulum back and throw more than 1.5 million men, 5,500 tanks, 26,000 guns, and 3,400 aircraft against the Japanese *Kwantung* Army in Manchuria, destroying it in a truly Soviet-style *blitzkrieg*.[43] However, to apply the principle of "swing strategy" today appears unrealistic.[44]

It seems that the present massive build-up in the Far East is a strong indication that Soviet strategists, until fairly recently, were resigned to face here the worst-case eventuality of nightmarish proportions, namely, a simultaneous outbreak of hostilities against the United States in Europe, as well as in the Pacific, combined with the high probability of conducting a simultaneous war with 1 billion Chinese.

Yet, despite the conspicuous shift of military resources in the 1880s to the Far East, the Central Asian Question remained the main bone of contention in the relationship between the two great Eurasian powers as long as there was a British India. In the following years the British would learn with regular occurrence about new alarming Russian plans to invade India.

Such a plan, for instance, was General Kuropatkin's scheme of 1886, revived during the Boer (1899–1902) and the Russo-Japanese (1904–1905) wars as part of the now familiar diversionary game conducted by the Russians in Central Asia. These schemes must be seen as part of a massive media campaign to keep the British on their toes in Central Asia and to give the Russians a free hand in Manchuria. Despite the Anglo-Russian Entente of 1907, and the partnership between the two Eurasian superpowers during World War I, Kuropatkin retained his vision of Russian expansion in Greater Central Asia from Persia, Afghanistan, and Sinkiang to Mongolia. In his capacity as Governor-General of Turkestan, he outlined this vision in 1916 in a memorandum submitted to the Tsar.[45]

Lord Curzon, a well-established authority on Central Asia before his appointment as Viceroy of India (1898–1905), was in many ways responsible for the continuing British obsession with the forward defense of India. He did not believe that Russia was systematically following a master plan of inexorable expansion in Asia, inspired by the apocryphal will of Peter the Great; rather, she was "driven by the impulse of natural forces" and profiting from others' mistakes. Failing to realize Russia's shift to the Far East, he wrote incessantly that her presence in Central Asia was a direct menace to India and that her desire to obtain a "second Port Arthur" on the Persian Gulf must be resisted.

But how real was the Russian menace to India? This is the main theme of Curzon's eloquent book *Russia in Central Asia in 1889*. He refused to believe that "a single man in Russia, with the exception of a few speculative theorists, and a giddy subaltern here and there," ever dreamed seriously of conquering India. "The project was too preposterous to be entertained." But a Russian invasion of India, whether real or simulated, whose chances were steadily improving because of the rapid development of strategic railways in Central Asia, was another matter. The Russian object, Curzon implied, "is not Calcutta, but Constantinople, not the Ganges, but the Golden Horn." Quoting directly from General Skobelev, that Russia must rule the Bosphorus because not only her greatness as a power of first magnitude depended on it, but also her defensive security, Curzon illuminated the paradox of Russian military demonstrations in Central Asia as follows: "The keys of the Bosphorus are more likely to be won on the banks of the Helmund. . . . To keep England quiet in Europe by keeping her employed in Asia, that, briefly put, is the sum and substance of Russian policy."[46] That Curzon understood the Russian mind shows in the instruction the Russian consul in Bombay received from St. Petersburg in 1900.

> The fundamental meaning of India to us is that she represents Great Britain's most vulnerable point, a sensitive nerve on which one touch may perhaps easily induce her Majesty's Government to alter its hostile policy toward us, and to show the desired compliance on all those questions where our . . . interests may collide.[47]

Subversion

The second strategic element, subversion, was collateral to diversion in most Russian schemes; after all, both elements could be found as parts of a strategem as old as the arts of politics and war. General Duhamel's memorandum, mentioned earlier, predicted that on the way to Lahore and Delhi the Russian army "will stir up the Mohammedan population and carry rebellion into the very heart of the English territory."⁴⁸ General Skobelev's plan of 1877 put a great emphasis on inciting rebellions inside India, in the hope that they "might even produce a social revolution in England."⁴⁹ Yet, when the Great Indian Mutiny broke out in 1857, its causes had very little to do with Russian intrigue. Until the Bolshevik Eastern strategy, the image of India teaming with Russian agents could be more safely traced to Rudyard Kipling's inimitable hero *Kim* than to real events.

However, a truly aggressive pitch on the subversive scale was reached neither by Russian nor British schemers, but by Imperial Germany, who inserted herself into the Great Game of Central Asia between Britain and Russia through her extended bridgehead of the *Bagdadbahn*. Inspired by the leading German Orientalist, Max von Oppenheim, the Kaiser decided to lend his support to Pan-Islamism; already in 1898 he had proclaimed himself protector of 300 million Muslims in Damascus.⁵⁰ As Fritz Fischer has shown in his important book, the emperor willingly embraced the image of revolutionary possibilities that Islam offered in the event of a global war, including the idea of a *Jihad*.⁵¹

Germany, like Russia, faced the dilemma of a war on several fronts, and she developed diversion cum subversion as an effective and legitimate means of strategic warfare on the eve of World War I. But her promotion of independence in Egypt or India must also be regarded as a war aim in itself, because the disintegration of the British Empire was a precondition of Germany's rise to the status of the leading world power. At first these schemes were primarily directed to divert and delay troop movements of the colonial powers from reaching the European theater of war.

The promotion of revolution by strategic subversion, in which Imperial Germany became the real pioneer, was an incredibly wide-ranging and systematic operation launched by her general staff in cooperation with the foreign office.⁵² Their most spectacular coup de theater, with not entirely forseeable consequences, was, of course, the transfer of Lenin across Germany in 1917 in a sealed train. With regard to the Islamic world, the German planners developed no less than ten schemes, ranging from Lahore to Casablanca. "Revolution in India and Egypt, and also in the Caucasus," wrote General Helmuth von Moltke Jr., chief of the general staff, "is of the highest importance . . . to awaken the fanaticism of Islam."⁵³

The fact that German planners first selected India as a priority target may have been due to the influence of two extraordinary outsiders, each in his own way obsessed with the vision of Greater Central Asia. One was Enver Pasha (1881–1922), the pro-German Turkish Minister of War and leading Pan-Turanist; the other was Swedish explorer Sven Hedin (1865–1952), a Pan-German (as far as his *Weltanschauung* was concerned) and unquestionably the most knowledgeable Western traveler in Central Asia, who was to assist the German general staff through advice and his invaluable maps during both world wars.[54]

Using Indian revolutionaries residing in Germany, two expeditions were organized during 1914 and sent to Baghdad with the military assistance of the Turkish ally. Led by Werner Otto von Hentig and Oskar von Niedermayer, the Kaiser's messengers rode across Persia and finally reached Kabul without achieving their main political objective. In exchange for the verbal recognition of full independence and an unrealistic offer of military assistance, Germany wanted to draw Afghanistan into war with British India. By inciting a mass tribal uprising, they could tie down most of the Indian Army on the North-West Frontier and facilitate revolutionary subversion inside India itself.[55]

Another group of highly adventurous German agents, operating from Baghdad and Persia, wanted to achieve too many controversial aims at the same time: an anti-Russian uprising in Azerbaijan, Bukhara, and Khiva; the extension of the *Jihad* among the Shiites; and a promotion of Pan-Turanian ideas advocated by Enver Pasha, which the Shiites, however, had no reason to welcome.

The boldest scheme was put forward by Count von Kanitz, the German military attaché at Tehran. He made several proposals during 1915 to liberate 50,000 German and Austro-Hungarian prisoners of war believed held in Russian Turkestan and to use them not only to foment unrest inside Central Asia, but also to isolate Turkestan from the rest of Eurasian Russia by taking control of the railway network between the Caspian Sea and Orenburg. Furthermore, Kanitz proposed to take control of the railway bridges across the Irtysh and Ob rivers and suggested that an operation against India be launched via Afghanistan.[56] The idea of controlling a large portion of the Russian Empire by seizing the main communications east of the Volga was not at all fantastic. In fact, only three years later the Czech Legion, also composed of former prisoners of war, seized control of the entire Trans-Siberian Railway.

It should not come as a complete surprise, therefore, that the Bolsheviks, and especially Lenin, were keen to adapt the German revolutionary strategy with its subversive tactics vis-à-vis what is today called the Third World. It is also no exaggeration to emphasize in this context that Wilhelmine Germany, in order to undermine the political cohesion of the Entente Powers and their colonial empires, pursued a more radical and consistent revolutionary strategy than did Hitler's Third Reich.[57] After all, the transfer of Lenin and his companions to Russia after the February Revolution of 1917 was a sufficient demonstration of Germany's cynical determination to promote revolution, in order to paralyze Russia, and get rid of the two-front war problem while fighting against the Entente. As for the subversive schemes to foment upheavals in India via friendly Afghanistan, this was by no means an original Bolshevik idea. The messianic ideology was already there; tactics were adopted from the earlier Tsarist scenarios, as documented in this text, and amplified by the fresh German experience gathered during World War I.[58] The first Bolshevik emissaries to Afghanistan, comrades Nicolai Bravin and Yakov Surits, followed in the footsteps of their German predecessors, Herren von Niedermayer and von Hentig.

When Amir Amanullah of Afghanistan launched an attack against British India in May 1919 (Third Anglo-Afghan War), he was convinced that the Russian Bolsheviks would hurry to his side. But Lenin could offer only lofty promises of military aid and recognition of Afghanistan's sovereignty, thereby conforming to the old German demands stipulated in the Brest-Litovsk Peace Treaty. Among the chief causes of the abortive Afghan-Bolshevik coordination was failed communication: the Orenburg-Tashkent Railway remained cut off for most of 1919, and although Tashkent could communicate with Moscow by radio, only horse-riding messengers could be used to and from Kabul.

The two Russian revolutions of 1917 caused great disruptions in the geopolitical framework of the Tsarist empire, resulting in the cession of its borderlands (Finland, Baltic provinces, Poland, Bessarabia, and temporarily the Ukraine and Transcaucasian Federation); yet they could not fundamentally change the geopolitical foundations of the Anglo-Russian rivalry in Central Asia.

Russian Turkestan, too, seemed to be drifting in the same irresistible direction of separation and disintegration. The Bolshevik power, resting solely on the maintenance of the only direct rail connection with central Russia via Orenburg, a connection cut off for most of the first two years of the Civil War, remained confined to Tashkent, the only larger Russified city in Turkestan. The central authorities in Petrograd and later in Moscow could hardly reach Turkestan, which in any case occupied a low military priority in the eyes of the Bolshevik government struggling to survive against a multitude of internal uprisings and foreign interventions.

From early on, however, the Bolsheviks possessed two major advantages. First, they were the only force in Central Asia capable of maintaining, repairing, and using the railway network for their own military aims. Second, they took full advantage of the only professional force of military value available in Turkestan after the dissolution of the old Russian Army. These were the prisoners of war, mostly Austro-Hungarians, estimated to number more than 40,000 in the fall of 1917. As indicated earlier, they had constituted an important element as early as 1915 in the calculations of German schemers who wished to unseat the British Raj in India by provoking a Muslim uprising.[59] In 1918 this remote threat suddenly became real. With the tacit agreement of the Bolsheviks under the terms of the Brest-Litovsk Peace Treaty, it was not impossible to imagine the Turco-German sweep originating from Transcaucasia across Transcaspia, northern Persia, and Afghanistan. These prisoners of war, suffering from malnutrition and boredom, were volunteering in increasing numbers to join the Red Guards in Turkestan as *internatsionalisty* and throughout 1918 they constituted the backbone of troops commanded by the Tashkent government. As a result the British became greatly alarmed by the additional gloomy prospect of watching "these potential recruits of an army of world revolution" getting loose in the direction of India.[60]

This was just one of many important factors that, in the period of the great upheavals in Central Asia between 1917 and 1922, created multiple political options in this region, options that could have shaped the future of Turkestan, as the main core of Central Asia, in a different way from what we know today. This state of continuous flux in Central Asia created an unpredictable series of challenges and responses for all participants in the division of spoils. Because there was hardly a similar dramatic cleavage during the last 100 years of Central Asian history, comparable with the years of 1917 to 1922, it is useful to sum up these options in more or less chronological order:

1 German designs concerned primarily with disrupting British control over India. By exploiting the Turkish connection Berlin hoped to stir up the Muslim population of India via Afghanistan through a mass tribal uprising on the North-West Frontier, tying down the British Indian Army and thereby preventing troop reinforcements from India from reaching other theaters of war. As a useful vehicle of religious and ethnic propaganda for Turkestan, the Germans hoped to exploit the Pan-Turanian movement (Enver Pasha). Although these German plans had been hatched since 1914 (for example, the Hentig-Niedermayer Expedition), preparations intensified after the Brest-Litovsk Peace Treaty during the short period between March and November 1918.[61]

2 British interventionists entering Baku in the late summer of 1918 to prevent the oil fields from falling into German hands and occupying Transcaspia between 1918 and 1919 to deny Turco-German forces control of Russia's South-East Passage toward India.

Although some prominent Muslims, like the Aga Khan, urged the British Empire, already "the greatest Muslim power in the world," to include additional Muslim states, "stretching from the Bosphorus to Chinese Turkestan," the temptation was wisely avoided in London. It was feared that the effect of Pan-Islamism "might easily be paralyzing." If the former Russian Empire were to disintegrate, the India Office thought that Turkestan "should look rather to Omsk than to Petrograd or Moscow as its focus." In other words, it was not in the British interest to encourage the reunification of the former Russian Eurasian Empire. If an Asiatic Russian government centered on Omsk, and controlling all the railway systems up to Orenburg, could survive the Civil War, then Central Asia, the India Office reflected, should be divided into four autonomous units under Siberian suzerainty: Bukhara and Khiva should retain their nominal independence; the rest of Turkestan should be organized into two local administrations, one based in Tashkent, the other in Kokand, with a mixed Muslim and European representation.[62]

3 Intermittent centrifugal movements created with German encouragement within the disintegrating Tsarist Empire. One such movement was the Southeastern Union, stretching from the Don region to Orenburg and Semirechie, which might have significantly influenced events in Turkestan, pending the control and maintenance of the Orenburg-Tashkent Railway.[63] The Cossack autonomists, however, proved even less coherent and short-lived than Admiral Kolchak's separatist government of Siberia.

4 The Balkanization of Central Asia, which might have led to the temporary extension of life for the ex-Russian protectorates, the Khanates of Bukhara and Khiva.

5 Alternatively, the conservative Khanates replaced by the forces of modern Islamic revival (*Jadids*), as epitomized by the short-lived existence of the Provisional Government of Autonomous Turkestan under Mustafa Chokaiev in Kokand. This government claimed authority over Russian Central Asia in competition with the Bolshevik Tashkent government (all-European). The Kokand experiment was savagely smashed by the Red Guards dispatched from Tashkent in February 1918.[64]

6 An attempt to create a larger Islamic federation in Central Asia, led by the ambitious Amir Amanullah. Apart from Afghanistan, it was to consist initially of Bukhara and Khiva. Because Persia was too weak, it was assumed that she would have to accept Kabul's leadership. Amanullah was hoping that further disintegration of the Russian Empire would increase the chances of incorporating the rest of Turkestan. In the event of British power collapsing in India, Kabul undoubtedly would have tried to reclaim the historic Afghan holdings across the Durand Line down to the Indus river to secure the integration of all Pashtun tribes (cf. the Third Anglo-Afghan War of 1919 and the origins of Pashtunistan), An inseparable part of Afghan territorial claims against British India was the maritime province of Sindh, with the port of Karachi as its center. This projected Islamic federation, however, would have rested on the leadership of Farsi or Dari-speaking traditional Persian elites; sooner or later, they would have clashed with the Pan-Turanist movement, rallying all Turkic-speaking groups of Central Asia.[65]

7   A Muslim Pan-Turanist federation in Central Asia—a lifelong dream of Enver Pasha who, after disastrously failing to lead Turkish troops to Central Asia through the Caucasus in 1915, with Lenin's encouragement would eventually arrive in Turkestan via Moscow in November 1921. But instead of helping promote an anticolonial revolution from near the Indian border and helping the Bolsheviks consolidate their control over the Central Asian Turks (as he must have promised Lenin), Enver Pasha at the first opportunity joined the anti-Bolshevik guerrillas (*basmachi*). Despite all his superb credentials (son-in-law of the last Turkish Sultan and *Khalif*; ex-Minister of War, etc.), Enver's claim to overall leadership was never recognized by the *basmachi*. After his death amid fighting in August 1922, the incoherent *basmachi* resistance would linger on for years into the 1930s, incapable, however, of offering a constructive solution for a viable political alternative in Central Asia.[66]
8   A Socialist Pan-Turan, as envisaged by the "red" Tatar, Sultan Galiev, Stalin's confident in the Commissariat for Nationalities. This perspective was exploited by the Bolsheviks during the Civil War, especially among the Tatars and Bashkhirs. It was also useful as a propaganda vehicle bearing anti-imperialist slogans to rally non-European revolutionaries.[67]
9   Finally, the option that materialized when all others had failed, the old *status quo ante bellum*, that is the *reconquista*[68] of Turkestan by the Bolsheviks. Only after repelling interventionist forces in central Russia could the Bolsheviks turn their attention to Turkestan, which hitherto had occupied only a secondary place on the list of strategic priorities. The essential prerequisite was to secure control over the entire length of the Orenburg-Tashkent Railway, which the Bolsheviks achieved in mid-September 1919. Finally, in November 1919, the so-called *Turkkomissiya*, led by the prominent Bolshevik military leader, M. V. Frunze, arrived in Tashkent declaring that its main task was "to strengthen the links between the toiling masses of the Russian and Turkestan peoples . . . to help to strengthen Soviet power . . . and to fulfill the Leninist national policy."[69]

The meaning of this was soon demonstrated. The second step of the Bolshevik *reconquista* terminated the political proviso hitherto tolerated by the Bolsheviks in allowing the existence of two living political anachronisms in Central Asia, the Khanates of Khiva and Bukhara. In a series of operations combining a tough military thrust and a soft subversion from inside, Khiva was absorbed in February 1920 to become the People's Republic of Khorezm; the People's Republic of Bukhara followed in September of the same year.[70] Furthermore, in May 1920 Soviet troops landed in the northern Persian port of Enzeli, and the region was soon proclaimed Soviet Socialist Republic of Gilan.[71]

The third step of the Bolshevik *reconquista* of Turkestan consisted of mopping-up operations to wipe out the *basmachi* guerrillas, a task that was not accomplished until 15 years later. In spite of the protracted struggle with the *basmachis*, however, the Bolsheviks could not postpone their anti-imperialist strategy and the promotion of world revolution through subversion from the Turkestan *platsdarm* (*place d'armes*). The failure of communist takeovers in Western Europe, which had been the prime target of their previous strategy, gave the advocates of anticolonial rebellions a chance to advance their own schemes, through which they could couple the Civil War in Russia with cross-border subversions to undermine the colonial empires. In this the Bolsheviks showed no scruples in enlisting the assistance of every potential ally, for example, Amir Amanullah, who eagerly sought Soviet support to disentangle his country from British bondage, and Enver Pasha, who had encouraged the massacre of the Armenians and was still pursuing the grand Pan-Turanian dream.[72] Following the second Komintern Congress and the Congress of the Eastern Peoples in Baku, which took place in July and September 1920 respectively, the Bolshevik strategy seemed to have radically switched, at least temporarily, from pursuing revolutionary takeovers in the West to supporting anticolonial uprisings in the East. Gregory Zinoviev, president of the Komintern who also chaired the Baku Congress, urged the participants to declare "a true Holy War against the English and French robber-capitalists." "If Persia is the door," he went on, "through which one has to go in order to invade the citadel of the revolution in the entire Orient, that is to say India, we must foment the Persian revolution." This quasi-Rawlinsonian image received the finishing touch when Zinoviev invoked the parable of falling dominoes:

The Persian uprising will give the signal . . . for a series of revolutions that will spread through all of Asia and part of Africa. . . . All that is needed is an impulse from outside, an external aid, an initiative, and a resolute decision.[73]

Following the decision of the Komintern, scores of Indian revolutionaries and Muslim *muhajirs* were to be trained and provided with weapons on Soviet territory. At a propitious moment they were to be launched via friendly Afghanistan to infiltrate the Indian border. At Tashkent, the prominent Indian Marxist, M. N. Roy, set up a military and propaganda training center.[74] Indian revolutionaries, who worked for the German Emperor during the war, were suddenly keen to transfer their allegiances to Lenin and conduct propaganda at the gates of India (for example, Maulavi Barakatullah, V. N. Chattopadhyaya, and the eccentric Raja Mahendra Pratap).[75] India now acquired a new dimension as the major external target for the Bolshevik strategy to enhance world revolution by striking at the most vulnerable spot in the edifice of the British colonialism.

Both Lenin and Stalin were anticipating the great anticolonial upheaval in the East from as early as 1918, though they still seemed to consider Europe the major playground of the future world revolution. Dzhugashvili, alias Stalin, himself an Asiatic from the Caucasus, went beyond the official Bolshevik appeals, stressing self-determination and renunciation of the former unequal imperialist treaties concluded by the Tsarist government with its weaker neighbors. In the first anniversary article in *Pravda* of 7 November 1918, Stalin stressed that the October Revolution "built a bridge between the socialist West and the enslaved East . . . against world imperialism." Two more articles followed in the journal of the Nationalities' Commissariat (*Narkomnats*), of which Stalin was in charge: "Do Not Forget the East" and "Light From the East."[76]

Did other Bolshevik leaders spread the same message? Nikolai Bukharin, for instance, expressed himself on the subject with cynical frankness in March 1919: "If we propound the self-determination for the colonies, the Hottentots, the Negroes, the Indians, etc., we lose nothing by it. On the contrary, we gain since it contributes to the destruction of English imperialism!"[77] Five months later, writing to the Central Committee, Leon Trotsky exploited the idea of a subversive thrust in terms of military strategy:

> The sort of army, which at the moment can be of no significance in the European scales, can upset the unstable balance of Asian relationships, of colonial dependence, give a direct push to an uprising on the part of the oppressed masses and assure the triumph of such a rising in Asia....
> One authoritative military official already some months ago put up a plan for creating a cavalry corps (30,000–40,000 riders) with the idea of launching it against India. It stands to reason that a plan of this sort requires careful preparation, both material and political. We have up to now devoted too little attention to agitation in Asia. However, the international situation is evidently shaping in such a way that the road to Paris and London lies via the towns of Afghanistan, the Punjab and Bengal.[78]

This "authoritative military official" could well have been the ex-Tsarist General Snesarev, whom Trotsky selected to head the Academy of General Staff in Moscow between 1919 and 1921.[79] However, such an ambitious invasion of India was never launched by the Bolsheviks in the early 1920s, when the political situation seemed most propitious. By 1923 the revolutionary enthusiasm, whether inspired by socialist ideas or Pan-Turanian or Pan-Islamist beliefs, seems to have evaporated, and the Soviet government became more inward looking, more cautious and calculating. The Bolsheviks turned against the Socialist Pan-Turan movement, headed by Sultan Galiev, which it originally wanted to use as a springboard for launching communist agitators into the neighboring Islamic countries.[80] By the time of the Curzon Ultimatum (May 1923), the Bolshevik Eastern strategy directed against India and emphasizing the connection with Islam, was effectively terminated. The abolition of the Caliphate by Kemal Ataturk caused the Khilafat Movement in India to die a natural death.[81]

Bolshevik forces did infiltrate Sinkiang and Outer Mongolia, trespassed on several occasions deep into Manchuria and Afghanistan (for example, in May 1929), and continued to fight against the *basmachi* guerrillas well into the 1930s. Their main task, however, was to consolidate Soviet power over the ex-Tsarist territories of Central Asia rather than to confront the British inside Afghanistan by applying diversion with subversion. The Komintern activists felt frustrated by the lack of success in India through subversive activities, underlined by the elimination of the most capable communist agitators and collaborators of M. N. Roy in the Cawnpore Conspiracy case.[82] Following these reverses in India, the Komintern's Asian strategy moved from the Muslim world and India to a new objective, China.

Nevertheless, the specter of communist subversion inside India, coupled with the phantom of a Soviety military invasion across Iran and Afghanistan, would continue to haunt the government of India, both its civilian and military branches, for the entire interwar period.[83] Military planners from the Indian General Staff and the War Office in London definitely viewed the Soviet Union as the number one threat to the security of India. The *casus belli* clause of 1907, which stipulated that a Russian attack on Afghanistan was to be answered by a British declaration of war on Russia, was retained in the Defence of India Plan (War with Russia in Afghanistan), drafted in 1929 by the War Office. During the previous year, the Chiefs of Staff (COS) concluded "that the present policy of Soviet Russia towards India is identical with that adopted in the past by Imperial Russia."[84]

Although the War Office scenario for a foward offensive policy in the event of a Soviet invasion took the cooperation of the Afghan government and the frontier tribes for granted, the Indian General Staff believed in neither. Their own contingency plans for the period, carrying the codes "Blue," "Pink," and "Interim" (1927, 1931, 1938), anticipated a Russian penetration coupled with Afghan hostility and guerrilla actions of the cis- and transfrontier tribes against the British. Even when the Axis threat became predominant toward the end of the 1930s, the British planners could never entirely divert their attention from the assumed Soviet menace in Central Asia until the day of Hitler's attack on the Soviet Union on 21 June 1941.[85]

Notwithstanding the enormous geographical and logistical difficulties facing a Soviet-sponsored invasion of India in the 1920s and 1930s, at least five hypothetical preconditions would have had to be fulfilled, more or less simultaneously, to bring about the demise of the British Raj over India: (1) the elimination of British naval supremacy in the Indian Ocean; (2) an outbreak of civil rebellion or communal unrest inside India; (3) a mutiny of the Indian Army; (4) an external challenge in the form of a tribal uprising on the North-West Frontier supported by Afghanistan;

and (5) collusion with an overland advance against India by a major power. Between 1918 and 1920, however, only two of these preconditions appeared to be fulfilled (2 and 4). But they did not occur simultaneously, and the Bolsheviks were either incapable of exploiting them, because of the distance and logistics involved, or late.

By contrast, between 1940 and 1942, when World War II created a series of parallel but not strictly analogous crises along the Eurasian rimland for the Western colonial powers, none of the serious challengers, that is, the Soviet Union (prior to June 1941), Nazi Germany, or Imperial Japan, were eager to shift their priorities to Central Asia to exploit several unique opportunities. This in spite of the fact that all five preconditions seemed to have been to some extent fulfilled. Moreover, in addition to these five preconditions, the Axis Powers could have cooperated more efficiently in transferring the outstanding Indian revolutionary, Subhas Chandra Bose, from Berlin to the Indian border, either to Afghanistan or Burma (as Imperial Germany had done in 1917 by sending Lenin from Switzerland to Russia). This would have decisively enhanced the collusion of all five elements needed to undermine the security of British India. When Bose finally arrived on the Asian scene in 1943 to take over the Japanese-sponsored Indian Independence Movement and command of the Indian National Army (INA), it was too late; all five preconditions, which had still existed throughout the early part of 1942, had either evaporated or turned in favor of the Allies.[86]

Drive to Warm Waters

Unlike diversion and subversion, which have been accepted more or less as irrefutable elements of Russian/Soviet imperialist policy in Central Asia, the drive to warm waters remains the strategic component that continues to arouse considerable controversy. It is branded with the stigma of historical forgery, namely, the fraudulent "testament" of Peter the Great.[87] Yet the testament, which fueled Russophobia well into the 1940s, does provide, in the recent words of a historical analyst, a rather "good synopsis of Russia's past and potential territorial expansion"[88] since the death of Tsar Peter.

Although Peter the Great devoted the best part of his life to the

20-year struggle for the domination of the Baltic area, he did aspire to secure a genuine warm water outlet for his expanding Russian Empire. At that time, however, it could only be the Black Sea, which is not ideal from a strategic point of view because its only outlet, the Bosphorus, is too narrow and is permanently controlled on both shores by a hereditary enemy, the Turks. But at least one contemporary Soviet strategist took Peter's putative geopolitical design as a given. He is Admiral Sergei Gorshkov, the architect of the present phenomenal Soviet naval expansion. Commenting on Peter's Azov campaign (1695–96), Gorshkov writes approvingly that "further development of the state and its economy could have proceeded only with the establishment of outlets to the sea."[89] Gorshkov's remark also exemplifies the notable fact that whereas the Soviet government goes to great lengths to disavow the internal policies of the Tsarist regime, the external expansionism is being legitimized as part of a "progressive heritage." It allegedly enabled the less advanced peoples on the periphery to receive the fruits of a higher civilization from the elder Russian brother.[90]

Tsar Peter's name is also associated with two military expeditions (1722–24) that attempted to gain access to the Indian Ocean through the Indo-Persian corridor to establish trade links with Persia, India, and China. These expeditions, and numerous others that followed under Peter's successors, were unsuccessful until the conquest of the intermediate zone—Transcaucasia (between 1800 and 1850) and Turkestan (1860 to 1880). Of decisive importance, however, was the introduction of railway transport in Central Asia by the Russian military. Waterless deserts and long distances were no longer major natural obstacles. Gradually, as rail spurs were extended deeper into Central Asia and closer to the Persian and Afghan borders, Russian troops filled the power vacuum up to the mountain rim of the great Central Asia divide. After establishing themselves in the Pamirs, it was logical that the next wave of Russian Cossacks would overflow the Amu Darya and seize the Hindu Kush ridge. The Cossacks were followed by European settlers from mother Russia, whose arrivals multiplied as soon as the new railways were completed. Thus, not only Semirechie, which opened to Russian colonists because of the Trans-Siberian Railway, but also Transcaspia and Turkestan, which had opened earlier, became more closely attached to the expanding Russian Eurasian Empire, regardless of the will of the subjected indigenous population.[91]

Even then, however, the essential logistical prerequisites for a successful penetration to the Persian Gulf did not exist until the completion of Russia's strategic railheads to the Indo-Persian Corridor. This is why the entire question of Russia's problematic drive to warm waters in the modern era, if it is to be considered more than a chimera, cannot be understood without a discussion of the significance of strategic railroads in Central Asia in general, and the plans for the Trans-Persian Railway in particular.

Railroad Imperialism in Central Asia

The era of railway imperialism did not have to wait long for the first perceptive geopolitical observations. Before the American Brooks Adams and the Englishman Halford Mackinder, French economist Paul Leroy-Beaulieu was a leading advocate of railway constructions overseas as an instrument of colonization.[92] He was one of the first Westerners who visited the construction site of *Le Grand Trans-Sibérien*. He regarded the establishment of the first Eurasian transcontinental railway as the decisive shift of the "world political axis" in favor of a new power constellation. The Trans-Siberian became for him a political railway because it brought Russia in direct contact with the Chinese Empire, from which she had previously been separated by deserts. It also offered the Tsar a new operational basis in the Far East to challenge other imperialist rivals and, therefore, significantly stimulated the process of modernization and great power self-awareness in Japan.[93]

The coming of the Railway Age seems to have intoxicated many contemporary authors. We have already quoted Dostoevsky's vision that Russia's civilizing mission in Asia was closely connected to the two strategic railroad projects, one reaching into Central Asia, the other into the Far East. But it was left to the French apostle of modern science fiction, Jules Verne, to devote a whole novel, *Claudius Bombarnac* (1894), to the fictitious continuation of the Transcaspian Railway (constructed in the 1880s). From Samarkand across the Tien-Shan Mountains to Kashgar, *Le Grand Trans-asiatique* was to follow the ancient Silk Road across the Gobi Desert to Peking and end at the Pacific coast. Jules Verne's inspiration might have come directly from the noted German expert on China, Ferdinand von Richthofen, who in 1874 had published his lecture proposing an optimal rail route between Europe and China.[94] The future Viceroy of India, George Nathaniel Curzon, who traveled twice on the Transcaspian Railway, described with enthusiasm the technological progress and the intricacies of power politics: "A railway train, lit by electric light and speeding through the sand-deserts of Central Asia, would add one more of the startling contrasts in which this extraordinary region abounds. ... This railway is a far more potent weapon to Russia in her subjugation of Asia than half a dozen Goek Tepes or a dozen Panjdehs. It marks a complete and bloodless absorption."[95]

Thus, the Transcaspian Railway (1880–88) was rightly seen as an obvious military threat to British India, bringing Russian troops menacingly close to the North-West Frontier. The man who built this strategic railway, the extremely efficient General M. N. Annenkov, compared the finished product to the sword of Damocles, suspended over the British in India "in order to keep them on their good behavior toward Russia in Europe."[96] As for the victims of this bloodless absorption, they did realize their dependence on the umbilical cord epitomizing their exploitation and dependence on the Russian metropolis. Only after the Russian Civil War did the clandestine Turkestan Socialist Party (ERK) stipulate in its 1924 program that the establishment of railway links between Turkestan and India, Iran, and China was one of the foremost tasks in the economic revival of Central Asia, thereby liberating Central Asian markets from the monopoly of the Russian railway network.[97] In this context the analogy with the systematic Soviet penetration of the transport infrastructure of today's Afghanistan, especially since the 1960s, is absolutely striking.[98]

By 1880 the British had constructed about 15,000 km of rail tracks in India, but Russia still had no single line in Asia. However, within 25 years after the construction of the Transcaspian Railway, Russia's military engineers built more than 4,300 km of spurs in Central Asia alone, including an extension from Merv to the Afghan border at Kushka (completed in 1900), which was less than 100 km from Herat and 770 km from Kandahar. After the completion of the Orenburg-Tashkent line in 1905, some British strategists predicted that Russia could flood the Afghan border with her unlimited supply of troops at the rate of at least 120,000 men per month. This 1907 estimate, perhaps one of the most pessimistic assessments ever produced by the British General Staff, concluded that India simply did not have the resources to compete on this level with Russia in Central Asia any longer. As far as chances for a strategic diversion mounted by the British themselves were concerned, the document was no less gloomy: "We cannot, by attacking Russia in other parts of the world, force her to let go her hold upon the northern provinces of Afghanistan."[99] Even in the event that Japan acted in alliance with Britain, the advantages of Russia's interior lines of communication seemed to give her a better chance for practicing strategic diversion. The construction of the future railway connection between Turkestan and Siberia, which was being surveyed at the time (although not completed until 1932 under the Soviets), would give Russia another parallel line of communication between the two potential theaters of war in the Far East and in Central Asia.

The increased German penetration along the *Bagdadbahn* in the Balkans and Asia Minor, however, convinced the Russians to sign the St. Petersburg Convention of August 1907 with the British. This temporarily suspended the Russian threat to invade India and lifted their veto on railway construction inside Persia by any power. "All plans for attack upon India are untenable and must be relegated to the field of fantasy," wrote I. A. Zinoviev, at that time the most senior Russian expert on the Middle East and ambassador in Constantinople. He recommended that the Black Sea Fleet be upgraded and efforts concentrated on the final push through the Bosphorus to secure access to the Mediterranean. Zinoviev seemed ready to overcome his notorious Anglophobia and make concessions regarding the Central Asian question, but only on condition that "England is prepared to assist in solving the problem of the Straits."[100] Thus, the partition of spheres of influence between the two major rivals, concerning Greater Central Asia as it covered the whole range from Persia to Tibet, contributed decisively to the formation of the temporary Anglo-Russian Entente (1907–17). Because Russia reluctantly, and only temporarily, recognized Afghanistan as lying within the exclusive sphere of British influence, the Committee of Imperial Defence retained the secret *casus belli* clause, which stipulated that in the event of a Russian invasion of Afghanistan, Great Britain would have to declare war on Russia.[101]

In the meantime, during the very years of the Anglo-Russian Entente, Russia succeeded along her Asian rimlands in converting northern Persia and Outer Mongolia into virtual protectorates and intensified her infiltration of Sinkiang. As for the new German participant in the Great Game of Central Asia, it seemed as if the century-old *Drang nach Osten* had shifted from the direction of the Baltic and the Ukraine to the more southerly latitude. The shift was earmarked by the growing German financial and military participation in the affairs of Ottoman Turkey, and epitomized in the new Hamburg-Basra axis, namely, the *Bagdadbahn* project.

The Trans-Persian Railway Dream

Among the essential logistical prerequisites for Russia's successful penetration toward the Indian Ocean was the establishment of three strategic railheads at the entrance to the Indo-Persian corridor: (1) in Azerbaijan, the Julfa railhead at the Iranian border (1907), with an extension of this line to Tabriz (1916); (2) the Kushka Fortress at the end of the branch line (1900) that joined the Transcaspian Railway at Merv; and (3) the second railhead on the Afghan border at Termez (1916), connected with the Transcaspian and the Orenburg-Tashkent lines (1905). The British, fully aware of their inadequate transportation during the Second Afghan War, responded to the Russian challenge by speeding up their own railway constructions on the North-West Frontier and in Baluchistan. After overcoming the treacherous Bolan Pass, the steam engine reached Quetta in 1887. Five years later the British completed the 4-km Khojak Tunnel, for many years the longest tunnel in Asia, which brought the rails to Chaman on the Afghan border, about 100 km south of Kandahar. The second British railhead in the Khyber Pass was not completed until 1925, although Peshawar had been attached to the Indian railway grid since 1883. In between a network of narrow-gauge military railways and roads was laid down in Baluchistan and in the nonadministered districts of what became, after 1901, the North-West Frontier Province. Finally, to undercut the anticipated Russian descent to the Indian Ocean via Khorasan and Seistan, a 700-km Quetta-Nushki Extension Railway was undertaken across the entire latitude of British Baluchistan, but it was not completed till the very end of World War I.[102] (See Figure 5.1.)

Critical to Russia's aspirations to project her power and

Figure 5.1 Railroad Map of Central Asia before World War I
Source: © Hauner and Canfield (1988).

influence to the warm waters of the Persian Gulf ports were the numerous schemes connected with the Trans-Persian Railway. This line was to provide the vital nexus for an alternative land route from Europe to India, making it possible to travel between London and Bombay in 8 days by rail instead of 33 days by boat via Suez. It was within this ambitious Indo-European land communication that the Trans-Persian Railway scheme achieved truly grandiose proportions, especially when the celebrated constructor of the Suez Canal, Ferdinand Lesseps, became one of its promoters. In his naively optimistic view, linking Russia and British India would facilitate trade and, as the construction of the Suez Canal had helped to alleviate the Anglo-French enmity, "this great project... will cause Anglo-Russian antagonism to vanish."[103]

This was precisely the right epoch when it became fashionable to believe that railways, rather than warships and mass armies, would decide the fate of India, and ultimately of Asia and Africa. By the mid-1890s Russian reconnaissance came up with three optimal routes for the Trans-Persian Railway, which were projected to serve exclusively Russian strategic interests: (1) the west-east axis, connecting Julfa, Tabriz, Tehran, Yazd, Kerman, and Bandar Abbas; (2) the Kurdistan route, linking Tabriz, Kirmanshah, and Khanaqin with the future Baghdad Railway; and (3) the north-south axis, cutting across eastern Persia from Ashkhabad and Meshed to Baluchistan and the Indian Ocean. Although the official choice favored the first route despite the heavy cost, the optimal alignment from the viewpoint of Russian military surveyors was a straight north-south track across Khorasan and Seistan to Bandar Abbas, whence the Strait of Hormuz could be easily overlooked, or farther east to Chah Bahar.[104] Russia, as Lord Curzon saw it, was bringing her forward frontier more than 300 miles nearer to the advanced frontier of India, thereby creating "unlimited opportunities from this base [that is, Seistan] of intriguing with trans-frontier tribes, and of nibbling at Baluchistan."[105]

"If Russia wants to assert herself at the very center of her empire in western Siberia and Central Asia," wrote Hermann Brunnhofer in the *St. Petersburger Herold* in 1895, and he was one of the most ardent promoters of Russian expansionism in Asia before the Western public, "she must above all keep the path open to a world ocean, i.e., the Indian Ocean... and construct a railway to Bandar Abbas, which will become the Russian Vladivostok in the Persian

Gulf."[106] However, in spite of the popular argument favoring the Trans-Persian Railway as a legitimate means to foster Russia's *Mission Civilisatrice* in Asia and eventually acquire the objective of supreme strategic significance, namely, a year-round naval base in the warm waters of the Indian Ocean, the official Tsarist policy was conservative and procrastinating. By obstructing any construction of railways in Persia, including, paradoxically, Russia's own, St. Petersburg reasoned that it could protect its trade interests in northern Persia against the more advanced British and German business competitors.[107]

The weakening of Britain's international position as a result of the Boer War, however, had increased Russia's temptation to overcome its siege mentality and push ahead (as in Manchuria) with railway expansion in Persia. One of the most active promoters was Captain P. A. Rittich, who had surveyed long stretches in Persia for purposes of railway development. He demanded that Russia exploit the opportune moment to achieve "our ancient dreams of reaching the open ocean in the Middle East," with Bandar Abbas, Qeshm, and other places like Chah Bahar acquired on the same basis as Port Arthur had been in the Far East.[108] Lord Kitchener, Commander-in-Chief India, regarded Rittich's scheme as the most dangerous yet contemplated by the Russians. It spurred Lord Curzon, the Viceroy, to submit yet another of his stirring memoranda on the Seistan question,[109] in which he pressed to forestall the Russian drive to the Persian Gulf by undercutting it with a new British strategic railway (the future 700-km Quetta-Nushki Extension Railway to Zahedan was not completed until 1918). On the Russian side, even such moderate liberal papers as *Russkaya Mysl'* joined the jingoist camp:

> What Russia wants is an outlet to the Indian Ocean, but the natural outlet is not through Afghanistan and India, but on the northern shore of the Persian Gulf.... Russia wants no territorial acquisitions in Persia. The uniting of many millions of Mussulmans under the Russian sceptre would only promote Pan-Islamism. We can reach the Persian Gulf without encroaching upon the integrity of Persia ... and without striking a blow we would acquire some port on the Persian Gulf suitable for the outlet of a railway running through Persia from north to south.[110]

Despite the temptation during that period to exploit British weaknesses caused by the war in South Africa, caution prevailed.

The Russians refrained from mounting a major diversionary operation in the Indo-Persian corridor. The Russian foreign ministry, the admiralty, and the war ministry all realized that without a naval squadron to defend it, and without a permanent rail link with the mainland, a Russian port in the Persian Gulf would be useless. The consensus in early 1900, seconded by Sergei Yu. Witte, the most able among Russian statesmen, was that instead of wasting money and energy on the Persian venture, Russia should concentrate her scarce resources on the vast enterprise in the Far East. By quickly completing the Trans-Siberian and Manchurian railway systems, she could make Port Arthur, free from ice and fog, a first-class naval base.[111] The fixation on the necessity of controlling an ice-free port, situated on an open sea shore and permanently linked by a rail with Russia's heartland, had been a characteristic feature of Russian geopolitical thinking.

The war with Japan had momentarily weakened Russia's determination to pursue her railway expansion schemes in Persia, but it strengthened her resolve to prevent railway constructions by others if she could not have it her own way. British opinion, nevertheless, still seemed greatly alarmed. Speaking at the meeting of the Royal Central Asian Society in March 1905, H. R. Sykes insisted that Russia still wanted to occupy Seistan, "in view of the contemplated development of her railway system to the Gulf or the Indian Ocean."[112] He warned, however, that Russia was not alone. While she was pushing from the north, Germany was pushing down through Mesopotamia on to the shores of the Gulf. Sykes clearly recognized why railways were much more important to Russia's expansion than to Britain's, as the latter relied primarily on sea power: "With Russia the case is wholly different. Her vast territorial possessions must be maintained and developed by railway. . . . seeking an outlet in a warm sea. . . . We cannot allow her to descend on to the Persian Gulf and establish there a second Port Arthur." In this he was simply echoing Lord Lansdowne's famous statement of May 1903.[113]

As both the British and Russians were pushing their rail spurs closer to the Afghan frontier, military experts became increasingly aware that occupation of Afghanistan would create tremendous logistic problems, despite the availability of railheads on the Afghan border, and that the fierce hostility of the Afghan tribesmen was a factor to consider. It might be of interest to recall that in 1904 the German Emperor William II encouraged his cousin, Tsar Nicholas II, to have Russian troops stage a provocation along the Afghan and Persian borders. The mighty Royal Navy would be useless against such diversion in Central Asia, and "the loss of India will give Great Britain the deadly blow," concluded the Kaiser. But even the Kaiser, with his developed sense of *Schadenfreude*, had to accept the verdict of his own General Staff, which argued, in a study produced at the end of 1904, that to invade India via Afghanistan with a large contingent of troops would take Russia years of preparations, during which Britain would find enough time to organize her defenses.[114] The India Command, however, with General Kitchener at its helm, continued to raise alarms that the Russian threat was real. The amount of troop reinforcements from England, which was always limited, and further financial assistance to the Indian Treasury for the construction of strategic railways became a hot issue between the Indian General Staff and the Committee of Imperial Defence.[115]

After signing the Anglo-Russian Convention of 1907, the British Government felt it no longer had the power to oppose the construction of railways in the Russian sphere of Persia (which occupied more than half of the distance from Russia to India). Moreover, the fear that Russia could reach an agreement with Germany on the extension of the Baghdad Railway into Persia (compare the Potsdam Agreement of 1911) also influenced British behavior. The British, in particular the Government of India, felt very strongly that the Trans-Persian Railway, if completed, would give Russia too many outstanding advantages in the commercial, financial, and, above all, strategic fields. The outbreak of World War I temporarily arrested the plans for the Trans-Persian Railway. Both powers, however, continued to push ahead with their extension spurs for military purposes—Russia in Azerbaijan and Turkestan, and Britain in Baluchistan. The discussion was resumed in earnest in 1916 under Russian initiative, only to be interrupted again in March of the following year by the Russian Revolution.[116]

However, none of the numerous Trans-Persian Railway schemes materialized during this entire period; the Russians were determined to prevent its construction by others if they could not have it on their own terms. Thus, all Russian/Soviet designs on the Persian Gulf failed to materialize. Several factors explain this: (1) external risks, exemplified by the British determination to remain the dominant power in the Indian Ocean; (2) serious geographical obstacles; and (3) the most important, Russian strategists never accorded Central Asia the same priority as the potential war theaters in Europe or in the Far East. Only a radical shift in the political and military balance affecting the whole of Eurasia could have altered what some schemers in Moscow and Berlin must have judged an unfavorable correlation of forces in southwest Asia.

Such a moment did occur, briefly, after the outbreak of war in Europe in September 1939. Great Britain, engaged single-handedly in a life-and-death struggle against Germany, and later against Italy also, had to appease Japan in the Far East and, consequently, could not effectively control the balance of forces in Asia. Between 1939 and 1941, there was thus a strong possibility that the Soviet Union, Germany's junior partner since August 1939, would join the Axis Powers, if she could only agree, according to the formula proposed in November 1940 by Hitler and Ribbentrop, to "center her territorial aspirations . . . in the direction of the Indian Ocean."[117] Because of the naval blockade around Europe, Soviet help was essential to the Axis Powers to maintain contact via the Trans-Siberian Railway. The Trans-Iranian Railway under Soviet and Axis control could have become the second branch of the Eurasian land bridge, thus accelerating the pace of political and military developments in Central Asia 35 years earlier than actually happened. But Stalin procrastinated. He was not anxious to give up claims on Finland, the Balkans, and the Turkish Straits, where Nazi and Soviet interests clashed, in exchange for the questionable privilege of attacking the British position in India as Hitler's vassal.

Nevertheless, Soviet policy was far from passive in the region at that time. The governments of Afghanistan and Iran were quick to realize the implications of Soviet-Nazi cooperation with regard to a very probable division of spheres of interests. And Soviet annexations before June 1941 confirmed their worst fears. The Afghan government regarded the Ribbentrop-Molotov Pact of 1939 as a green light for a Soviet invasion of its northern provinces.[118] As for Iran, evidence shows that for several months before the secret Molotov-Ribbentrop negotiations in Berlin (November 1940), the Soviets had pressed Tehran to permit the stationing of troops and air forces in important strategic locations inside Iran and to grant transit rights on the Trans-Iranian Railway together with free zones in the Gulf ports.[119] A captured Soviet contingency plan for the invasion of Iran, redrafted probably in early 1941, that is, just before the German attack on the Soviet Union, reveals that the Soviets had limited strategic objectives at that time. They were primarily interested in overcoming the anticipated resistance of Iranian and British imperial troops inside Iran along the main avenues of invasion, rather than seizing the Gulf ports; the Soviet Union then had no naval forces that could use these ports.[120]

Ironically, shortly thereafter in August 1941, the Soviet forces did actually invade Iran, but now they were partners of the British imperialists rather than their sworn enemies. The Soviets must have been immensely pleased that the great Trans-Iranian Railway, Reza Shah's most ambitious modernization project (1927–38), immediately became available to ferry vital American and British lend-lease supplies to the hard-pressed Red Army. Compared with other convoy routes to Russia, the Persian Corridor was the safest because the Indian Ocean was not infested by German and Japanese submarines. This link could operate year-round and offered the shortest route to Stalingrad, where the decisive battle of the Russian Front was about to begin. Almost 8 million tons of supplies were shipped to Russia via the Persian Corridor—a lesson in logistical efficiency and in the paramount importance of the "sea lane of communication" (SLOC) through the Indian Ocean, unlikely to have been forgotten in Moscow.[121]

Today, the 1,400-km Trans-Iranian Railway, consisting of more than 220 tunnels totaling 84 km, with countless bridges and heavy gradients rivaling the best that even Switzerland can offer, remains the single most impressive technological achievement in Central Asia. It is still the only rail link across the Indo-Persian corridor in the north-south direction. It intentionally avoided direct connection with either the Russian or the British Indian rail systems through its gauge and location of terminals.

In the 1970s Reza Shah's son initiated one of the world's largest expansion programs to modernize and extend the country's rail network. The purpose was to link up all major urban and industrial centers, not only in Iran but also outside that country, so that Iran could become the real communication and transportation hub of Central Asia, tremendously enhancing its geopolitical significance and hence its strategic value.

The multibillion-dollar railway expansion program provided for the creation of 10,000 km of new tracks, in addition to the existing rail-route length of 4,500 km, and for an extensive electrification and double-tracking of existing lines. The overheated pace of Iran's industrialization in the late 1970s put the state railways under great strain; perhaps no other rail system in the world showed such a steep increase in passengers and cargo. Although the Iranian Revolution of 1979 and the war with Iraq virtually arrested most projects in the Shah's ambitious agenda, it is worth recapitulating the late Shah's grandiose expansion plan.

The first project provided for the electrification of the Bandar Khomeini- (formerly Bandar Shapur) Tehran section of the Trans-Iranian mainline, which was to be double-tracked at the same time. The same provisions were to be applied to the Tehran-Tabriz-Julfa line and to the Tehran-Meshed line; the latter was supposed to be realigned to handle electric trains at speeds up to 240 km/h. The expansion projects provided for the following constructions:

1 A 550-km line connecting Kerman with Zahedan, with a bogie-changing depot at the new terminus (from the Iranian standard gauge of 1.435 m to the Pakistani broad gauge of 1.676 m).
2 A 700-km track to connect the Persian Gulf port of Bandar Abbas with Bafq via Sirjan on the Qom-Kerman line (itself completed in 1978).
3 A 150-km link between Shahrud-Gorgan and Bandar Shah.
4 A 300-km extension from Meshed to Sarakhs to connect with the Soviet network at Tedzhen, which would provide closer connection either with metropolitan Russia or with the Trans-Siberian Railway.
5 A line along the Caspian coast connecting Tehran with Astara on the Soviet border.
6 The longest stretch of new construction would have been a direct north-south line of more than 1,000 km from Meshed to Zahedan, and down to the Persian Gulf port of Chah Bahar—a project strongly reminiscent of the Russian Captain Rittich's aforementioned plan prepared at the turn of the century. (This particular option, which remains strategically the most attractive to the Soviets, figured prominently in the proposal deputy foreign minister Yuli Vorontsov brought with him from Moscow to Tehran during the summer of 1987.)[122]

Iran's ambitious expansion plans were to include Afghanistan in her extended network, thus making this landlocked country part of this first veritable Trans-Persian Railway, running in the west-east direction. About $1.7 out of $2 billion in credit, extended by the Shah to President Daoud of Afghanistan in 1975, was to go toward covering the cost of an over 1,800-km network inside the country. This network was to be completed during Afghanistan's seventh national plan (1976–80), according to a feasibility plan submitted by the French company *Sofrerail* in August 1977. Apart from linking the capital of Kabul with Herat via Kandahar, railheads were to be established at border points to connect:

1 With Iran at Islam Qala in the northwest (connecting also with the Soviet branch coming down from Sarakhs);
2 With the Kerman-Zahedan line at Tarakun in the southwest;
3 With Pakistan at Chaman in the southeast, which would allow through traffic to reach the Indian Ocean at Karachi.

Initial forecasts were for 1,300 million passenger-km and 1,300 million ton-km by 1985. The exploitation of the massive deposit of iron ore at Hajigak on the southern slopes of the Hindu Kush was of major significance; but ore was to be transported by cableway from the deposit to the railhead 100 km away, and thence to steelworks in Iran.[123]

Once completed, the Shah's new railway system would have redirected the flow of Afghanistan's trade away from the Soviet border back to the traditional markets in South Asia and the Middle East. In the absence of verifiable evidence, all speculations about the Soviet role in thwarting the Shah's new Trans-Persian Railway scheme must remain conjectural. But one can assume, nevertheless, that the Shah's ambitious dream of establishing a Tehran-Kabul-Islamabad alliance, welded by this important transportation link, was viewed in Moscow with little pleasure, especially as the new lateral axis would soon connect to China, which was close to completing the 1,200-km Karakoram Highway across the Himalayas from Kashgar to Islamabad.[124] (See Figure 5.2.)

There can be little doubt, certainly in Soviet thinking, that railroads have retained their unique importance, both strategic and commercial, in Central Asia. Almost certainly before the end of this century, the first through train from Europe will pass over the

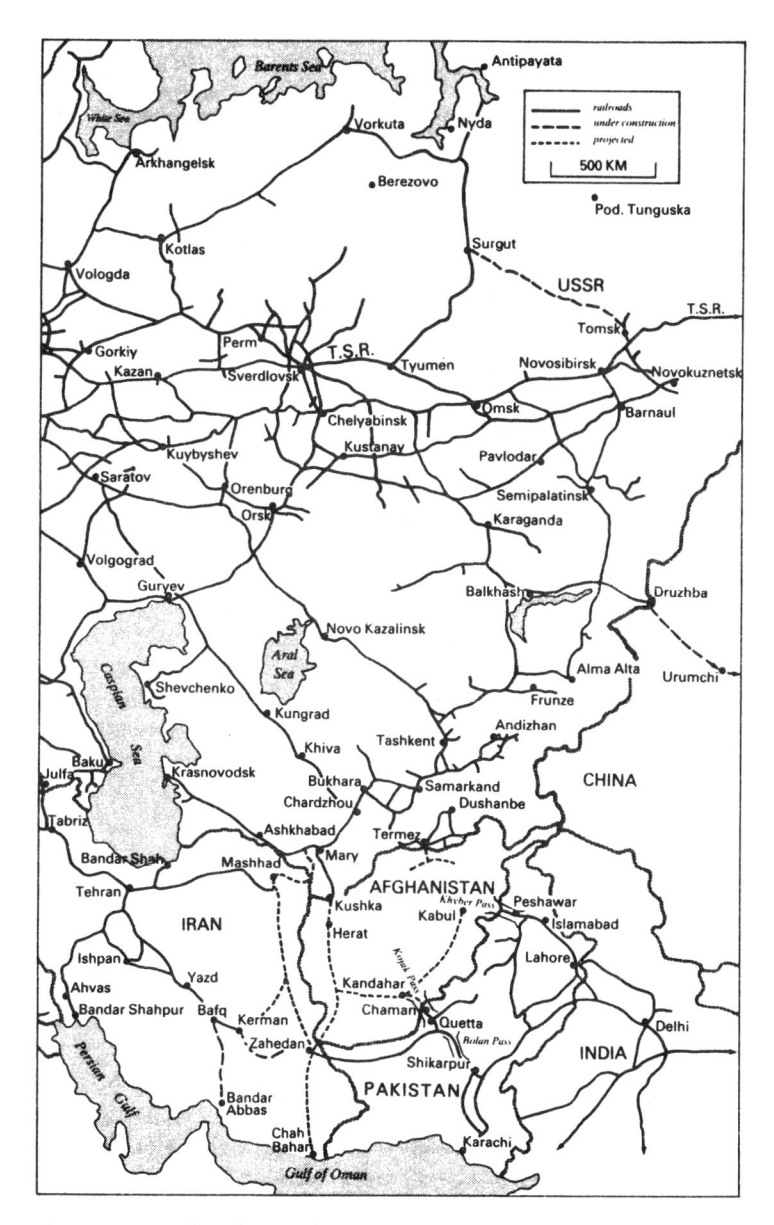

Figure 5.2 Railroad Map of Central Asia Today
Source: © Hauner and Canfield (1988).

completed Trans-Persian Railway, cutting through the heartland of the dual continent, as Ferdinand Lesseps predicted more than 100 years ago. This will not only increase "in an extraordinary degree the facilities of commerce," but will also remove "the ground for mutual distrust between the rival empires."[125] The persistent Russian pressure to expand railroads into Afghanistan as well bore fruit in May 1982, when the first Soviet train crossed into that country over the new Amu Darya bridge between Termez and Hayratan, almost 60 years after the Soviet government initiated the first survey and preliminary constructions.[126] Recent indications are that the former Shah's railway projects have been resumed, albeit on a much less ambitious scale. Because of the Gulf War, port facilities at Bandar Abbas and Chah Bahar began to be expanded. The leading South Korean construction firm, Daewoo, has been under contract since 1985 to complete the rail link to Bandar Abbas from Bafq, a distance of about 750 km; but completion is improbable as scheduled. Work has apparently also been resumed along the Kerman-Bam-Shur Gaz alignment in the direction of Zahedan.

Dual Soviet Strategy in the Indo-Persian Corridor

Tsarist absorption of Central Asia has certainly left its traces on Soviet strategic behavior in this region. But how does one reconcile the striking paradox in Russian strategic behavior? On one hand is General Skobelev's massacre of thousands at Goek Tepe (1881), which Dostoevsky tried to justify with so much eloquence and skill,[127] and on the other is "the utmost caution and temper" with which Russia had so far proceeded in her Central Asian movement—as even Rawlinson admitted with grudging admiration more than 100 years ago.

> Although steadfastly making progress year by year—whether from accident or design is immaterial—she has never placed her foot beyond that point from which she could, if required, conveniently withdraw it. ... Russia has always had her resources in readiness, and has not only secured her communications with her base, but has also looked to her lateral supports, so as to combine the whole forward movement in one harmonious operation.[128]

Is there a certain logic in Soviet strategic penetration of the Indo-Persian corridor in the light of recent history? How does one reconcile the apparent caution displayed by Moscow on the southern tier with other manifestations of Soviet great-power behavior in the same region, for example, the systematic build-up of the transportation infrastructure alongside the support of subversive activities.

The puzzle becomes clearer if one considers two inter-locking Soviet strategies. The first is the long-term projection of influence through the Indo-Persian corridor to the warm waters of the Indian Ocean, which has found its most consistent manifestation in the Trans-Persian Railway schemes. This approach avoids the application of direct force and combines diplomatic and economic pressure to gain control over the transportation infrastructure. One can trace this long-range policy on the part of the Soviet Union back to 1921, when bilateral treaties of supposed friendship were signed between Moscow on the one hand, and Kabul and Tehran on the other. In the Afghan case, it took the Kremlin more than 30 years to achieve the important breakthrough in influence that followed the visit of Nikita Khrushchev and Nikolai Bulganin to Kabul in 1955.[129]

The second strategy consists of seizing sudden opportunities and exploiting effervescent chances as they arise along the unstable frontier in Central Asia. This policy combines limited cross-border military intervention with political subversion and the support of separatist movements, for example: Soviet-sponsored propaganda and subversion vis-à-vis British India through Afghanistan (1919–22); attempts to set up the Soviet Republic of Gilan in northern Iran (1920–21); a brief armed incursion into northern Afghanistan in May 1929; preparations for the invasion of Iran and northern Afghanistan (1940–41); creation of the Soviet-backed autonomous republics of Azerbaijan and Kurdistan in Iran (1945–46); and the support of a communist coup in Afghanistan (1978) and the launching of a military invasion that followed (1979). In fact, the Soviet invasion of Afghanistan in December 1979 can be perceived as a consummation of these two seemingly contradictory yet interlocking strategies, even if the timing of the switch from one scenario to the other was not necessarily to Moscow's liking. Capitalizing on factional strife inside Afghanistan, Moscow invested its troops in the country, simultaneously putting itself in a better position to move toward "warm waters" through the systematic build-up of the transportation infrastructure. Roads and railways are the sinews of political and economic penetration. This is particularly true for the Russian/Soviet type of imperialism, in which expansion has generally involved contiguous areas and has been inseparable from railway transport.

Today, a modern transport infrastructure is being expanded from the southern USSR into Afghanistan,[130] which until recently had been the last remaining hiatus between the infrastructures of Soviet Central Asia, Transcaucasia, Iran, and the vast railway network of former British India. Hitherto impassable mountains, like the Hindu Kush or Karakoram, no longer represent technologically insurmountable obstacles. Long before the military occupation of Afghanistan, as we have noted, the Soviets had been preoccupied with the idea of linking Kabul with their own communication network. But it took them more than 30 years after completing the first survey in the 1920s to pierce the Hindu Kush with the Salang Tunnel (completed in 1965); indeed, without this tunnel they would not have been able to carry out the 1979 invasion and support themselves and the Kabul regime for another ten years.[131]

It remains to be seen whether the recently reported extensions of Soviet rail lines into Afghanistan—one south from Kushka and the other south from Termez across the new Amu Darya bridge—will eventually join the still incomplete Iranian and Pakistani networks, both of which operate on a gauge different from that of the Soviet system. If and when the Soviet intention becomes clear and a link-up is made, it would certainly constitute an event of major geostrategic significance. However, considering just the technical side of the question, it will take many years for Iran to complete the Bandar-Abbas-Zahedan link. Moreover, it is plausible that the Soviets would like to avoid any violent move against Iran and Pakistan for the time being, that is until the strategic rail link is completed "peacefully," preferably by the Iranians with the assistance of foreign (non-Soviet) companies. But direct Soviet involvement cannot be ruled out, as the revival of Soviet initiative in the almost century-old project of the Trans-Persian Railway from Transcaspia to the Indian Ocean demonstrated in the summer of 1987.

Other opportunities, such as insurrections and military coups stimulated or caused by Kurdish, Baluch, or Pashtun separatism; serious political upheavals in Afghanistan, Iran, and Pakistan; or a new crisis brought about by the unpredictable turns in the Gulf War, might tempt Moscow to seek a more forceful solution. Yet, Moscow's bitter experience in Afghanistan, where the recent agreement on Soviet troop withdrawals was achieved after almost 10 years of bloody fighting, must be rated as a definite setback for long-range Soviet political plans in the region. It seems that the Soviets, presently absorbed in their demanding task of internal reconstruction under Gorbachev's *perestroika*, might prefer to wait for a convenient fait accompli, that is, until the correlation of forces is restored in their favor.

The geostrategic significance of Central Asia cannot be determined in isolation from other security concerns of the Soviet Eurasian Empire. Historically, Central Asia dominated Russia's Asian strategy only infrequently, most particularly between the 1860s and 1880s. Thereafter, the Far East became the focus of Russian expansionism in Asia.

Yet, the southern tier assumed an important dual function at the beginning of the twentieth century. The first function was as a convenient platform, perfectly sheltered on the southern edge of the Eurasian heartland from any attack by hostile sea powers (this observation, incidentally, must have been a major inspiration, as we shall examine, for Mackinder's 1904 concept of the Eurasian Heartland), from which diversionary operations could be launched through the Indo-Persian corridor to threaten British India. The second function was to back up the vulnerable lifeline connecting the two extremities of the Empire, along what Winston Churchill would have called "the soft underbelly" of Russian Eurasia.

This west-east lifeline is epitomized in the construction and further improvement of the Trans-Siberian Railway (the line was completed in 1904, but improvements like double-tracking and electrification are still being carried out). Russia's decision to complete the Trans-Siberian Railway must be understood as a sign of irrevocable determination to hold on to the Far Eastern territories, come what may. The vital importance of this west-east lifeline created by the new transcontinental railway was underlined during the Russo-Japanese War of 1904–05, when the Russian Eurasian Empire was confronted with a new factor that henceforth haunted Russian strategists: the nightmare of a two-front war that had to be fought simultaneously at the two extremities of Eurasia.

Today, the Trans-Siberian landbridge links the two largest military complexes in the world, over a distance of more than 13,000 km; in comparison, the Southern Theater of Military Activities (*teatr voiennykh deistvyi*—TVD), which covers Central Asia, is a poor third. (See Table 5.1). Notwithstanding the continuous overriding importance of the Main (*glavnyi*) Theater of Military Activities (GTVD) opposing NATO in Europe, which contains more than 100 Red Army divisions or about 50 percent of Soviet ground forces, it is the Far Eastern TVD that has experienced a phenomenal expansion during the last 20 years.

After the Sino-Soviet split, Moscow doubled and then tripled the actual number of units in the Far East to an estimated current strength of 61 divisions. An entire logistical infrastructure, including new roads and rail spurs, ammunition and fuel depots, barracks, hospitals, and more had to be erected at the other end of the world. The strenuous effort to complete the Baykal-Amur Mainline (BAM), totaling more than 4,000 km and designed to alleviate the burden of the Trans-Siberian, must be seen as part of this enormous military build-up. In addition to ground and air forces, the Pacific Fleet has undergone massive expansion to become the largest of the four separate fleets of the Soviet Navy. It deploys smaller naval detachments in the South China Sea (from Cam Ranh Bay) and in the Indian Ocean (from Aden and the Dahlak Islands).

By contrast, no comparable military build-up has been observed along the southern tier, where an independent TVD was established in 1969. Its 32 divisions were estimated to have been at lower combat readiness than the average units at the two main TVDs. Until the invasion of Afghanistan, about three-quarters of the units from the southern TVD had been deployed in the North Caucasus and Trans-Caucasus military districts (MD), whereas the Turkestan MD has never had more than 6 divisions. Even the 40th Army, with its 6 to 7 divisions, which until mid-1988 operated inside Afghanistan, had been composed of units of different combat readiness. However, between 1979 and 1988 Afghanistan became the only "active front" for the Soviet military. The battered country provided an invaluable combat experience for the Soviet Army and its officer corps.

Table 5.1 Deployment of Soviet Armed Forces 1986

Region and TVDs	Western GTVD				Southern TVD	Far Eastern GTVD	Strategic Reserve	Cuts[g] 1989–90
	Northwestern TVD	Central European TVD	Southwestern TVD	NSWP[a]				
Divisions[b]	10	63	27	(24)	32	56	18	500,000[h] men 56,000 NSWP
Tanks	1,400	19,460[e] (9,800)	6,850 (5,300)	(15,100)	5,400	14,900	4,590	10,000 tanks 2,000 NSWP
APC[c]	3,130	20,400	5,400	(17,200)	9,100	17,300	3,600	?
Artillery	2,000	15,000 (5,800)	5,900 (3,850)	(9,650)	5,600	13,400	4,175	8,500 guns 630 NSWP
Tactical SSM[d]	100	580 (230)[f]	200 (155)	(385)	185	375	120	?
Aircraft	225	2,320 (1,600)	910 (750)	(2,350)	965	1,730	150	800 planes 130 NSWP

Sources: Compiled from *Soviet Military Power 1986* (Washington: Department of Defense); IISS, *The Military Balance 1985–1986, 1986–1987, 1987–1988, 1988–1989*. The figures up to 1988 are not substantially different.

[a] Non-Soviet Pact members taken together.
[b] Figures include motor-rifle, tank, airborne, and artillery divisions. Soviet divisional strength varies from 7,000 men (airborne) to 11,000 (armored) and 14,000 (mechanized). By comparison, the U.S. ratio is 16,800, 18,300, 18,500. Only about one-quarter of Soviet units are in category A (75% to full strength) of combat readiness. The rest are in category B (50–75%), C (20–50%), or even below those levels.
[c] Armored Personnel Carrier.
[d] Surface-to-Surface Missile.
[e] IISS gives different figures: 10,500 tanks, excluding those in reserve.
[f] Figures in brackets belong to NSWP (Non-Soviet Warsaw Pact).
[g] Following Mikhail Gorbachev's UN speech of 7 December 1988, the Soviet Union and the NSWP members announced unilateral cuts in armed forces to be executed until the end of 1990. With the exception of footnote *h*, all figures concern cuts in the Western GTVD. See Douglas Clarke, RFE-RL: *RAD Background Report/32*, "Warsaw Pact Arms Cuts in Europe," 22 February 1989.
[h] Of which 240,000 are in the Western GTVD, 200,000 in the Far Eastern GTVD, and 60,000 in the Southern TVD.

© M. Hauner (FPRI 1986–updated).

During the 10 years of the Soviet military build-up along the southern tier, rumors persisted that the new enforcements might be used to penetrate further toward the Indian Ocean. In fact, even the improved logistical infrastructure of Afghanistan, much of it with direct Soviet assistance prior to the invasion (for example, the Salang Pass Highway between the Soviet border and Kabul), could not sustain supplies for more than 120,000 troops. This was believed to be the maximum Moscow could afford to keep inside the country, which had only a few roads and no railways. In addition, 80,000 troops of the pro-communist Kabul government depended on the Soviet supply system. The reliance, therefore, on these extended and overloaded lines of communication could hardly help in more ambitious military operations against Iran and/ or Pakistan, let alone in the seizure of oil terminals in the Persian Gulf.

Under its new leader, Mikhail Gorbachev, the Soviet government decided in the spring of 1988 to put an end to the unpopular and unwinnable war in Afghanistan. By August of the same year, half of the Soviet garrison had been pulled out; the rest of the troops were gone by mid-February 1989. It remains to be seen whether Moscow can entirely surrender its stakes in Afghanistan, recall all its advisers, and relinquish its massive economic investments, especially in northern Afghanistan directly across the Soviet border. Nonetheless, the current Gorbachev leadership seems determined to withdraw from dangerous foreign adventures and to concentrate all human and material resources of Soviet Eurasia on the ambitious task of restructuring the Empire's obsolescent economic and political system. It seems plausible, therefore, to assume that Gorbachev must have prevailed on his military commanders, who were incapable of winning the war over the *mujahidin*. Recalling Rawlinson's wise observation cited earlier, which at the moment seems exemplified by Gorbachev's "foot withdrawal" from Afghanistan, we now turn our attention to the global aspects of Soviet strategy.

A Breakout to the Indian Ocean?

The Soviet Eurasian Empire frequently has been portrayed as a predominantly land-based power, obsessed primarily with the security of its own borders, its extended glacis. Thus, the Empire has appeared inherently defensive to the outside world. This is a naive approach that ignores the paradoxical mixture of both the defensive and offensive strategies displayed by both superpowers.[132]

As far as the Central Asian heartland is concerned, at least two relatively recent elements that can hardly be interpreted as strictly defensive are present in the Soviet geostrategic equation. A modern transport infrastructure has been steadily expanding from the USSR's southern tier into Iran and Afghanistan, an area that until recently constituted the last hiatus between the transportation network of Soviet Central Asia and the extensive railway grid of former British India. Thanks to modern technology hitherto impassable mountains are no longer obstacles for the swift transit of goods and people. The steadily expanding transport infrastructure along the southern tier remains the prerequisite for Soviet economic penetration in the southerly direction. This penetration must continue, in one form or another, regardless of the military debacle in Afghanistan. Moreover, in the event of a serious regional crisis—which cannot be excluded as much as Gorbachev's reign in the Kremlin cannot be guaranteed forever—Moscow might be compelled to make any number of strategic advances southward to deny the Western world and Japan further access to Gulf oil. Furthermore, this source has retained its long-term strategic attraction for Moscow because of steadily dwindling Soviet oil reserves.

The second element connected with Moscow's strategy in Asia is the phenomenal growth of the Soviet Union's Navy and its merchant marine during the last 30 years. The USSR is no longer merely a land power with an auxiliary coastal navy, but a sea power that ranks second only to the United States. However, because of the physical and climatic limitations of the Eurasian landmass in the northern hemisphere, the Soviet naval power does consist of four separate fleets in four separate seas. A glance at a map tells us that only the Indo-Persian corridor, with Afghanistan at its center, can give the Soviets access to a major, year-round naval base situated on the open sea, which eventually might be connected with the Soviet heartland through a rail link. Soviet submarines and surface vessels could leave from and return to such a base without hindrance and be kept at optimal combat readiness throughout the year. Furthermore, assuming that the Trans-Siberian Railway would be disrupted in the event of a protracted Sino-Soviet war, the Soviet Navy must establish a sea lane of communication (SLOC) running across the Indian Ocean to supply the Far Eastern TVD. In peacetime Soviet convoys must cover 10,000 nautical miles between the Black Sea ports and Vladivostok, passing through two critical choke points, the Turkish Straits and Suez, both of which are in hostile hands. Were the starting point for the southern SLOC established on the northern shore of the Indian Ocean, anywhere between Bandar Abbas and Karachi, the distance to Vladivostok would be reduced to some 6,000 miles.

This extraordinary expansion of Soviet naval power should be seen in parallel with Moscow's diplomacy of "collective security." Since the 1960s both elements of Soviet global strategy, that is, sea power and collective security, have complemented each other in efforts to establish a Soviet-controlled maritime passage from the Black Sea, via Suez and the Indian Ocean, to the Far East. Moreover, the Sino-Soviet split compelled the Kremlin leadership to rethink the function of the west-east nexus within the broader correlation of forces scenario. On the one hand, it appeared imperative to close the security gap between the western and eastern defense complexes. On the other, the dual objective of the Soviet global strategy, namely, to erode the U.S. naval predominance in the coastal waters of the Indian and Pacific Oceans and to encircle China, could also be pursued. In this arch, India remains the keystone.[133]

Undoubtedly, the loss of Egypt in 1976, after President Sadat's abrogation of the friendship treaty with the USSR, was a serious setback, only partially compensated for by the establishment of Soviet *points d'appui* in the Red Sea and the Gulf of Aden. The initial Soviet naval presence in the Indian Ocean in 1968 was directed against the anticipated U.S. deployment of Polaris submarines; but since the early 1970s the main concern has been the protection of the SLOC. Although the Soviets do not seem to want to challenge the U.S. naval predominance in Southwest Asia, especially in the Persian Gulf, it must be assumed that they will try to gain more basing facilities to the detriment of the West, an objective they have been pursuing with greater vigor recently in the Asia-Pacific region. In this respect the Indo-Soviet naval cooperation, exemplified in the steadily broadening Indian access to Soviet naval technology (including nuclear submarines), is an essential prerequisite. Before Gorbachev assumed power the Kremlin had been pushing hard, as in the case of Ethiopia, Afghanistan, and South Yemen, when no countervailing Western pressure was present. In addition, the Soviet and Indian proposals for transforming the Indian Ocean area into a "Zone of Peace" must be understood as part of the same global strategic design, which has clearly demonstrated the advantages of the long-range correlation of forces approach.

At this point we can sum up the Soviet geostrategic dilemma in Asia: alongside the new opportunities for breaking out toward the Indian Ocean from the geographic enclosure in Central Asia remains the geostrategic problem of first magnitude—the specter of a two-front war. Notwithstanding the importance of all other factors mentioned earlier, it is fair to predict that the Central Asian nexus will assume an increasing geostrategic significance. It finds itself approximately equidistant from the two main TVDs at the western and eastern extremities of the Empire, and it is located in close proximity to what remains perhaps the most politically unstable region in the world. Furthermore, if the Trans-Siberian Railway were cut off from the Far Eastern TVD, then the Indo-Persian Corridor would be the only passage through which the Soviets could gain access to the shores of the warm waters of the Indian Ocean, and from there to East Asia via a SLOC.[134] They have no other year-round alternative.

Moreover, as the invasion of Afghanistan has demonstrated, only in the Indo-Persian corridor can the Soviet Union still intervene without risking a major war accompanied by the danger of nuclear escalation. Whether the Soviets will behave more aggressively in the Indo-Persian corridor in the near future depends not on some sort of master plan for world domination, but on the outcome of the internal political struggle between the Gorbachevites and their opponents. Whatever the outcome—and it is far from obvious that Gorbachev will prevail in reimposing firm control over the centrifugal ethnocultural forces of the non-Russian peoples within the Empire—those in charge of the Soviet Eurasian Empire stretching from "sea to sea" will have to redefine their geostrategic relationship with their two major rivals, the United States and China. There can be no voluntary renunciation of superpower status by whoever happens to be master in the

Kremlin. It was achieved at high cost and after enormous sacrifices, the latter always linked in the Russian mind with the standard reference to those 20 million Soviet citizens killed in the course of the Second Great Patriotic War.

Is there an alternative to the superpower syndrome, to a potential right-wing coup supported by the military? Let us suppose that Gorbachev's domestic *perestroika* maintains its priority over foreign ventures in the near future. What will happen to the Soviet Eurasian Empire in 5 or 10 years? Will it maintain its cohesion without using brutal force against the centrifugal forces of political and ethnic nationalism in the borderlands, that is, in the Baltic republics, Eastern Europe, the Ukraine, the Caucasus, and Central Asia?

Furthermore, what will be the consequences if the Indian Ocean area, which already today has a population of 1.5 billion, one day becomes the world's third geostrategic region?[135] Should the breakout to the warm waters succeed, what advantages could Moscow possibly derive from controlling this new geostrategic realm? Although the assets are considerable (for example, access to cheap oil and minerals, a year-round control of sea lanes), they would be offset by Moscow's reluctance to take on more millions of devout Muslims and tens of millions of hungry people. Unable at present to feed their own population, today's masters of the Kremlin would presumably prefer not to revive the ancient Tsarist dreams of one day ruling over the entire Eurasian Continent.

Before the introduction of Gorbachev's "New Political Thinking," the Indo-Persian corridor was of largely derivative importance for the Soviet Eurasian Empire. It maintained, nevertheless, its geostrategic importance stemming from the continuing stress on the western and eastern fronts and the fear that war with China was inevitable. This focus on the west-east axis is all the stronger given the shift of the Soviet economic center of gravity to the east of the Urals, where nearly 90 percent of the Empire's mineral and energy resources are located.

Given time, circumstances will endow Greater Central Asia with growing importance in international affairs. The region has already been the major supplier of oil to Western Europe and non-communist East Asia for a number of years, and since the late 1970s also has been a major zone of war activities and revolutionary upheavals. It could become again the "geographical pivot of history," as Mackinder characterized it at the beginning of the century—a fulcrum of power bearing weight to the east, west, and south. In 1904 Mackinder stressed that the inaccessibility of "Heartland Russia" to hostile sea powers was a prime geostrategic advantage (discussed in the next chapter). The major lessons since then have been not only the ascendancy of air power, together with the existence of nuclear missiles as weapons of absolute destruction, but also the prosaic fact that the future belongs to economies with maritime rather than transcontinental forms of transportation.

If the Soviet Eurasian Empire wants to maintain its superpower position vis-à-vis its multiple rivals (the United States, Western Europe, China, and Japan), it must not only rely on its pivot area, which offers the traditional strategic advantage of controlling the hub of Eurasia's west-east and north-south axes of communication, but also break out of this enclosure and reach out to the warm waters that are the arteries of international trade. The second option, which would be more in harmony with the philosophy of the "New Political Thinking" developed in Moscow's think tanks during 1988,[136] would be to restructure the Empire along non-military and anti-autarkic principles before it is too late. The restructured Empire would then resemble a chain of decentralized states, joined in a kind of confederacy, organized on a strictly regional (both economic and ethnocultural) basis. As discussed in the following chapters, this is a scenario that was familiar to geopolitically minded intellectuals at the turn of the century.

Notes

1 Vladimir Solovyov and Elena Klepikova, "Russia's Geographic Imperialism," *The Washington Post*, March 30, 1980. Reprinted as "A Lesson in Russian Geography," *The Christian Science Monitor*, July 30, 1986.
2 Ibid. See also Roger Dow, "Prostor: A Geopolitical Study of Russia and the United States," *The Russian Review* (November 1941).
3 Compiled after J. P. Cole, *Geography of the Soviet Union* (London: Butterworths, 1984), 9.
4 John J. Stephan, "Asia in the Soviet Conception." In *Soviet Policy in East Asia*, Donald Zagoria ed. (New Haven: Yale University Press, 1982), 31.
5 W. H. Parker, *An Historical Geography of Russia* (Chicago: Aldine, 1969), 18.
6 Ibid., 18–29.
7 Klyuchevsky, *Kurs russkoi istorii* (1956), I:46–65.

8 Richard Edes Harrison, *Look at the World*. *The Fortunes Atlas for World History* (New York: Knopf, 1944); Gerard Chaliand and Jean-Pierre Rageau, *Strategic Atlas*. *A Comparative Geopolitics of the World's Powers* (New York: Harper & Row, 1985).
9 M. Hauner, "Soviet Eurasian Empire and the Indo-Persian Corridor," *Problems of Communism* (January–February 1987), 25–27.
10 Alexander von Humboldt, *L'Asie Centrale*, 3 vols. (1843), Russian trans. of vol. 1 (1915); Berthold, *Découverte* (1947), 185; E. M. Murzaev, *V dalekoi Azii. Ocherki po istorii izucheniya Srednei i Tsentral'noi Azii v XIX–XX vv* (Moscow: Akademiya Nauk, 1956), 9–10; Denis Sinor, *Inner Asia. A Syllabus* (The Hague, 1969).
11 Lawrence Krader in *Encyclopaedie Britannica*, Macropaedia 3 (1982), 1119.
12 According to Robert L. Canfield (ed.) *Greater Central Asia* (Santa Fe: American School of Research, in preparation 1989), introduction.
13 See Solzhenitsyn's letter to the Soviet leaders of 1973 quoted in chapter 2.
14 A. E. Snesarev, *Anglo-Russkoe soglashenie 1907 goda* (St. Petersburg, 1908), 12.
15 According to Charles Simond, *L'Afghanistan: Les Russes aux portes de l'Inde* (Paris, 1885), 323.
16 Snesarev's two lectures presented on 4 and 12 January 1905 at the joint meeting of the Russian Oriental Exploratory Society and representatives of the General Staff in St. Petersburg; published as *Indiya kak glavnyi faktor v sredneaziatskom voprose* (St. Petersburg: A. S. Suvorin, 1906), 7–13. See also his *Afghanistan* (Moscow: Gosizdat, 1921), 15.
17 Snesarev, *Afghanistan* (1921), 212–15.
18 According to Emil Ludwig's biography (*Napoleon* [Berlin: Rowohlt, 1927], 18–19), at the age of 17 Napoleon's reading notes were amazingly detailed: their printed version numbered around 400 pages and showed passionate interest in Egypt and India, abstracted mainly from abbé Guillaume Thomas de Raynal's popular *Histoire philosophique et politique des etablissements et du commerce des Européens dans les deux Indes* (Amsterdam, 1770). Alas, we have no such record about Hitler's reading list, though witnesses confirmed his lifelong fascination with Karl May's adventurous novels, which also deal extensively with the Near and Middle East, and with the popular editions of Sven Hedin's explorations of Central Asia. For example, Bradley F. Smith, *Adolf Hitler: His Family, Childhood and Youth* (Stanford: Hoover, 1967); J. Sydney Jones, *Hitler in Vienna 1907–1913* (New York: Stein & Day, 1982); Sven Hedin, *German Diary 1935–1942* (Dublin: Euphorion, 1951).
19 Snesarev, *Afghanistan* (1921), 10, 218.
20 Ibid., 216–20; G. N. Curzon, *Persia and the Persian Question* (London: Longmans Green, 1892), I:219, 577.
21 India Office Records (hereinafter IOR): L/P&S/20/A 100.
22 Snesarev, *Indiya kak glavnyi faktor* (1906), 173.
23 A. E. Snesarev, *Severo-indiiskiy teatr: voienno-geograficheskoe opisanie* (Tashkent: General Staff of the Turkestan Military District, 1903), I:9.
24 Snesarev, *Indiya kak glavnyi faktor* (1906), 172.
25 Snesarev, *Afghanistan* (1921), 3–19, 243.
26 Ibid., chapter 8. See also Alexandre Barmine, *One Who Survived. The Life Story of a Russian under the Soviets* (New York: Putnam, 1945), 85–87.

27 Barmine, *One Who Survived* (1945), 231; George S. Agabekov, *OGPU, the Russian Secret Terror* (New York, 1931), 179–80, and *Cheka za rabotoi* (Berlin: Strela, 1931), 276–83; issues of *Pravda* (Moscow) from May 7–10, 1929.
28 Sir Cecil Kaye, David Petrie, Sir Horace Williamson, *Communism in India*. Unpublished documents from the National Archives of India, 1919–33, 3 vols. (Calcutta, 1971–76).
29 Bisheshwar Prasad, *Defence of India, Policy and Plans* (New Delhi: Orient Longmans, 1963), 1–90.
30 See chapter 3.
31 H. S. Edwards, *Russian Projects Against India from the Czar Peter to General Skobelev* (London: Remington, 1885).
32 Malcolm Yapp, in his massive *Strategies of British India: Britain, Iran and Afghanistan, 1798–1850* (Oxford: Clarendon Press, 1980), considers that the external threat to India, first from the French, and then from the Russians for much of the nineteenth century, was a chimera, meaningful only in the sense that the Russian advance to India via Iran and Afghanistan might arouse British fears of an internal uprising, through the fomenting of unrest among the Muslims of the Indian Army. When the Great Indian Mutiny broke out in 1857, its causes had little to do with Russian instigation.
33 General A. O. Duhamel, "The Road to India"; Sir Louis Mallett, "Historical Summary of the Central Asian Question," April 30, 1874. Both in IOR Confidential Memoranda, L/P&S/18/C 9.
34 Yapp, *Strategies of British India* (1980), 439–40; Gerald Morgan, *Anglo-Russian Rivalry in Central Asia: 1810–1895* (London: Frank Cass, 1981), 56–58, 103–106. The notorious work on the Russian threat to India was General C. M. MacGregor's *The Defence of India* (Simla, 1884).
35 C. T. Marvin, *The Russians at the Gates of Herat* (New York: Scribners, 1885); A. E. Snesarev, *Afghanistan* (1921), 192, 219. For the criticism of Rawlinson's deterministic fixation on Herat as the gateway to India, see G. J. Alder, "The Key to India? Britain and the Herat Problem, 1830–1863," *Middle Eastern Studies* 10/2–3 (1974), 186–209, 287–311, and *British India's Northern Frontier 1865–1895* (London, 1963).
36 H. C. Rawlinson, "Memorandum on the Central Asian Question," July 20, 1868, IOR: L/P&S/18/C 3; see also Rawlinson, *England and Russia in the East. Political and Geographical Condition of Central Asia* (London: John Murray, 1875), 294–95.
37 Snesarev, *Anglo-Russkoe* (1908), 14; P. N. Savitsky, "Geopoliticheskie zametki po russkoi istorii." In *Nachertanie russkoi istorii*, by G. V. Vernadsky (Prague, 1927), 254–60. Certain strong residuals of the Herat fixation, I suspect, must have been present in the decision-making process of the Soviet leadership during 1979, which culminated in the full-scale invasion of Afghanistan by the end of the same year. Despite the absence of prima facie evidence from Soviet sources, there are strong indicators that the Soviets must have been extremely outraged by the anti-Russian uprising in Herat in mid-March 1979, during which an estimated 50 to 100 Soviet advisers and members of their families were mercilessly massacred. In revenge, squadrons of Soviet bombers and numerous military personnel helped loyal Afghan troops

suppress the Herat rebellion. See E. Girardet, *Afghanistan: The Soviet War* (New York: St. Martin's, 1985), 115–116.
38   A. L. Popov, "Ot Bosfora k Tikhomu Okeanu," *Istorik-Marksist* 3/37 (1934), 15–16.
39   "Indian Officer," *Russia's March towards India* (London: Sampson Low, 1894), II:79–100; G. N. Curzon, *Russia in Central Asia in 1889 and the Anglo-Russian Question* (London: Longmans Green, 1889), 307, 322–30. In February of the same year (1877), a certain Colonel Matveev was sent by the Russian general staff to reconnoiter the future line of supply to Russian troops in the event of their advance from Herat to the Punjab. Matveev's study was published several years later in the *Sbornik geograficheskikh, topograficheskikh i statisticheskikh materialov po Azii*, published by the Imperial General Staff, vol. 5; Warren B. Walsh, "The Imperial Russian General Staff and India: A Footnote to Diplomatic History," *The Russian Review* 16/2 (April 1957), 53–58.
40   *General Staff: The Military Resources of the Russian Empire* (1907), 188, confidential print, War Office Records: WO 33/419.
41   *Soviet Military Power 1988* (Washington: Department of Defense); *The Military Balance 1987–1988* (London: IISS, 1987).
42   John Erickson, *The Soviet High Command* (New York: St. Martin's, 1962), 767; A. D. Coox, *Nomonhan: Japan Against Russia, 1939* (Stanford University Press, 1985), I:84; Jonathan Haslam, *Soviet Foreign Policy, 1930–33* (New York: St. Martin's, 1983), 71–96.
43   P. H. Vigor, *The Soviet Blitzkrieg Theory* (London: Macmillan, 1983), 102–21; Michael Sadykiewicz, "Soviet Far East Command: A New Developmental Factor in the USSR Military Strategy toward East Asia," *Asian Perspectives* 6/12 (1982), 29–71.
44   Harry Gelman, *The Soviet Far East Buildup and Soviet Risk-Taking against China*, R–2943–AF (Santa Monica: Rand, 1982), 111.
45   A. Lobanov-Rostovsky, *Russia and Asia* (New York: Macmillan, 1933), 295; Hermann Oncken, *Die Sicherheit Indiens* (Berlin: Grote, 1937), 66.
46   Curzon, *Russia* (1889), 313–23.
47   A. L. Popov, "Angliiskaya politika v Indii i Russko-Indiiskie otnosheniya v 1897–1905 gg.," *Krasnyi Arkhiv* 19 (1925), 53–63.
48   See note 33.
49   See note 39.
50   R. L. Melke, "Max Freiherr von Oppenheim: Sixty Years of Scholarship and Political Intrigue in the Middle East," *Middle Eastern Studies* 9 (1973), 81–93.
51   F. Fischer, *Germany's Aims in the First World War* (New York: Norton, 1967), 121.
52   T. G. Fraser, "Germany and Indian Revolution, 1914–1918," *Journal of Contemporary History* 12 (1977), 255–72.
53   Fischer, *Germany's Aims* (1967), 126.
54   Ulrich Gehrke, *Persien in der deutschen Orientpolitik während des Ersten Weltkrieges* (Stuttgart: Kohlhammer, 1960), I:23–5; M. Hauner, *India in Axis Strategy* (London & Stuttgart: Klett-Cotta, 1981), 161, 166, 236.
55   W. O. von Hentig, *Mein Leben eine Dienstreise* (Göttingen, 1962); O. von Niedermayer, *Im Weltkrieg vor Indiens Toren* (Hamburg, 1942); R. Vogel,

Die Persien-und Afghanistan-expedition Oskar Ritter v. Niedermayer 1915/16 (Osnabrück, 1976), see also Hentig's private papers: Aufzeichnungen 1934–69, 3 vols., Institut für Zeitgeschichte, Munich.
56 Gehrke, *Persien* (1960), I:137.
57 M. Hauner, "The Professionals and Amateurs in Nazi Foreign Policy: Revolution and Subversion in the Islamic and Indian World." In *The Führer State—Myth and Reality. Studies on the Structure and Politics of the Third Reich*, ed. L. Kettenacker (London & Stuttgart, 1980), 305–28; D. Dignan, *The Indian Revolutionary Problem in British Diplomacy 1914–1919* (New Delhi: Allied Publisher, 1983).
58 See chapter 2.
59 See note 56. At the time of the October Revolution, there were more than 2 million prisoners of war in Russia, mostly Austro-Hungarians; their numbers in Turkestan by mid-1918 were estimated at 41,000. In Siberia as much as 75 percent of the Bolshevik forces consisted of foreign nationals. See V. M. Fric, *The Bolsheviks and the Czechoslovak Legion* (New Delhi: Abhinav, 1978), I:128–32; Alexander G. Park, *Bolshevism in Turkestan* (New York: Columbia University Press, 1957), 20–21.
60 Compiled from the *Journal of the Royal Central Asian Society*, vol. 6 (1919), 3–11, 119–36; vol. 7 (1920), 42–58; vol. 8 (1921), 46–69; vol. 9 (1922), 96–110.
61 W. Baumgart, *Deutsche Ostpolitik 1918* (Vienna: Oldenbourg, 1966).
62 See note 60. L. C. Dunsterville, *The Adventures of Dunsterforce* (London: Cape, 1920); F. M. Bailey, *Mission to Tashkent* (London: Cape, 1946). Quotes from "The Future of Russian Central Asia," a memorandum by the India Office, December 3, 1918, IOR: L/P&S/18/C 186.
63 Anonymous, "Russia, Germany and Asia," *The Round Table* 8 (1917–18), 526–64.
64 Mustafa Chokaiev, "Turkestan and the Soviet Regime," *Journal of the Royal Central Asian Society* 18 (1931), 403–20.
65 Ikbal Ali Shah, "The Federation of the Central Asian States," *Journal of the Royal Central Asian Society* 7 (1920), 29–49; L. W. Adamec, *Afghanistan 1900–1923. A Diplomatic History* (Berkeley: University of California Press, 1967), 108–68.
66 Essad Bey, *Die Verschwörung gegen die Welt* (Berlin, 1932); Azade-Ayse Rorlich, "Fellow Travellers: Enver Pasha and the Bolshevik Government 1918–1920," *Asian Affairs* (October 1982), 288–96.
67 Alexandre Bennigsen and S. E. Wimbush, *Muslim National Communism in the Soviet Union. A Revolutionary Strategy for the Colonial World* (Chicago: University of Chicago Press, 1979).
68 Why the Spanish term *reconquista* fits better than any other is convincingly explained in Guy Imart's highly stimulating *The Limits of Inner Asia: Some Soul-Searching on New Borders for an Old Frontier-Land* (Bloomington: Indiana University, 1987), 14.
69 Quoted from Yu. S. Akhtyamova, *Istoriya Bukharskoi Narodnoi Sovetskoi Respubliki 1920–1924 gg.* (Tashkent: FAN, 1976), 467.
70 Richard Pipes, *The Formation of the Soviet Union. Communism and Nationalism 1917–1923* (Cambridge: Harvard University Press, 1954), 174–84.

71 Dietrich Geyer, *Die Sowjetunion und Iran, 1917–1954* (Tübingen: Bohlau, 1955), 14–16.
72 G. Fraser, "Basmachi," *Central Asian Survey* 6/1 & 2 (1987), 1–73, 7–42. The most perceptive study on the position of the Russian minority in Central Asia during the Revolution is D. B. Yaroshevski's "Russian Regionalism in Turkestan," *Slavonic and East European Review* 65/1 (1987), 77–100.
73 *Baku: The Congress of the Peoples of the East, Baku, September 1920.* Stenographic Report. Trans. and ed. B. Pierce (London, 1977), 36; R. A. Ulyanovsky et al., *The Comintern and the East*, 2 vols. (Moscow, 1969 and 1978). See chapter 2.
74 M. N. Roy, *Memoirs* (Bombay: Allied Publishing House, 1964); C. S. Samra, *India and Anglo-Soviet Relations* (London: Asia Publishing House, 1959); G. D. Overstreet and M. Windmiller, *Communism in India* (Berkeley: University of California Press, 1955), 33–44.
75 A. C. Bose, *Indian Revolutionaries Abroad* (Patna, 1971); H. Kapur, *Soviet Russia and Asia, 1917–1927* (Geneva, 1966).
76 E. H. Carr, *The Bolshevik Revolution 1917–1923* (London: Penguin, 1966), III:236–37; C. B. McLane, *Soviet Strategies in Southeast Asia* (Princeton University Press, 1966), 9.
77 Carr, *The Bolshevik Revolution* (1966), 238.
78 *The Trotsky Papers, 1917–1919*, ed. J. M. Meijer (The Hague: Mouton, 1964), I:623–25.
79 Snesarev, *Afghanistan* (1921), 17–19, 188–210, 243. See chapter 5, "General Snesarev and the Central Asia Question."
80 Bennigsen and Wimbush, *Muslim National Communism* (1979), 66–68.
81 G. Minault, *The Khilafat Movement* (New York: Columbia University Press, 1982), 201–207.
82 See note 74; McLane, *Soviet Strategies* (1966), 32–34.
83 See note 28.
84 Prasad, *Defence of India* (1963), 15, 22–28, 28–33, 35–36.
85 Ibid.; M. Hauner, "The Soviet Threat to Afghanistan and India 1938–1940," *Modern Asian Studies* 15/2 (1981), 287–309.
86 Discussed in detail in Hauner, *India in Axis Strategy* (1981).
87 Kerner, *The Urge to the Sea* (1942); Eugene Schuyler, *Peter the Great, Emperor of Russia* (New York: 1884), II:512–14; John A. Morrison, "Russia and the Warm Waters. A Fallacious Generalization and Its Consequences," *U.S. Naval Institute's Proceedings* 78/11 (November 1952), 1172–79.
88 Albert Resis, "Russophobia and the 'Testament' of Peter the Great, 1812–1980," *Slavic Review* (Winter 1985), 692.
89 Sergei Gorshkov, "Russia's Road to the Sea, Peter I to Napoleon." In *Red Star Rising at Sea*, ed. Herbert Preston (Annapolis: U.S. Naval Institute, 1974), 14.
90 This is exemplified in the work of N. A. Khalfin, *Prisoedinenie Srednei Azii k Rossii* (Moscow: Nauka, 1965), who describes the process as "joining" rather than conquest—in contrast to the M. N. Pokrovsky school of the 1930s (see chapter 3).
91 Pierce, *Russian Central Asia* (1960), 184–9; B. H. Sumner, *Tsardom and Imperialism in the Far East and Middle East 1880–1914* (London: British Academy, 1942).

92 Paul Leroy-Beaulieu, *De la colonisation chez les peuples modernes* (Paris, 1882).
93 Leroy-Beaulieu, "La Sibérie et le Transibérien," *Revue des Deux Mondes* 68 (1898), 808–44.
94 Ferdinand von Richthofen, "Über den natürlichsten Weg für eine Eisenbahnverbindung zwischen China und Europa," *Verhandlungen der Gesellschaft für Erdkunde zu Berlin*, vol. 1, July 1873–August 1874 (Berlin, 1875), 115–26. Richthofen recommended following the Ili River valley to the western end of Lake Balkhash. The joint Sino-Soviet project of the 1950s foresaw the passage through the Dzhungarian Gates, a slightly more eastern route passing by the eastern shore of Lake Balkhash. Today, the Xin-Lan Railway (1955–61), which ends up in Urumchi, is being extended again toward the Soviet border railhead Druzhba, which has been awaiting the arrival of the first Chinese train for the last 20 years, when construction stopped due to the Sino-Soviet schism. The linkup, which is not expected to be completed before 1992, will thus become the third Sino-Soviet rail connection, in addition to the Trans-Mongolian Railway (1952–56) and the former Chinese Eastern Railway in Manchuria (1897–1904).
95 Curzon, *Persia* (1892), I:73, 79.
96 George Dobson, *Russia's Railway Advance into Central Asia* (London-Calcutta: 1890), 423–26.
97 See *Programs of the Muslim Political Parties 1917–1920* (Oxford: Society for Central Asian Studies, 1985), 113. See also Bennigsen and Wimbush, *Muslim National Communism* (1979), 67, 170.
98 Victor Mote, "Afghanistan and the Transport Infrastructures of Turkestan." In *Afghanistan and the Soviet Union: Collision and Transformation*, ed. M. Hauner and R. L. Canfield (Boulder: Westview, 1989), 120–59.
99 War Office Records, WO 33/419: *General Staff* (1907), 289–95, 303–306.
100 Quoted in I. M. Reisner, "Anglo-Russkaya Konventsiya 1907 g. i razdel Afganistana," *Krasnyi Arkhiv* 10 (1924), 54–66; see also Walsh, "The Imperial Russian General Staff" (1957), 58.
101 N. H. Gibbs, *Grand Strategy* (London: HMSO, 1976), I:825; Berryl J. Williams, "The Strategic Background to the Anglo-Russian Entente of August 1907," *The Historical Journal* 9/3 (1966), 360–73.
102 Compiled from IOR: L/P&S/10/54 and 1188; L/P&S/18/A 169, A 200, C 152. See also M. Hauner "Seizing the Third Parallel: Geopolitics and the Soviet Advance into Central Asia," *Orbis* (Spring 1985), 17–19, and "Soviet Eurasian Empire and the Indo-Persian Corridor," *Problems of Communism* (January-February 1987), 25–35.
103 IOR: L/P&S/18/D 229.
104 The discussion between the India Office and the Government of India concerning the Trans-Persian Railway schemes, with particular emphasis on the Russian plans and British countermeasures, is contained in the India Office Records, secret memoranda files: L/P&S/18/C 124, 128, 129, 130, 131, 133, 134, 135, 152, 153, 154, 179. Contemporary British opinion is comprehensively reflected in public lectures delivered before the Royal Central Asian Society and subsequently published in the Society's Proceedings of 1904, 1905, 1911. For the discussion on the Russian side, see N. Shavrov, "O

torgovykh putyakh v Aziyu," *Trudy Obshchestva dlya sodeistviya russkoi promyshlennosti i torgovli* 3 (St. Petersburg: 1873), and "O kitaiskoi i indiiskoi zheleznykh dorogakh," *Trudy Obshchestva* 9 (1987), 96–119; P. M. Romanov, *Zheleznodorozhnyi vopros v Persii i mery k razvitiyu russko-persidskoi torgovli* (St. Petersburg: Yu. N. Erlikh, 1891); P. A. Rittich, *Zheleznodorozhnyi put' cherez Persiyu* (St. Petersburg: Porokhovshchikov, 1900), and *Otchet o poezdke v Persiyu i persidskyi Baluchistan v 1900 g.* (St. Petersburg: General Staff, 1901). A good survey appears in Curzon, *Persia* (1892), I:613–39. For more updated literature, see Sumner, *Tsardom* 1942; Wilhelm Treue, "Russland und die persischen Eisenbahnbauten vor dem Weltkrieg," *Archiv für Eisenbahnwesen* 2 (1939), 471–94; F. Kazemzadeh, "Russian Imperialism and Persian Railways," *Harvard Slavic Studies* 4 (1957), 355–73; Derek W. Spring, "The Trans-Persian Railway Project and Anglo-Russian Relations 1909–1914," *Slavonic and East European Review* 54 (1976), 60–82.
105 Curzon, *Persia* (1892), I:236.
106 Brunnhofer, *Russlands Hand* (1897), 42–47.
107 Sumner, *Tsardom* (1942), 32–35.
108 Rittich, *Zheleznodorozhnyi* (1900) and *Otchet o poezdke* (1901).
109 IOR: L/P&S/18/C 152.
110 Firuz Kazemzadeh, *Russia and Britain in Persia, 1864–1914* (New Haven: Yale University Press, 1968), 333.
111 Ibid., 334–39. See also *Krasnyi Arkhiv* 18 (1926), 4–29; Sumner, *Tsardom* (1942), 11, 20–35.
112 H. R. Sykes, "Our Recent Progress in Southern Persia and Its Possibilities," *Proceedings of the Central Asian Society* (March 1, 1905), 12–19.
113 See note 101. As a direct antecedent to the CID's *casus belli* clause on Afghanistan (and to the 1980 Carter Doctrine), one might consider the statement by Lord Lansdowne of 5 May 1903 in the Parliament: "We should regard the establishment of a naval base, or of a fortified port, in the Persian Gulf by any other power as a very grave menace to British interests, and we should resist it with all the means at our disposal." See J. C. Hurewitz (ed.), *The Middle East and North Africa in World Politics: A Documentary Record* (New Haven: Yale University Press, 1975), I:538–41.
114 Oncken, *Die Sicherheit Indiens* (1937), 101–102; Gehrke, *Persien* (1960), I:2–3.
115 Keith M. Wilson, *The Policy of the Entente: Essays on the Determinants of British Foreign Policy 1904–1914* (Cambridge: Cambridge University Press, 1985), 76–84.
116 See note 104. David Gillard, *The Struggle for Asia, 1828–1914. A Study in British and Russian Imperialism* (London: Methuen, 1977). As late as 1916 the Russians were keen to obtain British collaboration for the extension of their recently reached railhead at Termez in the direction of Peshawar across Afghanistan. The 650-km "missing link" would have included a 21-km tunnel in the Hindu Kush, which would have been the longest tunnel in the world, superceding the Simplon in Switzerland (IOR: L/P&S/18/D 229).
117 Hauner, *India in Axis Strategy* (1981), 185–86.
118 Ibid., 132–73, 306–39.

119 H. Glaesner, *Das Dritte Reich und der Mittlere Osten*, Ph.D. Diss. (University of Würzburg, 1976), 302–12.
120 *Soviet Command Study of Iran* (Moscow General Staff, 1941), Draft Foundation and Brief Analysis, Gerold Guensberg (Arlington: SRI International, 1980).
121 T. H. Vail Motter, *The Persian Corridor and Aid to Russia*. Series: *U.S. Army in World War II*, vol. 7/1, Washington, 1952, 6, 488.
122 See Milan Hauner and John Roberts, "Moscow's Iran Gambit: Railroading a Friendship," *Washington Post*, Outlook, August 16, 1987.
123 Compiled from *Jane's World Railways* 1979–80, 1985–86, 1986–87.
124 *The Middle East Economic Digest* 21/11 (March 18, 1977), 3–4; Alvin Z. Rubinstein, *Soviet Policy toward Turkey, Iran, and Afghanistan* (New York: Praeger, 1982), 149–50; *International Railway Journal* (August 1985), 14–15.
125 See note 103.
126 India Office, Political Department: Confidential memorandum on the Kagan-Termez Railway, Bridge and Road to Afghanistan, December 12, 1925, IOR: L/P&S/18/A 200.
127 See chapter 1.
128 Rawlinson, *England and Russia* (1875), 280.
129 *Khrushchev Remembers*, trans. by Strobe Talbot (London: Sphere Books, 1971), 465–66.
130 Mote in Hauner and Canfield, *Afghanistan* (1988). See note 98.
131 The Chinese, too, extended military roads across the Himalayas into the region, to Pakistan, and to Nepal between 1965 and 1978. China is a remarkable example of how even an underdeveloped land-based state was able to sustain three cross-mountain battlefronts—in India, and in both North Korea and North Vietnam against overwhelming U.S. air and sea supremacy.
132 See discussion in Hauner, *Orbis* (1985), 13.
133 Robert H. Donaldson, *Soviet Policy toward India: Ideology and Strategy* (Cambridge: Harvard University Press, 1974); Avigdor Haselkorn, *The Evolution of Soviet Security Strategy, 1965–1975* (New York: Crane, Russak & Co., 1978), 5; and "Gorbachev's Selective Expansionism," International Security Council: *Vulnerabilities of the Soviet Empire* (Geneva, September 1987).
134 Michael MccGwire, *Military Objectives in Soviet Foreign Policy* (Washington: Brookings Institution, 1987), 183–210, James T. Westwood, "Soviet Maritime Strategy and Transportation," *Naval War College Review* (November–December, 1985), 42–49.
135 The other two "geostrategic realms," according to Saul B. Cohen, are the "Trade-Dependent Maritime Realm," centered on the North Atlantic basin, and the "Eurasian Continental Realm," consisting of two cores—the Russian heartland with Eastern Europe, and the East Asian mainland, centered on China. See Saul B. Cohen, *World Divided* (1973), 66, 308–12.
136 See M. Hauner, RFE-RL Research Paper: "The New Soviet Political Thinking and Europe," January 1989.

Part III

The Heartland Debate

6

Mackinder's Concept of Heartland Russia in 1904

Land Power versus Sea Power

In Part II we examined various manifestations of Russian interest and presence in Asia from a historic perspective, focusing deliberately, but not exclusively (because spatial relationships must be visualized in a broader context), on the heartland of Eurasia. We now turn our attention to this intriguing and highly topical heartland concept.

The creation of the Russian Eurasian Empire, spreading from "sea to sea" (*ot morya do morya*), was the result of a relatively slow process of military expansion and colonization that lasted more than three centuries. The original fur traders and Cossacks who ventured deep into Siberia opened the path for the subsequent waves of peasant colonists of predominantly Slavic stock. With those settlements the Tsarist administration wished to create a solid population belt stretching to the Pacific shore. This could hardly be achieved without adequate means of modern transportation. Because the great Siberian rivers flow in the south-north direction, and there is no chain of mid-continental lakes as in North America, the only means of transport could be railroads. At the turn of the century this narrow west-east strategic corridor, in which European settlers soon outnumbered the sparce indigenous population of Turko-Mongolian origin, became identical with the steel tracks of the Trans-Siberian Railway.

The interlocking of the vast Eurasian space with railways, which could carry passengers and goods faster than ships from the interior to seaports, or troops and war *matériel* from one end of the double continent to the other, was an event of major geopolitical significance. Russia had to use railways to overcome her hopelessly adverse geographic conditions. Whereas other nations used ships as a major instrument of imperial expansion and integration, she had to turn to railways. Still, sea power continued to dominate the imperialist mind as the ultimate achievement of historical progress.

The archpriest of seapower expansion and domination at the turn of the century was the American ideologue of navalism, Admiral Alfred T. Mahan (1840–1914), who often has been juxtaposed with the British geographer, Halford J. Mackinder (1861–1947). A man no less brilliant but much less popular at home and virtually unknown abroad, Mackinder advocated a different view based on the future importance of land powers as against the relative decline of sea powers. Neither man, however, was a rigid doctrinaire; rather than citing their views in contrast one should see them as complementary.

The American admiral was certainly not blind to Russia's continental peculiarities, as he described "the vast, uninterrupted mass of the Russian Empire, stretching without break," so that "the Russian center cannot be broken." Mahan observed further that geography had made Russia much weaker on her flanks, because of the overextended lines of supply and the sparse network of communications. Russia's endeavor to reach the Persian Gulf via Khorasan and Seistan was, in his view, "a strictly analogous movement" with her penetration of Manchuria and the occupation of Port Arthur.[1] He also pointed out that, as in the Far East, Russia absolutely needed a railroad connecting her hinterland through the Indo-Persian corridor with the Gulf; otherwise, her contemplated naval presence there "would be most excentrically placed."[2]

Mahan was also one of the first strategic thinkers who clearly grasped the fundamental geostrategic dilemma of Russia as a unique Eurasian power: the difficulty of waging war simultaneously at both extremities of her territory. Moreover, he doubted whether she could expand at the same time in two different directions, in the Far East and toward the Persian Gulf. He suggested that it was less risky for Britain to allow Russia to expand in the Pacific, where the latter would inevitably be confronted by Japan, the United

States, and probably Germany, in addition to the British hostility. In contrast, if Russia expanded in the direction of the Persian Gulf, where Britain would be alone she would be more difficult to contain, especially because of the additional heavy burden of guarding the communication lines with India.

The substance of Mahan's message was that Britain should wrest the initiative for diversionary challenge from Russia, pay her back in her own coin, and stage a diversion in the Far East with the purpose of allowing "Russia to engage herself so deeply in Manchuria that she would have neither the time nor money to spend on Constantinople or the Persian Gulf."[3] This diversion became the primary function of the Anglo-Japanese Alliance of 1902 and of the subsequent Russo-Japanese War of 1904–05.

Although seen at the time as two irreconcilable concepts, Mahan's geostrategic observations on the role of Central Asia in relation to the Far East should be regarded as complementary to the heartland concept formulated in January 1904 by Mackinder. In his fascinating lecture, "The Geographical Pivot of History," delivered before the Royal Geographical Society, Mackinder heralded the arrival of a new era of geopolitical polarization between imperialist powers.[4] It was a propitious moment in Eurasian history, too. The Trans-Siberian Railway was almost completed, and Japan was about to attack Port Arthur, the principal Russian naval base on the Pacific, thereby starting the Russo-Japanese War.

What made Mackinder's bold thesis a landmark in the evolution of geopolitical thinking was his single-minded emphasis on land power as superior, in the long run, to sea power. A heretical opinion at the time, it challenged the majority's view, which was defended by A. T. Mahan. Mackinder's "grand theory" of 1904, which he was to modify twice (see Figure 6.1) at decisive historical moments (1919 and 1943),[5] was, according to Colin Gray (a leading advocate today of American strategy of nuclear deterrence), of "a devastating simplicity."[6]

First, Mackinder revised the comfortable Eurocentric view of history in favor of the geographer's simplified but fascinating vision. He requested his London listerners ". . . for a moment to look upon Europe and European history as subordinate to Asia and Asiatic history, for European civilization is, in a very real sense, the outcome of the secular struggle against Asiatic invasion."[7] He

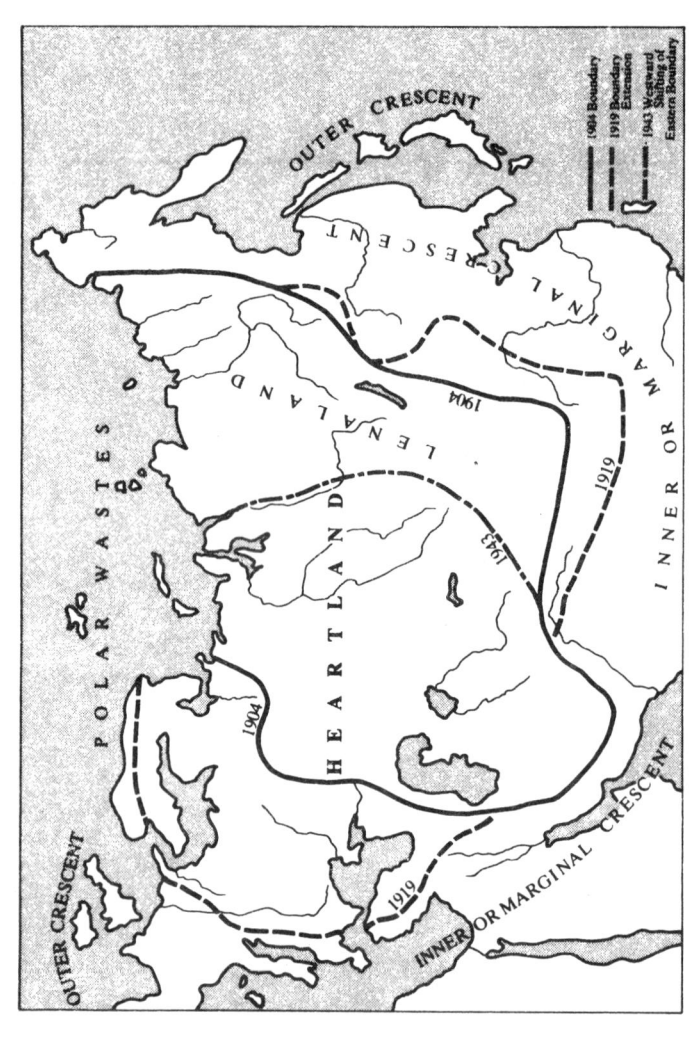

Figure 6.1 Modifications of Mackinder's Heartland Russia of 1904, 1919, and 1943
Source: © Hauner 1989.

wondered whether the Columbian Age, which had given Europe its pivotal role for the last four centuries, was not drawing toward its end, eclipsed by the ascendancy of the new "geographical pivot of history," namely, the "Heart-land" of "Euro-Asia."[8] The main geostrategic advantage of this imaginary center of a true world empire that, enlarged by the African continent, he would call the "World Island," was to be its invulnerability to the direct application of sea power (in 1904 this was still the pre-missile, even pre-airplane age).[9] Thus, in Mackinder's prophetic vision and lofty imagination, the fate of this future "Empire of the World" would depend on the control of its central core, the heartland.

Who Commands the Heartland?

The strategic control over the heartland would belong, Mackinder suggested, either to Russia exclusively or to a Russo-German combination. By shifting the center of power entirely from western to eastern Eurasia, however, it could be usurped by the "Yellow Peril" if China and Japan joined forces. From Mackinder's perspective it did not really matter whether the center of gravity was identical with the country's capital city or another important administrative or military center. The heartland could be commanded from Moscow as well as from Berlin, or for that matter from Peking or Tokyo. One did not need to reside in the heartland's pivotal point to control it.[10]

Because British sea power had encircled the Eurasian land mass along the circumferential maritime highway, thereby blocking Russia's attempts to break out and reach the warm seas, the rising naval might of Germany and Japan at the two extremities of the "inner and outer marginal crescents" of Eurasia might soon break the British naval monopoly. Or, alternatively, the coastal rimlands might be penetrated from inside the heartland by the Russian land power in its irresistible drive to gain access to a year-round naval base situated on an open sea frontage.

Thus, as early as 1904 Mackinder already visualized the Russian superpower of today, exercising essentially the same pressure on the rimlands of Eurasia as did the nomadic raiders from the steppes of Inner Asia. He regarded the Russian Eurasian Empire as uniquely endowed with "a correlation between natural environment and political organization so obvious as hardly to be worthy of description."[11] There are places in which Mackinder's imagination, described by a colleague as "a way of blending dreams and hard sense, subtlety and simplicity" so that "he never seemed to know when he passed from the one to the other,"[12] reached an extraordinary power of prophecy, as in this extract:

> Russia replaces the Mongol Empire. Her pressure on Finland, on Scandinavia, on Poland, on Turkey, on Persia, on India, and on China, replaces the centrifugal raids of the steppemen. In the world at large she occupies the central strategical position held by Germany in Europe. She can strike on all sides and be struck from all sides, save the north. The full development of her modern railway mobility is merely a matter of time. Nor is it likely that any possible social revolution will alter her essential relations to the great geographical limits of her existence.[13]

Mackinder's second argument for selecting the Central Asian "Pivot Area" in 1904 as the core of his heartland stemmed from the unique physical features of the Eurasian geography, determined primarily by the Arctic and the interior drainage of its river systems, including the Volga basin. Some of the greatest rivers of the world empty their waters into the Arctic Ocean, for example, the Ob, the Yenisei, and the Lena, but they are practically useless for year-round internal navigation. Other rivers and streams of Inner Eurasia, such as the Volga, the Oxus, the Jaxartes (Amu and Syr Daryas), the Tarim, and the Helmund fail to reach the ocean.

Mackinder depicted the heartland as measuring some 9 million square miles (out of 21 of the whole of Eurasia), more than twice the area of Europe, but having no available waterways to the ocean. On the other hand, except for the subarctic forest in the north, the heartland contained, according to Mackinder's optimistic vision, favorable conditions for the inner mobility of horsemen and camelmen to be replaced by modern railways; its potential for agriculture and extraction of raw materials seemed unlimited. The geographical location of the heartland coincided with its singular historical and cultural significance. To the east, south, and west, it was surrounded in a vast crescent by marginal regions, kinds of subcontinents that were, nevertheless, accessible to maritime traffic. Four in number, these regions corresponded to the great world religions: Buddhism, Hinduism, Islam, and Judeo-Christianity.[14]

This almost metaphysical meaning of the Eurasian heartland was reclaimed less than half a century later by Owen Lattimore, the renowned scholar of Inner Asia, who suggested that the world's new center of gravity was to be found within a 1,000-mile radius drawn around Urumchi, the capital of Sinkiang. To him this area represented "a whirlpool in which meet political currents flowing from China, Russia, India and the Moslem Middle East... encloses more different kinds of frontier than could be found in any area of equal size anywhere else in the world."[15] This was a vision much in the Mackinderian tradition, although Lattimore would never call himself a geopolitician.

Mackinder's peculiar genius consisted of his ability to reduce the complexity of world affairs to a single problem and to make his conclusions sound simple yet grandiose. As Strausz-Hupé correctly pointed out: "Mackinder reduced the sum total of world political questions to a fundamental one: Who will ultimately control the Heartland?"[16]

In 1919 Mackinder was to expand—and in my view depreciate—his heartland thesis by shifting the center of gravity radically westward to Europe, locating the "Pivot Area" in the contested zone lying between the historic German and Russian spheres of expansion (aptly called in German *Zwischeneuropa*). He believed this area would be critical to political developments worldwide. In his book *Democratic Ideals and Reality* Mackinder stipulated his new dictum: "Who rules East Europe commands the Heartland; who rules the Heartland commands the World Island [i.e., Eurasia plus Africa]; who rules the World Island commands the World."[17]

In 1943, just before Mackinder made the final modification to his heartland concept, Nicholas Spykman, an American geopolitician of Dutch extraction, reversed this dictum into: "Who controls the rimland rules Eurasia; who rules Eurasia controls the destinies of the world."[18] Some experts would argue that the "refashioned" Mackinder was to become, even after his death, the promoter of the U.S. strategy of containment against the USSR following World War II. However, the unwitting originator of this strategy, George Kennan, may not have realized that he had invoked the Mackinder legacy.[19]

Mackinder's view of Russia was originally founded on the typical perceptions of an Edwardian imperialist who contemplated Tsarist Russia as the perennial aggressor ready to seize the Dardanelles and decend on India. In addition, he was alarmed by the German *Drang nach Osten*, which threatened to reach the Persian Gulf via the Baghdad Railway, and the Bolshevik menace that arose after World War I. In 1920, Mackinder returned from Southern Russia, where he had been sent by the new Foreign Secretary Lord Curzon as British High Commissioner with the White Russian forces of General Denikin. He was convinced that Bolshevik propaganda must be neutralized and that Germany and Russia must be prevented from joining hands lest the world be confronted with a powerful new Eurasian alliance.[20]

Importance of Railroads

Blending history with geography, Mackinder visualized a metamorphosis of the arid steppes of Central Asia through a major transportation revolution. Impressed by the strategic role railways played during the Boer War, and by the completion of the Trans-Siberian Railway, he predicted that the empty spaces of Eurasia would be crisscrossed by new transcontinental railways before the end of the century (see Figure 6.2). The railways would transform this vast region of low economic yield into one potentially in "population, wheat, cotton, fuel, and metals so incalculably great, that it is inevitable that a vast economic world, more or less apart, will there develop inaccessible to oceanic commerce."[21]

Here was one principal contradiction of Mackinder's fascinating tableau: his unique talent to harmonize irreconcilable geographic realities with his own wishful political thinking. He wanted to have the heartland protected from sea powers by virtue of its geographic inaccessibility, while at the same time the heartland was to project its preponderant weight upon the coastal regions.

Perhaps Mackinder was also too optimistic, overrating both the capacity and scope of the railway expansion in Asia. His optimism in this respect was infectious. As late as 1942 one of his chief interpreters, Hans Weigert, could still write that according to Mackinder's prophecy all Asia would be covered by rails before the end of the century, a fact that was bound to have "the most radical effect on the fundamentals of a future military strategy." Weigert predicted the development of "a non-oceanic economic system of gigantic dimensions on the basis of the Russian railways"

Figure 6.2 Mackinder's Sketch of Future Railways in Eurasia (1919)
The World-Island united, as it soon will be by railways, and by aeroplane routes, the latter for the most part parallel with the main railways. Mackinder's wishful railway charter of the three continents (including a hint of the growing role of "aeroplane routes"—added for good measure), as sketched by himself for the 1919 book (pp. 144–45). It is interesting to notice that although not all of the transcontinental railways suggested by Mackinder for Africa and Asia have been completed, seventy years later, those completed in China and the Soviet Far East more or less fit Mackinder's forecast.
Source: Mackinder (1919): 144–145.

within the vast spaces of Soviet Eurasia and Mongolia, which are inaccessible to oceanic commerce.[22]

From the vantage point of the 1980s, one could easily make a case both for and against Mackinder. The positive side would feature the overwhelming economic and military significance of the Trans-Siberian Mainline for the tight coherence of the Soviet Eurasian land fortress. Its capacity has increased enormously since its opening in 1904. It is double-tracked along its entire length and electrified from the west as far as Chita. Furthermore, the rail network of Soviet Central Asia and Western Siberia has been vastly expanded.

On the negative side, one could argue that despite the prophecies of Mackinder and others, no radical step forward has occurred since the completion of the Trans-Siberian Railway, which remains today the only true west-east transcontinental railroad across Eurasia. As indicated in the previous chapter, all other railway projects in Asia, carried out since 1904, are so far unfinished: the Trans-Persian Railway has still not been linked up, nor is the Baykal-Amur Mainline yet operational, though it was originally scheduled for completion in 1983.

On the other hand, one could argue in favor of at least partial achievement with regard to transcontinental transportation: the completion of the Turk-Sib between Semipalatinsk and Tashkent in 1931; the Baghdad Railway (1940) and its extension to the Persian Gulf via Basra by standard gauge (1964); the Trans-Iranian Railway from the Caspian Sea to the Persian Gulf in 1938; and the Trans-Mongolian Railway connecting Ulan Ude with Peking via Ulan Bator in 1955. The Xinlan, the longest Chinese railway (almost 2,000 km), which connected Xinjiang (Sinkiang) with Lanchow in 1962, remains still to be linked up with a Soviet branch line via the Dzhungarian Gate, in order to form a second transcontinental railway across Eurasia.

Along with the railway building in Central Asia, especially after World War II, was road construction, mostly for military purposes in the high mountain areas. The most noticeable Soviet achievement was the completion of the more than 1,200-km circular military road in the Pamirs, between Dushanbe and Osh. The Salang Pass Road, which is more than 400 km and connects Amu Darya with Kabul across the Hindu Kush, was built between 1956 and 1966 (with a high-altitude tunnel almost 3 km in length at 3,500 meters above sea). Without this road the Soviet military occupation of Afghanistan would not have been feasible. Moreover, in May 1982 the Soviets completed a combined rail and road bridge across the Amu Darya from Termez to Hayratan on the Afghan shore.

The Chinese have been even more productive in building a mesh of military roads: three of those, totaling about 3,500 km and completed in the 1950s, led to Tibet; one branch was subsequently extended across the main Himalayan crest to connect Nepal's capital Kathmandu. Finally, after 20 years of construction, the 1,200-km Karakoram Highway was completed, connecting Kashgar in western Sinkiang with Islamabad in Pakistan.[23]

In the ensuing debate following Mackinder's exposition in 1904 before the Royal Geographical Society, Leopold Amery (1873–1955), the future secretary of state for India, argued very convincingly against Mackinder that nothing could replace the seagoing ship as a bulk and troop carrier "except fifteen or twenty parallel lines of railway," and that the advent of air transportation, which Amery boldly forecast, would render the geographical location of the military power less important.[24] Mackinder replied by specifying three fundamental criteria for the establishment of a world empire: "I ask for an inner land mobility, for a margin densely populated, and for external sea forces."[25] He tried eloquently to uphold the case in favor of what he called "the non-oceanic economic system." On the other hand, he was quick to admit that the "great industrial wealth of Siberia and European Russia and a conquest of some of the marginal regions would give the basis for a fleet necessary to found the world empire," and that with the help of railways, which would take the place of camelmen and horsemen, thus exploiting the advantage of internal communications, "you will be able to fling power from side to side of this area." "My aim is not to predict a great future for this or that country," he repeated to Amery, "but to make a geographical formula into which you could fit any political balance."[26]

Notes

1 Alfred T. Mahan, *The Problem of Asia* (Boston: Little & Brown, 1900), 24–27, 43–45, 118–19.
2 Mahan, *Retrospect and Prospect*, ch.: "The Persian Gulf and International Relations" (Boston: Little & Brown, 1902), 232–33. See also Paul Kennedy, *The Rise and Fall of British Naval Mastery* (London: Macmillan, 1983), especially ch. 7, "Mahan versus Mackinder."
3 Robert Seager and Doris Maguire (eds.), *Letters and Papers of Alfred T. Mahan* (Annapolis: Naval Institute Press, 1975), III:226.
4 Halford J. Mackinder, "The Geographical Pivot of History," *The Geographical Journal* 23/4 (1904), 421–44.

5 Mackinder, *Democratic Ideals and Reality* (London: Constable, 1919), and "The Round World and the Winning of Peace," *Foreign Affairs* (July 1943), 595–605. See the next chapter.
6 Colin S. Gray, *The Geopolitics of the Nuclear Era: Heartland, Rimlands, and the Technological Revolution*, National Strategy Information Center (New York: Crane, Russak, 1977), 21, and "Keeping the Soviets Landlocked: Geostrategy for a Maritime America," *The National Interest* (Summer 1986), 26.
7 Mackinder, "The Geographical Pivot" (1904), 423. It is interesting to note that Mackinder never used the term *geopolitical*; the approach in his 1904 article is more geohistorical.
8 Ibid., 430–31. Both terms are used here in the original transcription as applied by Mackinder himself in 1904—despite later comments to the contrary.
9 Mackinder, "The Geographical Pivot" (1904), 441. See also notes 24 and 25.
10 Ibid., 436–37. See also W. H. Parker, *Mackinder—Geography as an Aid to Statecraft* (Oxford: Clarendon Press, 1982), 220.
11 Mackinder, "The Geographical Pivot" (1904), 423.
12 W. M. Childs, *Making a University: An Account of the University Movement at Reading* (London: Dent, 1933), 11; according to Brian Blouet, *Halford Mackinder. A Biography* (Drawer: Texas A&M University Press, 1987), 199.
13 Mackinder, "The Geographical Pivot" (1904), 436.
14 Ibid., 431.
15 Owen Lattimore, *Pivot of Asia. Sinkiang and the Inner Asian Frontiers of China and Russia* (Boston: Little, Brown, 1950), 3.
16 Strausz-Hupé, *Geopolitics* (1942), 154.
17 Mackinder, *Democratic Ideals* (1919), 194.
18 Nicholas J. Spykman, *The Geography of the Peace* (New York: Harcourt, Brace & World, 1944), 44.
19 Robert E. Walters, *The Nuclear Trap. An Escape Route* (Penguin Books: 1974), 178; Gray, "Keeping the Soviets Landlocked" (1986), 24.
20 Blouet, *Halford Mackinder* (1987), 172–77.
21 Mackinder, "The Geographical Pivot" (1904), 434.
22 Hans W. Weigert, *Generals and Geographers. The Twilight of Geopolitics* (New York: Oxford University Press, 1942), 131.
23 Compiled, among others, from: George Cleinow, *Roter Imperialismus. Eine Studie über die Verkehrsprobleme der Sowjetunion* (Berlin: Julius Springer, 1931); Hugh C. Hughes, *Middle East Railways* (Harrow: Continental Railway Club, 1981); Oswald S. Nock, *Railways of Asia and the Far East* (London: Adam & Charles Black, 1978) and *World Atlas of Railways* (Bristol: Victoria House, 1983); *Jane's World Railways 1985–86*.
24 Mackinder, "The Geographical Pivot" (1904), 441.
25 Ibid., 443.
26 Ibid.

7

Mackinder and the Russian Quest for a New Center of Gravity

A Conspiracy of Silence?

One would assume that Mackinder's seminal article of 1904 would have been eagerly read and immediately commented upon by the Russians themselves. After all, his bold concept directly implicated Russia in many ways; no other country was so vitally affected by the heartland concept. But nothing of that sort happened. Not a whisper. It was as if a silent conspiracy took place among the Russians to ignore completely the unintentional but provocative challenge made by the British geographer. Why? It is not easy to answer this question for a number of complex reasons. For example, the peculiarities of the Russian national psyche did not encourage public discussions on the topic of Russian expansionism as forecast by some unfriendly foreigners. In addition, three more general but interrelated causes seemed to prevail.

The first was certainly the unsatisfactory level of theoretical discussion on the relationship between geographical environment and human action. Briefly, it was a question of geographical determinism, which in prerevolutionary days many Russian intellectuals took for granted, even with enthusiasm, as long as the subject was not Russia. They could discuss Henry T. Buckle's *History of Civilization in England* (1861),[1] but would most likely avoid discussing Mackinder's heartland concept. The second reason had to do with the ambivalent nature of Russo/Soviet-German relations, the principal vehicle for intellectual contact between Russia and Europe, which is discussed in the following chapter. Finally, the imposition of Marxist ideology on Russia after 1917, we must assume, twisted the whole Soviet approach to geopolitics, which became, in the eyes of the regime's propagandists but *not* genuine experts, primarily an anti-Soviet pseudoscience. Whereas geopolitics seemed to stress people's dependence on geographic factors, the Bolshevik utopians wanted to prove exactly the opposite; they wanted to liberate man from the bondage of environmental determinism. In sum, more than 80 years have passed since Mackinder first formulated his heartland concept, and we are still waiting to hear an adequate Russian/Soviet response.

However, there is no logical premise in Marxism-Leninism to detest political geography as a bourgeois pseudoscience. Only an accident of history kept from Lenin's attention those 20 odd pages of text on the "Geographical Pivot of History," written by a certain Mackinder in 1904. Had the highest theocratic authority of Soviet Marxism read and liked Mackinder, Soviet geographers and political scientists would have felt infinitely less embarrassed to comment on the subject. Certainly Soviet military historians and theoreticians have quoted the Prussian general, Carl von Clausewitz, because his works caught Lenin's fancy (Lenin read very carefully and approved enthusiastically of Clausewitz).

One example of how environmental determinism was not only accepted but also worshipped in the Soviet Union was the extraordinary career of the infamous charlatan of Soviet agrobiology, Trofim D. Lysenko (1898–1976), a protégé of Stalin and Khrushchev. Lysenko denied the existence of genes, the special role of chromosones in Mendelian genetics, and advocated instead that heredity was the result of environmental changes. Scientists who did not convert quickly to "Lysenkoism" not only lost their positions but also could have been exiled to Siberia, like the distinguished geneticist, N. I. Vavilov, who died there.[2]

What seems particularly surprising, however, was that total silence on the subject of Mackinder prevailed during the last years of the Tsarist regime; one would think that a limited amount of discussion among Russian geographers and other scholars would have been in order without much personal risk for the individuals involved. Ladis Kristof has conducted extensive and painstaking research into Russian and early Soviet periodicals that might have discussed Mackinder's concept of heartland Russia—but all in vain.³

Our astonishment becomes even more acute when we consider the flow of foreign books and specialized periodicals to Russia, as well as the presence in England of Russians who should have been interested in Mackinder. London at the time had an important colony of Russian revolutionaries, several of whom later became Soviet diplomats (Litvinov, Maisky, Rothstein). Moreover, in an unusual coincidence, the renowned Russian anarchist and geographer, Prince Kropotkin, was scheduled to speak on Central Asia at the same Royal Geographical Society only a few days after Mackinder's historic lecture. It seems inconceivable that Mackinder and Kropotkin were unaware of each other. One can, therefore, understand why Kristof reached his rather paradoxical conclusion, stating that whereas "Mackinder's famous 1904 article must have come to the attention of a goodly number of Russians, scholars and politicians, living inside and outside of Russia . . . for some reason Mackinder's writings, despite their particular relevance to Russia, did not appeal to Russians whether before or after the Revolution."⁴

The Elusive Center of Russian Eurasia

To elucidate the enigma of an almost perpetual silence over Mackinder's heartland concept in the old and new Russia, it might be useful to clarify two interconnected problems. First, what was the essence of the specific Russian interpretation of Eurasia, and was there any room for it in Mackinder's heartland concept? Second, how important in this context was the Russian/Soviet attitude to geographical determinism, and to what extent was this peculiar attitude chiefly responsible for the reluctance of the Russians to be involved in geopolitical speculations about the future of their empire?

As indicated earlier, the Russians had never considered Central Asia the pivotal spot for their imperialist theories. The only aspects that acquired a certain notoriety appeared to be the mystico-utopian theories of such individuals as Yuzhakov and Fyodorov or certain anthropo-ethnographic interpretations (Venyukov, Brunnhofer) mentioned earlier. The latter were founded on similar idolized preconceptions shared with Western racial theories that contemplated Central Asia as the cradle of the Euro-Aryan race (Gobineau). In the opinion of many Russian patriots, however, the spiritual heartland of Holy Russia, derived from its Christian-Orthodox tradition as well as from its self-image as the legitimate successor of the Greco-Byzantine civilization, could never be perceived as outside the sacred triangle of Kiev-Novgorod-Moscow. This concept was accepted at least as long as either Jerusalem, "the navel of the earth" (*pup zemli*),[5] or Constantinople (*Tsargrad*), regarded by the leading Pan-Slavist Danilevsky as "something very like the ontological center of the world"[6] as well as the most important crossroad of world routes and the Gordian knot of the Eastern question, remained outside the Russian Empire. The exiled Russian socialist (Menshevik), Boris Nikolaevsky, in analyzing the ideological roots of Soviet imperialism, singles out Danilevsky as "the first geopolitician of our epoch," having preceded Mackinder, Kjellén, and Haushofer, by four decades on average. The other two subcurrents that Nikolaevsky believed existed in Russian imperialism, in addition to the idea of a Pan-Slav empire centered on *Tsargrad*, were the fear of the yellow peril and the vision of invading India.[7]

The decision of Peter the Great to transfer the capital from Moscow to the new western city on the Baltic founded by him constituted at that time the most radical geopolitical challenge to the Russian Idea, whose guardians remained hostile to the St. Petersburg Idea. Three hundred years later, the Bolsheviks moved the capital back to Moscow, a decision primarily motivated by military considerations amidst a raging civil war and foreign intervention. The move, however, was grudgingly welcomed for different reasons even by their enemies, the Orthodox believers as well as the Eurasianists in exile. As Mikhail Agursky explains in his original book *The Third Rome*, Lenin's decision to move the capital in March 1918 was welcomed by all genuine Russian patriots: Petrograd was created as a symbol of German and foreign influence, whereas "Holy Moscow" was to remain always an authentic Russian city.[8] Had Trotsky, for instance, become Lenin's successor instead of Stalin, his view that the world's center of activity was shifting to the Pacific might have shaped the fortunes of the nascent Soviet state in a much more decisive way. In a considerably stronger and more forceful argument than that of

Gorbachev 60 years later,[9] Trotsky spoke in 1927 in unambiguous military terms about the new front lines emerging on the Pacific coast and the necessity of Russia making an "about face" in 10 to 20 years to reverse the 1,000-year dependence of the rest of the world on Europe. Perhaps unwittingly echoing Herzen, who had boldly predicted the ascendancy of the United States and China in the Pacific, Trotsky argued that there was no avoiding the incontrovertible facts that Europe had been relegated to second place and that the Atlantic was losing its significance to the Pacific.[10]

In spite of the Pan-Slavist obsession regarding the Balkans, Constantinople, and the control of the Straits, the pull of Russian expansionism was eastward, beyond the Urals, where the empty spaces of Siberia outweighed the old cis-Ural dominions of Moscovy. Where did Russia belong? To Europe or to Asia? To many historians the artificial dividing line of the Ural Mountains between Europe and Asia did not make much sense. Yet, as a philosophical concept, it was one of the most entrenched prejudices to overcome, especially among the geographers who, at the same time, had no difficulties recognizing the uniformity of the Eurasian climate, its geological structure, internal river drainage system, and the like. Thus, dissecting Eurasia along the Urals makes just as much sense as dividing North America into two continents along the line of the Appalachians.

Apart from solving the growing spatial imbalances along the west-east and north-east axes of the Russian Eurasian Empire, the quest for the optimal locational center of this enormous lump of territories had its theoretical rationale. This was the so-called concept of "relative location," pioneered by the renowned German geographer, Friedrich Ratzel (1844–1904), the originator of the infamous *Lebensraum* idea. Ratzel implied that the centrality of places was subject to constant change caused by the technological revolution, especially in mass transportation and communication, which, in turn, directly affected social, political, and economic principles of behavior.[11] As a standard historical example the impact of the Suez Canal on the Eastern Mediterranean is often cited. In the case of Eurasia the opening of the great Trans-Siberian Railway and of the two strategic railways in Russian Central Asia would arguably have produced even greater impact.

The Empire from Sea to Sea: Mendeleev and Semyonov-Tyan-Shansky

The most radical proposal for the establishment of a new symbolic center of Russia came from the celebrated Russian scientist, Dimitriy I. Mendeleev (1834–1907). Known better for his achievements in chemistry, this true *Sibiryak* (Mendeleev was born in Tomsk) was also a passionate statistician. Evaluating the results of the first general census of the Russian Empire of 1897, completed only in 1905, which indicated a most satisfactory healthy birth rate with a high percentage of young population, superior to all other great powers, Mendeleev optimistically made demographic projections up to the end of the century of almost 600 million tsarist subjects, a fourfold increase from 150 million at the beginning of 1906. His demographic optimism left him undeterred that the absolute increase at a 1.5 percent net annual growth rate could drive up the Empire's population to more than 1,280 million by the year 2052 (by 2026 at 1.8 percent annual growth). Even then, Mendeleev argued in an undisturbed, somewhat Malthusian fashion, every Russian subject would have on average more arable land at his disposal than the contemporary Englishman or Chinese in 1905.[12] Furthermore, Mendeleev, by birth a genuine Eurasian, was unconcerned that by the end of the nineteenth century close to 60 percent of the Empire's subjects were non-Russians, a higher percentage than today.[13] A strong believer in the powerful trend toward assimilation, Mendeleev argued that, as a whole, the Slav element within the Empire had shown the vitality to increase steadily its share of 72 percent at the expense of the Tatar-Turkic races, which then accounted for about 11 percent.[14]

Another major theme that Mendeleev pursued in his perceptive work, *Toward Understanding of Russia*, was the irresistible eastward shift of the Empire's center of gravity (*tsentr tyazhesti*).[15] He identified what he called the "mean center of population" (adopting the same term American demographers used at the time), which he located near the town of Kozlov (today's Michurinsk) in the Tambov province. This was some 600 km west of Samara (today's Kuibyshev, which became the USSR's mean center of population in the early 1960s). In order to correlate this mean center of population with the Empire's median point of surface (*tsentr poverkhnosti*), which was south of the little town of Turukhansk, between the great Siberian rivers, the Ob and the Yenisei (about 63° northern latitude), Mendeleev suggested a slightly more hospitable "center of Russia" (about 8° lower), along the river Tara just northeast of the city of Omsk (see Figure 7.1). He predicted that Russia's mean center of population would gravitate eastward in the future toward this imaginary focus—with a slight southward tilt (*s uklonom na yug*).[16] The conservative reaction was furious, and it continued after Mendeleev's death. "There was a Russia of Petersburg," wrote one critic indignantly, "but there can be no Russia of Omsk!"[17]

The closest Mendeleev unwittingly came to genuine geopolitical thinking was in his posthumously published *Legacies*, in which he examined the relationship between space and population statistics of six major powers.[18] After World War I the new Soviet regime recognized Mendeleev's outstanding contribution to solving the spatial and population dilemma of Russian Eurasia and allowed the existence of a Centrographical Laboratory, set up in Leningrad under the auspices of the Geographical Society by a group of young enthusiasts, mostly statisticians by training. Not surprisingly, their vision of Russia's modernization did not fit into Stalin's concept of forceful industrialization and collectivization, and the entire Laboratory was "liquidated" in 1933.[19] Because the new territorial and administrative subdivision of the USSR into 21 economic regions required some degree of statistical supervision, a modest degree of discussion on spatial reorganization had been going on within the *Gosplan*, the state supreme planning agency. It became known as "regioning" (*rayonirovanie*).[20]

The second and most original geopolitical analysis that emerged from Russia under the *ancien régime* was developed by Veniamin P. Semyonov-Tyan-Shansky (1870–1942). He was a geographer and statistician, one of the chief driving forces behind the first general census of the Empire's population of 1897—very much like his father, Pyotr P. Semyonov (1827–1914), who was the renowned explorer of Central Asia (hence the title "Tyan-Shansky," given to him by the Tsar), and for 40 years (1873–1914) the vice-president of the Imperial Russian Geographical Society. Veniamin Semyonov's article "About the Great Power Territorial Dominion Applied to Russia," published in the Society's main periodical in 1915 when the belligerent great powers were redrawing the borders of their future empires, went nevertheless against the prevailing trend of

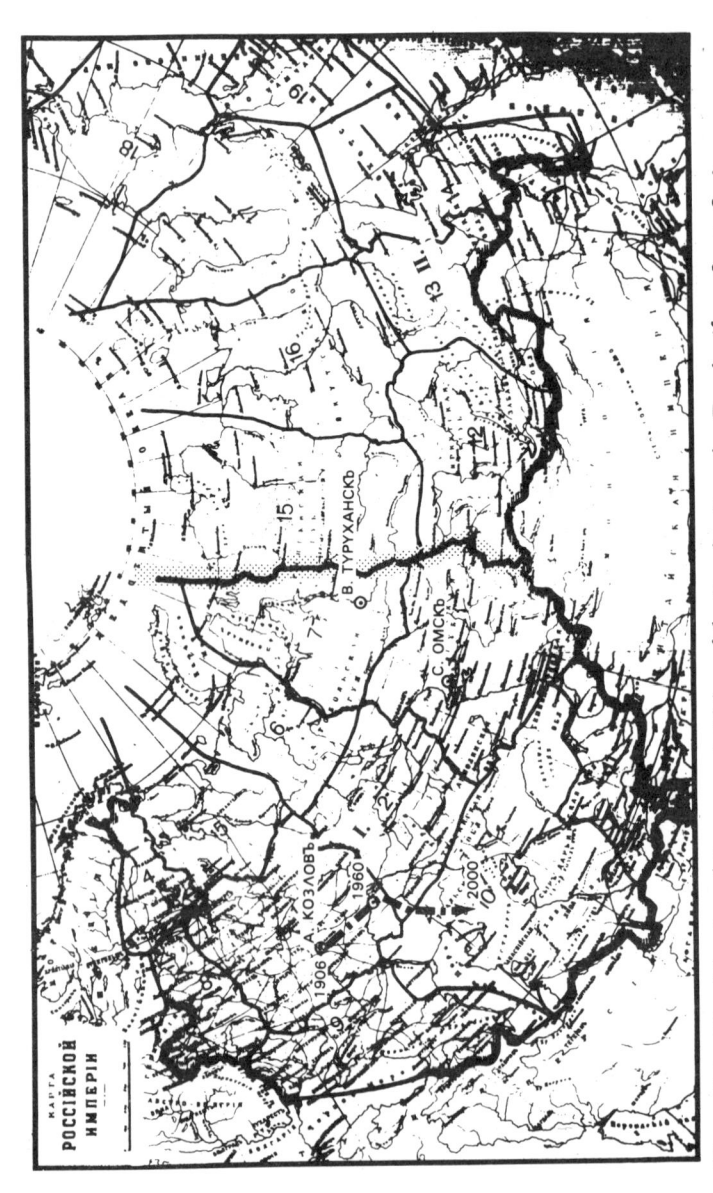

Figure 7.1 Mendeleev's and Semyonov's Vision of the Russian Eurasian Empire 'from Sea to Sea'
Source: V. P. Semyonov-Tyan-Shansky in *Izvestiya Imperatorskago Russkago Geograficheckago Obshchestva* (1915).
Key: A—Russia's Mean Center of Population in 1906 (Kozlov, today's Michurinsk), according to Mendeleev—and its

Russian imperial thinking, which favored the resumption of the traditional drive to the Balkans and the Turkish Straits.[21] Instead, he advocated an eastward expansion, with the ultimate aim of strengthening the empire "from sea to sea" (*ot morya do morya*), which he wanted to restructure so that the existing imbalances between its western and eastern extremities could be reduced. Semyonov saw an analogy with the empire of Alexander the Great, which once stretched from the Greek Archipelago to the Indian Ocean, and was inspired even more by the contemporary American effort to achieve "Manifest Destiny from coast to coast" through improved communications and internal colonization. He believed that the great Russian Eurasian Empire of the future should first consolidate its enormous territory stretching eastward from the Atlantic to the Pacific, rather than follow the adventurous drive south and west.

Semyonov's typology of colonial empires distinguished among three types: "circular" (like ancient Rome and Carthage in the Mediterranean and contemporary Japan in the Yellow Sea); "scattered" (Portugal, Spain, and England); and "from sea to sea" (modeled on Alexander the Great and adopted by all three potential superpowers in the northern hemisphere, that is, Russia, the United States, and Britain in Canada). The Russian task, however, was much more arduous. The sheer size of the space and the harsh climate were against her. There also were many more yellow Asians opposing the Russian colonizers than there were Indians in North America, inhabitants who were wiped out by the white race, which, in turn, applied the Monroe Doctrine to the American continents. This was something an ambitious Russian imperialist could only envy. Like Mendeleev, Semyonov vehemently opposed the artificial division between Europe and Asia along the Ural Mountains; but unlike the former, he did not feel confident about Russia's future in the vast spaces of East Asia, where the European settlers would always be outnumbered by the yellow race demanding "Asia for the Asians." He suggested restructuring the Empire, according to a novel geopolitical vision, into 19 "states and territories," organized like the Dominions of Australia and Canada and falling into two major zones. The western zone, between 15° and 95° eastern longitude, could be subdivided into 2 halves along 55° east, that is, the old Ural line; the eastern zone would stretch from the Yenisei River to 170° western longitude. This eastern zone, with the exception of territories numbered 12, 13 and 14 along the southern border, was mostly unsuitable for human habitation and further colonization (see Figure 7.1). Therefore, according to Semyonov, it could never develop into proper "states."[22]

Another common issue between Mendeleev and Semyonov was the center of gravity concept. Like Mendeleev, whom he, nevertheless, does not mention in his article, Semyonov strongly believed that the pull of Russian Eurasia needed to replace St. Petersburg with a new focal point of gravity to be established east of the Volga, such as Ekaterinburg (today's Sverdlov) in the Urals. A less radical method, elaborated by Semyonov, would have been the creation of four new cultural-economic-colonial bases between the Urals and the Pacific, around which the European settlers could cluster (that is, the Urals, the Altai, Turkestan-Semirechie, and the Baykal zones). According to Semyonov, if the Russian colonization failed to acquire the Baykal zone, Russian expansion would be diverted southward to the Mediterranean and the Persian Gulf, whereby the drive from sea to sea would shift from its west-east latitudinal axis to a new north-south longitudinal axis of expansion (Caucasus-Asia Minor).

Semyonov's strong emphasis on further expansion of transcontinental railways as the main sinews of Russian colonization in Asia and the Empire's military capabilities echoed Mackinder's own vision. Although it is difficult to imagine that Semyonov was not familiar with the important 1906 book of his famous compatriot, Mendeleev, speculation that he might also have been familiar with Mackinder's 1904 article must remain a mere conjecture. However, like Mackinder, Semyonov visualized a whole new network of strategic railways crisscrossing the Russian Eurasian heartland. He explicitly mentioned the future Turk-Sib, connecting Turkestan and the Altai region (surveyed at the time but completed under the Soviets in 1934), and the Baykal-Amur Mainline, connecting the northern tip of Lake Baykal with Nikolaevsk on the Amur, a line still under construction today.[23]

Voeikov, Savitsky, and Lamansky

A survey of Russian geopolitical interpretations of Eurasia would not be complete without mentioning the views of a renowned

Russian climatologist, Aleksandr I. Voeikov (1842–1916). His article "Will the Pacific Ocean Become the World's Main Trade Route?"[24] was published about the time that Mackinder expressed his bold vision of the emerging Eurasian heartland as the pivot region of the world and Mendeleev marshaled his vital statistics to demonstrate the irresistible eastward shift of the center of gravity within the Russian Eurasian Empire. Voeikov's interpretation comes closest to Nicholas Spykman's "rimlandic" view of Eurasia (mentioned earlier), which was formulated 40 years later. On a tentative basis Voeikov analyzed the formation of seven commercial regions, three in Europe and four in Asia, which were to depend entirely on the oceanic trade. They would, therefore, gravitate toward the coastland (rimland), rather than toward Mackinder's hypothetical pivotal "Heartland" of Eurasia or toward a purely theoretical "center of gravity" in the middle of the Siberian wilderness, as suggested by Mendeleev. Although Voeikov did not deny the major significance of the Trans-Siberian Railway connecting Russia with China by land, he doubted that it could successfully compete on commercial terms with maritime transport. The railway would carry passengers and mail faster across Eurasia, Voeikov conceded, but never heavy goods.[25]

The most strenuous effort to present Russian Eurasia as a unified continent, as a kind of third world between Europe and Asia proper, was surely made by the Eurasianist Movement during the 1920s. The leading geographer among the Eurasianists, Pyotr N. Savitsky, advocated the concept of "topogenesis" (*mestorazvitie*) as particularly appropriate for interpreting the uniqueness of Eurasia. Savitsky was equally aware of the fundamental importance that transportation had always played in Eurasian economics, but he realized, like Voeikov, that movements of goods by land over long distances could not rival shipments by sea. With the major Siberian rivers running into the ice-bound Arctic Sea, he could not envisage a bright economic future for Central Asia within a free world market. Although distinctly less optimistic than Mackinder on this question (Savitsky does not appear to know Mackinder's works), he saw a way out in the development of an integrated Eurasian continental market, independent of the world oceanic trade, which could be further diversified to satisfy regional requirements and specifications. But Russia could not afford to be totally isolated from the world maritime trade. She still needed, Savitsky insisted, a new port on the Persian Gulf.[26]

Savitsky and the Eurasianists might also have been inspired by the works of several earlier Russian writers. Linguist Vladimir I. Lamansky (1833–1914) pioneered the idea of the "Middle World," neither exclusively European nor Asiatic.[27] There was also the outstanding pedologist, Vasilii V. Dokuchaev (1846–1903), and the remarkable economist, Pyotr B. Struve (1870–1944), under whom Savitsky studied in St. Petersburg.[28] The idea of a middle world originated in the works of militant Pan-Slavists, like General Rostislav A. Fadeev (1824–84) and Nikolai Ya. Danilevsky, in the context of discussing the Eastern question.[29] The Pan-Slavists regarded the Russian Orthodox Empire as the only rightful successor to the Islamic realm of the Ottomans, who had controlled the Middle Empire between Asia and Europe proper for 500 years.

The Eurasianists wanted to be persistent also in terms of geographic references and rejected the established habit of subordinating the rest of the world to the assumed central location of Western Europe. Although it was not Savitsky who first replaced the 0° Greenwich meridian with the Pulkovo meridian (30° east of Greenwich), since 1839 the seat of Russia's principal observatory near St. Petersburg, he nevertheless refers to the "0° Pulkovo meridian" throughout his work. He designates the entire territory between Pulkovo and 90° eastward (120° east of Greenwich) as Eurasia proper. Thus, west of the Pulkovo line Savitsky pinpointed Europe, whereas east of the Lena River was the genuine Asia (China, Japan).[30] Savitsky, who faithfully followed his scheme of four climatic zones, divorced the strategically important Russian Far East and Manchuria from Eurasia.

The imperialistically minded Russian colony in Kharbin, which also housed Russia's most active fascist movement, was terribly upset by their exclusion from the schemes of the Eurasianists domiciled in Europe. Conscious of their location facing the Pacific Ocean, they demanded, like the *Vostochniki, sliyanie* (merger) of Russian and Chinese cultures at the expense of the European linkage.[31] But Europe proper, that is, Western Europe, was not to be considered part of Eurasia, wrote Savitsky from his Prague exile. Thus, the dispute about Eurasia's proper demarcation line at its western and eastern extremities was unavoidable the moment the debate started. Slogans like "Russia is not only the West, but also the East, not only Europe but also Asia, and not at all Europe, but Eurasia,"[32] were difficult to reconcile with reality. This was especially so when the crucial question of who were the proper inhabitants of Russian/Soviet Eurasia could not be satisfactorily answered. For the time being the majority of inhabitants were still Russians, on both sides of the Urals. But what were the differences between the Eurasians and the Europeans and Asians? These were much more difficult questions to resolve than the vague assertion that the proper frontiers of Eurasia should correspond roughly with the political boundaries of the Tsarist Empire.

Thus, the quest for the new center of gravity for Russian Eurasia must remain inextricably linked not only with the shifts of economic and strategic factors, but also with the self-awareness of the Eurasians themselves in the true geopolitical sense—an outcome that is still not visible on the horizon. So far, the only true Eurasian characters are those that have appeared in works of fiction.[33]

Mackinder's Heartland Russia in 1919 and 1943

With regard to Mackinder's concept of heartland Russia mentioned previously, the Eurasionist image stretched beyond the confines of the Volga basin and the internal and Arctic drainage. Furthermore, Mackinder shared with many Westerners the fear of Russia's fast-growing population, which no other great power could match at the time.[34] In scope Mackinder's original Euro-Asia of 1904 measured nearly half of Asia east of the Urals and a quarter of Europe west of the Urals. But in 1919, in light of the geopolitical changes brought about by World War I and the Russian Civil War, Mackinder decided to modify his heartland scheme by extending it farther westward. Now the Russo-German cooperation, especially the very real threat of a military partnership between the two strongest continental nations, seemed to him a much more decisive factor than did the Anglo-Russian rivalry of 1904 along the rimlands of Asia. He therefore included the whole of Eastern Europe because of its buffer-like position between Germany and Russia and assigned it the role of a real pivot in his new, rather asymmetric, Eurasian heartland.

This was not, however, Mackinder's last modification. At the height of World War II, Mackinder proposed a third version of the heartland, the most complete so far, making it roughly coterminous with the USSR territory, but wisely leaving the edges at both extremities blurred. Thus he left people guessing how much of non-Soviet Eastern Europe should be included. On the other hand, he excluded more than half of Siberia, east and south of the Yenisei River, the so-called "Lenaland." Thus he unwittingly accepted the same approach that Semyonov had recommended some 30 years earlier—that the northeasternmost territories of Russian Asia were unfit for human habitation and, therefore, for further development. Moreover, without realizing it, in his last modification Mackinder came close to the prevailing Eurasionist vision as defined by Savitsky in the 1920s. Mackinder's 1943 description of the heartland refers to three basic features of physical geography that, while reinforcing each other, are not exactly coincidental:

> First of all, we have in this region by far the widest lowland plain on the face of the globe. Secondly, there flow across that plain some great navigable rivers; certain of them go north to the Arctic Sea and are inaccessible from the ocean because it is encumbered by ice, while others flow into inland waters such as the Caspian, which have no exit to the ocean. Thirdly, there is here a grassland zone which, until within the last century and a half, presented ideal conditions for the development of high mobility by camel and horse-riding nomads. . . . The water divide which delimits the whole group of Arctic and "continental" rivers into a single unit does isolate neatly on the map a vast coherent area which is the Heartland according to that particular criterion. The mere exclusion of sea mobility and sea power, however, is a negative if important differential; it was the plain and the grassland belt which offered the positive conditions conducive to the other type of mobility, that proper to the prairie. The grassland traverses the whole breadth of the plain eastward and westward but does not cover its entire surface. Notwithstanding these apparent discrepancies, the Heartland provides a sufficient physical basis for strategic thinking. To go further and to simplify geography artificially would be misleading.[35]

Although not interested in the Lenaland, Mackinder's main attention belongs to the territory west of the Yenisei, which he calls *Heartland Russia*, a plain extending 2,500 miles north and south, east and west, of four and a quarter million square miles and a population of more than 170 million. It was this vast plain of the

Russian heartland that offered Soviet troops in World War II a formidable defense in depth and further enormous space for strategic retreat toward the "inaccessible Arctic coast, the Lenaland wilderness behind the Yenisei, and the fringe of mountains from the Altai to the Hindu Kush, backed by the Gobi, Tibetan and Iranian deserts." All things considered, Mackinder spelled out the inescapable conclusions:

> If the Soviet Union emerges from this war as conqueror of Germany, she must rank as the greatest land Power on the globe. Moreover, she will be the Power in the strategically strongest defensive position. The Heartland is the greatest natural fortress on earth. For the first time in history it is manned by a garrison sufficient both in number and in quality.... I have described afresh my concept of the Heartland, which I have no hesitation in saying is more valid and useful today than it was either twenty or forty years ago. I have said how it is set in its mantle of broad natural defenses—ice-clad Polar Sea, forested and rugged Lenaland, and Central Asiatic mountain and arid tableland. ... And upon and beneath the Heartland there is a store of rich soil for cultivation and of ores and fuels for extraction, the equal—or thereabouts—of all that lies upon and beneath the United States and the Canadian Dominion.[36]

This is as far as Mackinder would go in defining the heartland. Still, many critics came to regard this as inadequate because it lacked a more precise demarcation of its boundaries.[37] As W. H. Parker rightly points out in his absorbing book, Mackinder was always more concerned with the heart of the matter than with its precise definition, with metaphors and generalizations rather than with pedantic measurements and detailed analyses, with cores rather than with boundaries.[38]

As for the general delimitation of Eurasia, Mackinder did, in fact, suggest in his seminal 1904 study that Russia should form, rather like India, a subcontinent in her own right. His World Island—apart from the odd protrusion of Africa—consisted of four appendices attached to the Eurasian heartland: peninsular Europe, Southwest Asia, China, and India.[39] To those who still criticize Mackinder claiming that his heartland theories were full of vague definitions and blurred boundaries, Mackinder might reiterate what he wrote in 1942 to the exiled German geopolitician, Hans Weigert: "The desire for a precise definition of the Heartland is futile—it is a strategical concept on the map."[40] Finally, it is helpful to know that Mackinder personally would do anything to avoid definitions, for "in this country we define nothing if we can help it."[41]

Notes

1. Henry Thomas Buckle, *History of Civilization in England* (London: Routledge, 1861), 22–86. Buckle's *History* became immensely popular in prerevolutionary Russia, where it was published in translation many times over (see also note 3).
2. Zhores A. Medvedev, *The Rise and Fall of T. D. Lysenko* (New York: Columbia University Press, 1969). See also the recent Soviet criticism (at last!) of Lysenko by Valeriy Soifer in *Ogonëk*, no. 1, 26–29, and no. 2, 4–7, 31 (January 1988); and the article on N. I. Vavilov in *Ogonëk*, no. 47 (November 1987), 10–15.
3. Ladis K. D. Kristof, "Mackinder's Concept of Heartland and the Russians" (unpublished paper delivered at the 23d International Geographical Congress in Leningrad in July 1976). The relevant Russian periodicals Kristof concentrated on are, in particular: *Izvestiya Imperatorskogo Russkogo Geograficheskogo Obshchestva* and *Morskoi Sbornik*. I am thankful to Professor Kristof for allowing me to see his paper and for discussing with me topics of common interest.
4. Ibid., 4–5.
5. Nikolai Ya. Danilevsky, *Rossiya i Evropa* (St. Petersburg: Panteleev Brothers, 1895), 398.
6. Robert E. MacMaster, *Danilevsky. A Russian Totalitarian Philosopher* (Cambridge: Harvard University Press, 1967), 271–73.
7. Boris Nikolaevsky, "O ideologicheskikh kornyakh sovetskogo imperializma," *Sotsialisticheskiy Vestnik* 2 (New York, 1954), 29–32.
8. Agursky, *The Third Rome* (1987), 192–93; see chapter 2, "The Russian Idea Today."
9. See chapter 1.
10. According to Mark Bassin, *A Russian Mississippi? A Political-Geographical Inquiry into the Vision of Russia on the Pacific 1840–1865*, Ph.D. Diss. (Berkeley: University of California, 1983), 316.
11. Ronald Abler et al., *Spatial Organization. The Geographer's View of the World* (Englewood Cliffs: Prentice-Hall, 1971), 571.
12. D. I. Mendeleev, *K poznaniyu Rossii* (St. Petersburg, 1906), 12. A 1924 edition, published in Munich and introduced by A. Saltykov, has been used here.
13. In the posthumously published condensed summary, *Zavety D. I. Mendeleeva: Rossiya i chto iei nado* (Berlin: Russkoe Tvorchestvo publishers, w.d.), 11, Mendeleev calculated that although the share of Great Russians was 43.5 percent (lower than today), together with the other Slavs, mainly Ukrainians (Little Russians), Belorussians, and Poles, the percentage climbed up to 72

[same as 1979 census]. See also Richard Pipes, *The Formation of the Soviet Union* (Cambridge: Harvard University Press, 1954), 2, who thinks that the true proportion of non-Russians at the end of the nineteenth century was rather close to 60 percent. See also *Nationality and Population Change in Russia and the USSR. An Evaluation of Census Data, 1897–1970*, ed. Robert A. Lewis et al. (New York: Praeger, 1976), and *Research Guide to the Russian and Soviet Censuses*, ed. Ralph S. Clem (Ithaca: Cornell University Press, 1986).
14 *Zavety Mendeleeva*, 5–10.
15 Mendeleev, *K poznaniyu Rossii* (1906/1924), 124–42 (chapter 2, "On the Center of Russia").
16 Mendeleev, *K poznaniyu Rossii* (1906/1924), 142. The Turukhansk region ranks among the most inhospitable regions of Siberia. Between 1913 and 1916 this geometric center of the Eurasian empire became the place of exile for Iossif V. Dzhugashvili—the future absolute master of the empire (Adam B. Ulam, *Stalin—The Man and His Era* [London: Allen Lane, 1973], 121–9).
17 Mendeleev, *K poznaniyu Rossii* (1906/1924), intr. 99.
18 D. I. Mendeleev, *Dopolneniya k Poznaniyu Rossii* (St. Petersburg: A. S. Suvorin, 1907), 3–17, 98–99.
19 E. A. Semyonov (ed.), *Geograficheskoe Obshchestvo za 125 let* (Leningrad: Nauka, 1970), 168. On recent Soviet developments in this field see Mason H. Soule and Robert N. Taaffe, "Mathematical Programming Approaches to the Planning of Siberian Regional Economic Development," *Soviet Economy* I/1 (1985), 75–98.
20 For further references see: Oskar von Niedermayer and Juri Semjonow, *Sowjet-Russland. Eine geopolitische Problemstellung* (Berlin: Kurt Vowinckel, 1934), 69–88; Bruce Hopper, "Eastward the Course of Soviet Empire," *Foreign Affairs* (October 1935), 37–50.
21 V. P. Semyonov-Tyan-Shansky, "O moguchestvennom territorial'nom vladenii primenitel'no k Rossii," *Izvestiya Imperatorskogo Russkago Geograficheskago Obshchestva* 51/8 (1915), 425–57.
22 Ibid., 446–48. See also chapter 5, "Geographic Projections."
23 Ibid., 449–55.
24 A. I. Voeikov, "Budet-li Tikhyi Okean glavnym torgovym putyom zemnogo shara?" *Izvestiya Imper. Russkago Geograf. Obshchestva* 40/4 (1904), 482–556.
25 Ibid. For a contemporary discussion see Albert Wohlstetter, "Illusions of Distance," *Foreign Affairs* 46/2 (January 1968), 242–55.
26 P. N. Savitsky, *Rossiya—osobyi geograficheskyi mir* (Prague, 1927), 40, 47.
27 V. I. Lamansky, *Tri mira Aziisko-Evropeiskago materika* (St. Petersburg: 1892).
28 Richard Pipes, *Struve: Liberal on the Right, 1905–1944* (Cambridge: Harvard University Press, 1980), II:351–57; Otto Böss, *Die Lehre der Eurasier* (Wiesbaden: Harrassowitz, 1961), 25–33.
29 R. A. Fadeev, *Mnenie o Vostochnom Voprose* (St. Petersburg: Udelov, 1869); Danilevsky, *Rossiya i Evropa* (1869); Böss, *Die Lehre* (1961), 25–33; Kristof, "Mackinder's Concept" (1976), 9.
30 P. N. Savitsky, "Kontinent-Okean. Rossiya i mirovoi rynok." In *Iskhod k Vostoku. Predchuvstviya i sversheniya. Utverzhdenie Evratziitsev* (Sofia,

1921), 104–25. Savitsky drew inspiration from Mendeleev (1906/1924), 140–6. Analogous with the Russian case is the post-1945 movement in the United States to create an American-centered world, underlined by the new zero (0) meridian running through Washington, DC, rather than Greenwich, and advocated in the works of Henry Luce and others. See Alan K. Henrikson, "America's Changing Place in the World: From Periphery to Center," in *Centre and Periphery: Spatial Variation in Politics*, ed. Jean Gottman (Beverly Hills: Sage, 1980), 75.

31 Vsevolod N. Ivanov, *My: Kul'turno-istoricheskie osnovy russkoi gosudarstvennosti* (Kharbin: 1926); Böss, *Die Lehre* (1961), 25–33. For more details about the extraordinary phenomenon, namely the Russian fascist movement in the Far East, whose center was Kharbin in Manchuria, see John J. Stephan, *The Russian Fascists. Tragedy and Farce in Exile 1925–1945* (New York: Harper & Row, 1978).

32 P. N. Savitsky in *Iskhod k Vostoku. Predchuvstviya i svercheniya. Utverzhdenie Evraziitsev* (Sofia: 1921), 2; Böss, *Die Lehrer* (1961), 26.

33 Unfortunately, there is no space here to analyze even some of the most important works of Russian literature dealing with Eurasian themes (e.g., the symbolist schools led by Aleksandr Blok and Andrei Belyi). Some critics believe that Pasternak's great novel, *Doctor Zhivago*, should be regarded as the major Eurasian work (Nicholas V. Riasanovsky, "The Emergence of Eurasianism," *California Slavic Studies* 4 [1969], 68–69). I consider Vladimir K. Arseniev's remarkable book, *Dersu—The Trapper*, the nearest to the ideal Eurasian symbiosis between the European geographer and explorer of the Ussury region in the Russian Far East, Arseniev himself, and his Asian counterpart, the unforgettable trapper Dersu Uzala. The autobiographic book is available in English (New York: Dutton, 1941). In 1975 the great Japanese film director, Akira Kurosawa, made a motion picture (*Dersu Uzala*) based entirely on Arseniev's book.

34 Mackinder, "The Geographical Pivot" (1904), 443; Mackinder *Democratic Ideals* (1919), 149–90.

35 Mackinder, "The Round World" (1943), 598.

36 Ibid., 601, 604.

37 Parker, *Mackinder* (1982), 215–17.

38 Ibid., 217.

39 Mackinder, *Democratic Ideals* (1919), 143; W. H. Parker, *An Historical Geography of Russia* (Chicago: Aldine, 1969), 29.

40 Weigert, *Generals and Geographers* (1942), 253.

41 Parker, *Mackinder* (1982), 217.

8

German *Geopolitik*, Haushofer, and the Russians

Russia and German Mediators

If we have failed so far to establish a direct string of evidence showing that Mackinder's 1904 heartland concept found its way to the minds of the Russians, who, nevertheless, developed their own geopolitical tradition, it might be helpful to look for some other clues and indicators. The first obvious choice is German culture, with which Russian intellectuals were most familiar. Even if there is no evidence that Mackinder's ideas attracted the Russian mind during the remaining years of the Tsarist regime, surely, following the Bolshevik Revolution, Russo-German contacts were so numerous that it seems reasonable that the Russians encountered Western geopolitical ideas in one form or another.

Because of their proximity and long-established cultural links following the emergence of the modern Russian state under Peter the Great, the Germans had been the most conspicuous intermediaries between Western Europe and Russia proper. One has to be reminded that the Russians for centuries used the words *Niemoy* and *Niemets* (that is, the "mute"—ignorant of Russian language) for Germans, often meaning all Western foreigners in general, simply because the Germans were the first Westerners with whom the Russians had most contact. As a result of the Russian acquisition of the Baltic provinces and the colonization policy of settling

German immigrants in the Ukraine and elsewhere, there were already around 2 million German-speaking Tsarist subjects and residents by the end of the nineteenth century. The dynastic links between the Romanovs and German princely houses were unusually strong because all Russian emperors were married to German princesses; Ekaterina II (Catherine) was, of course, a German-born princess. Among Western universities, those in Germany attracted the majority of Russian students going abroad, notwithstanding the fact that there was a German-speaking university at Tartu (Dorpat). Even the Slavophiles, let alone Russian Marxists, were influenced primarily by German culture (Herder, Hegel). The Imperial Academy of Science in St. Petersburg had many distinguished German scientists, as did the Russian Geographical Society. Broadly speaking, throughout the nineteenth century, one-third of all high government officials, army and navy officers, and Senate members were of German origin. In some ministries, like foreign affairs or war, they often constituted more than 50 percent; all that at a time when the Germans constituted slightly more than 1 percent of the Empire's population. Military leaders, geographers, and explorers of German descent in Tsarist service played a leading part in the conquest of new territories and in the acquisition of knowledge about Central Asia, the Far East, Siberia, and the Pacific.[1]

This was resented, naturally, by many ordinary Russians, making the Russo-German relationship one of deep reciprocal ambivalence. No wonder that many educated Germans adopted the notion of Germany's *Kulturmission* in Russia and visualized, in particular, the German *Kulturträger* in the *Drang nach Osten* as the guiding element exercising a civilizing influence on their Russian companions, whom they taught to westernize the "Asiatic barbarians."[2]

And yet, the notion of racial superiority that certain German nationalists, and later National Socialist ideologues like Alfred Rosenberg,[3] tried to impose on Russo-German relations was easily refuted, even by experts from their own ranks. For instance, Erich Obst, a leading German geopolitican specializing on Russia, wrote in 1928 that the concept of race would lead nowhere if applied to Russia. He noticed a natural symbiosis between the Russians and other ethnic groups, like the Tatars and Germans, who, while maintaining their language, were quickly adopting Russian customs.[4]

One must also bear in mind the extraordinary influence of German Oriental studies (*Orientalistik*) in Russia.⁵ Both German and Russian explorers showed a remarkable fascination with Central Asia. Karl Haushofer, about whom more will be said, appeared genuinely intrigued by the long catalog of distinguished Germanic names connected with the explorations of Central Asia. The first was Alexander von Humboldt (1769–1859), considered the true founder of modern geographic science, who conducted the first systematic survey of Russian Asia in 1829. His *Zentralasien* (1843) was later translated into Russian.⁶ Next came Carl Ritter (1779–1859), under whom Pyotr Semyonov studied in Berlin and whose *Erdkunde Asiens* he subsequently translated into Russian.⁷ Ferdinand von Richthofen (1833–1905) was also highly regarded in Russia as the leading authority on China.⁸

However, it was Richthofen's pupil, the famous Swedish explorer, Sven Hedin (1965–1952), who helped among the Germans to "demonize the attraction of Central Asia as the ancient cradle of the Aryan race."⁹ His ruthless ambition was to conquer rather than to discover Central Asia. To the average German he embodied the Teutonic spirit, and later, especially during the Nazi era, he was often portrayed as the epitome of the Nordic *Übermensch*. If the Austrian Hitler and the ex-Tsarist subject Rosenberg became Germans by choice, the Swede Hedin felt like one by temperament.¹⁰

The Nazi Connection

In understanding the roots of anti-Semitism in National Socialism, Walter Laqueur observed more than 20 years ago that not enough attention had been paid to the impact of specific Russian sources, such as the sinister *Protocols of the Elders of Zion*, or to prominent individuals of German ethnic origin who came from Imperial Russia to postwar Germany during the revolutionary turmoil.¹¹ Three Balts, in particular, played an important part in the rising Nazi movement: Max Erwin von Scheubner-Richter, Alfred Rosenberg, and Arno Schickedanz. They helped forge a Russo-German popular front, called *Aufbau* (Reconstruction), which gathered together right-wing German nationalists and Russian monarchists, united in their anti-Semitism and hatred of Bolshevism.

In spite of courting their favors, "Alfred Valdemarovich," as Rosenberg was affectionately called by his Russian friends, despised them as racially inferior because he was convinced of their mixed Turanian and Mongolian origins.[12] Although it is generally accepted that Hitler's anti-Bolshevik views were to some extent influenced by the Baltic Germans, neither Rosenberg nor Scheubner-Richter argued that Germany might benefit territorially from the dismantling of the Russian Empire. The latter, killed while at Hitler's side at the *Feldherrenhalle* during the Munich putsch of 9 November 1923, could hardly have advocated the disintegration of Russia if his stated program was to unite all Russian forces opposed to Bolshevism.

Scheubner-Richter established his reputation among Hitler's followers, General Ludendorff, and other right-wing elements because of his active part in the Kapp-Luttwitz putsch of March 1920, having earlier collaborated with the German forces of occupation in Latvia. Even more interesting, from our point of view, was his "Oriental" connection, which he acquired during World War I as a German liaison officer (because of his knowledge of Russian) with the Turkish Army in Eastern Anatolia and Persian Azerbaijan. Moreover, during 1920 he also headed a mysterious trading mission, divised by Alfred Rosenberg in Munich, to General Wrangel in the Crimea, the political purpose of which was to establish proper contact with the White Russian forces determined to rid Russia of Bolshevism.[13]

In the early 1920s Alfred Rosenberg was probably Hitler's most important single source of information about Russia and the Slavs in general. Although Rosenberg would concede that Slavs might eventually become fascists, he denied them the questionable privilege of calling themselves "National Socialists"—this "last honor" being reserved for Nordic Aryans only. From 1922 on Rosenberg advocated the dismemberment of Soviet Eurasia along ethnic lines, the separation of the Baltic and Caucasian states with an "independent" Ukraine as the future Nazi pivot within the Russian state. The Russians must fulfill their "racial mission" inside Asia, as far away from Europe as possible, Rosenberg insisted. The British Empire, on the other hand, must be preserved, and India was to remain under British rule for the benefit of the superior Nordic race.[14]

With regard to the Jews, Rosenberg was without pity; the

"Judeo-Bolshevik" elements were the "Asiatic pestilence" orchestrating the new Mongol invasion of the West. As John Stephan has described in his fascinating book *Russian Fascists*, Rosenberg owed a special debt to a fellow Balt for devising an "efficacious method" of handling the Jewish problem. This Balt fugitive was a certain Fyodor V. Vinberg (1861–1927), a truly sinister ex-Tsarist colonel and a former active member of the Black Hundreds. From him Rosenberg presumably received the Russian original of the *Protocols of the Elders of Zion*, a forged blueprint purporting a Zionist world conspiracy, which he used for the first German edition in 1923. He may have been inspired by the colonel's insistence, disseminated in anti-Semitic periodicals, that the shipment of Jews to Kolyma, the easternmost tip of Siberia, was not enough, and that the only "Final Solution" to the Jewish question lay in their total physical extermination.[15] While enthusiastically supporting "from the Nordic as well as the German standpoint" the British domination over India, Rosenberg warned against the "racial chaos" in Russia and against any appearance of German "Easterners," who might be seeking a kind of Eurasian fusion of Germany with Russia to spread the 'Asiatic-Eastern Spirit" from Vladivostok to the Rhine.[16]

The remarkable philosopher, Oswald Spengler, was more explicit than Rosenberg on the notion of the yellow peril, which one can trace from Danilevsky and Solovyov into German writings. In his final pronouncements Spengler had a vision of Europe threatened by the "colored world revolution" from outside, in which class and racial wars would merge together.[17]

A German Lawrence among the Bolsheviks

At the other end of the Russo-German cultural spectrum was the increased political intercourse between German Communists and Bolsheviks, epitomized by the behavior of Lenin, who never ceased to hope for a German revolution. In Moscow the newly founded Communist International (Komintern) purposely used German as the official "language of the Revolution."[18] It was the Komintern agent for Germany, the highly gifted and eccentric Karl Radek (1885–1939?), who can be described as having provided the geopolitical link between Germany and Soviet Russia in the early 1920s. He pursued this line, even after Hitler's seizure of power, well into 1936 when he was arrested and tried, ironically, for treason. After failing to gain the support of the German military for a joint attack against Poland, Radek not only wanted to promote communist revolution in Germany, but also, pragmatically, was instrumental in forging the clandestine joint ventures between the *Reichswehr* and the Red Army. This effort enabled Germany to develop and manufacture tanks and military aircraft inside Russia, thereby bypassing the prohibitive clauses of the Versailles Treaty.[19]

The chief liaison between Radek and General von Seeckt in Moscow during the 1920s was a "Major Neumann." The unofficial *Reichswehr* representative with the Red Army, whose real name in fact was Oskar von Niedermayer (1885–1948?). A colleague of Karl Haushofer on more than one level, because he was not only a fellow Bavarian and a professional officer with a passion for geopolitics, Niedermayer also was later to become, like his master, a university professor of (military) geography and a major-general.[20] In addition, however, Niedermayer outdid Haushofer as the great practitioner of geopolitics, having led, together with Werner Otto von Hentig, the most adventurous subversive action ever mounted by the Central Powers during World War I. This extraordinary expedition to Afghanistan in 1915, which earned him the name of fame: "German Lawrence," was organized from Berlin with the purpose of convincing Amir Habibullah to take an anti-British stand.[21]

In his frequent dealings with Radek, the Commissariat for Foreign Affairs (for example, with Karakhan), and the Red Army General Staff, Niedermayer noticed how popular among them were Haushofer's recent books, especially *Dai Nihon* (1913), *Geopolitik der Selbstbestimmung in Süd-Ost Asien* (1923), and, above all, *Geopolitik des Pazifischen Ozeans* (1924). The last had even been translated into Russian without the author's permission and used as a college course book, under the title *Tikhookeanskaya Problema*, by the Soviet military and foreign affairs experts.[22] Niedermayer urged his master to accept the repeated requests of the Soviet General Staff to write analytical assessments of recent Japanese books and articles on strategic topics for an adequate fee.[23]

Haushofer and Mackinder's Heartland

In view of the strong criticism of geopolitics in general, and of German *Geopolitik* in particular, in official Soviet statements, it may seem far-fetched to stress the extraordinary influence that Karl Haushofer (1869–1946), its chief advocate and propagator in Germany, seemed to have during the 1920s on a restricted Soviet audience. Nevertheless, it seems reasonable to assume that Mackinder's 1904 heartland concept, rather than his second modification of 1919, became the intellectual property of the Soviet experts precisely through the Haushofer-Niedermayer connection. However, it is virtually impossible to support this claim by additional written evidence.

Haushofer, who became acquainted with Mackinder's 1904 thesis sometime around 1921, never hesitated to pay the highest tribute to the Englishman's originality and boldness ("Never have I seen anything greater than these few pages of a geopolitical masterwork!").[24] Although *Democratic Ideals and Reality* (1919), in which Mackinder elaborated his second thesis, must have been disliked intensely by patriotic Germans. The book's central message contained a warning to the peacemakers at Versailles that any spatial rapprochement between Germany and Russia, regardless of the political systems prevailing there, must be prevented by setting up a sort of *Cordon Sanitaire* between them, composed of the small but genuinely anti-German and anti-Russian independent states. But Haushofer would still justify his highly favorable references to Mackinder by citing Ovid's *Fas est ab hoste doceri* (It is right to learn from the enemy).[25]

Paying tribute to Mackinder's genius did not mean that Haushofer adopted the heartland concept as the centerpiece of his own geopolitical vision of the world. After all, Mackinder's view of the world was that of a British imperialist whom a patriotic German must have considered an enemy.[26] The major difference, often overlooked and underestimated in recent comparative studies, was that Haushofer's foremost interest belonged to East Asia. His lifelong fascination remained Japan, the only foreign country of which he had firsthand experience. He lived in Japan long enough (1909–12) to become acquainted with her culture and language and devoted his first full-scale monograph to her.[27] After World War I his focus extended to what he then began to describe as the "Indo-Pacific space" (*Indopazifischer Raum*), thus leaving interpretations of Central Europe (*Mitteleuropa*), Russo-German relations, and Russian Eurasia to other colleagues. Haushofer thereby abandoned the prewar bias among German imperialists and replaced the *Drang nach Osten* with a *Drang nach Süden*, epitomized by the construction of the Baghdad Railway to the Persian Gulf, literally circumnavigating the Central Asian pivot area through the Indo-Pacific maritime link. Although strongly influenced by Ratzel's concept of the state as a living organism (*Lebensraum*), which was superficially incorporated by Adolf Hitler into his *Mein Kampf*,[28] and by Rudolf Kjellén's theory of the organic state,[29] Haushofer's eyes remained fixed on the Far East.

The Indo-Pacific Space

In contrast to Hitler's and Rosenberg's racially motivated foreign policy advocating the establishment of a "Nordic Bloc," wherein a 100-million-strong Greater Germany and Scandinavia allied with England would protect Europe from being overrun by the "Russo-Mongolian military power,"[30] Haushofer's outlook and inspiration were completely different. Although he would later occasionally use some of the anti-Semitic catchwords, after the war he justified his moral degradation as a concern for the life of his Jewish wife.[31] But during the 1920s Haushofer's *Weltanschauung* was by no means determined by an anti-Semitic or anti-communist stand. He shared the view that Germany as a defeated and humiliated power should assist the have-nots in the Indo-Pacific sphere (that is, India and China but not Africa),[32] whose legitimate aspirations to achieve self-determination against the Anglo-Saxon colonial and maritime powers he found worthy of support, even at the cost of cooperating with Soviet Russia. Despite his admiration of Mackinder, he advocated the disintegration of the British Empire prompted by the rise of Japan, the demographic explosion along the Indo-Pacific rimlands, and by the spreading of nationalist, anti-colonial, and communist ideologies. One might say that Haushofer felt almost a malicious delight in watching the British decline. It is noticeable, nevertheless, that he did not feel the compulsion to use such racist terms as the yellow or brown peril.[33]

Haushofer's geopolitical vision thus contrasted with Mackinder's heartland concept in the sense that the British geographer remained transfixed by the menace of an emerging Russo-German alliance, whereas the formation of a Russo-Japanese bloc seemed to him much less probable. For Haushofer, on the contrary, the existence of a Berlin-Tokyo axis was essential for the later inclusion of Russia. He appears, therefore, more radical than Mackinder, who, in this respect, shared the traditional outlook of Whitehall officials who visualized the Russian threat as coming primarily via Eastern Europe, the Mediterranean, and Central Asia. Mackinder offered three options for the coming world empire (the World Island), all based on the control of the pivotal Eurasian heartland: (1) by Russia alone, (2) by Germany, and (3) by the Sino-Japanese "Yellow Peril." Haushofer offered only one synthetic but overwhelming alternative, directed against the maritime supremacy of the Anglo-Americans, the *Transcontinental Bloc*. The latter was to be composed of all the major victims and opponents of the interwar Versailles Peace system (Germany, Italy, the Soviet Union, Japan), enlarged gradually by the have-nots of the Third World (China and India).

Haushofer anticipated that the decisive showdown between the great powers would take place in the Indo-Pacific sphere. Germany, lacking either sea power or direct overland access, should support Japan and ally herself with the Soviet Union, both of which would step in alongside Germany to champion the anticolonial and anti-Western revolt.[34] From the Soviet vantage point of the early 1920s these were the opinions worth exploring, and perhaps pursuing. Whether they carried the imperialist label of geopolitics was immaterial, nor did it seem to matter how much of the original Mackinder was smuggled in this way by Haushofer to Soviet Russia.

When interrogated by U.S. officers after the war, Haushofer freely admitted that as a geopolitician he would acknowledge two major influences on his life: first, Mackinder's heartland concept of 1904, with the implications it carried for the rimlands and maritime powers, and second, the inevitable political emancipation of Southeast Asia, that is, the Indo-Pacific space, which he tried to link with the emergence of "Pan-ideas." In the latter case it would have been the spread of the Pan-Asiatic movement armed with the slogan "Asia for the Asians."[35] The combination of these two major influences led Haushofer to formulate the idea of the Transcontinental Bloc, an alliance formed by Germany, Russia, and Japan (and hopefully China). In contrast to Hitler's racial vision of the subjugated Eastern *Lebensraum*, Haushofer envisaged Russia as an equal partner constituting the Eurasian landbridge to Japan. To repeat Strausz-Hupé's masterful summary: "Haushofer saw the Eurasian axis with its fulcrum balanced on the Heartland and its German and Japanese extremities joined by secure land communications."[36]

Haushofer's Transcontinental Bloc versus Hitler's *Lebensraum*

From the vantage point of Hegelian dialectics the Transcontinental Bloc would appear to be a new synthesis "abolishing" and "elevating" ("*aufheben*" is Hegel's key word) both extreme options Mackinder predicted for the future formation of the Russian Eurasian Empire, namely, the German and the Japanese "antitheses." There are occasional hints in Haushofer's first book, which he wrote after returning from Japan and before reading Mackinder,[37] but he fully developed his thesis ten years later in his perhaps most original work *Geopolitics of the Pacific Ocean* (1924). This is the same work the Soviets translated and published in an expurgated version without the author's permission.[38]

Thus, close Russo-German cooperation aimed at undermining the Anglo-Saxon monopoly of power, and founded on the spirit of the Rapallo Treaty of 1922, became the leitmotiv of the monthly *Zeitschfrift für Geopolitik*, which Haushofer edited between 1924 and 1944. And the presence in Moscow of Major Oskar von Niedermayer ("Neumann"), a keen geopolitician and friend of General Haushofer, was sufficient proof that as far as Russo-German relations were concerned German geopoliticians did not allow much discrepancy between theory and practice. Certainly there was an element of ill-concealed vengeance in this demonstration of solidarity with the Bolsheviks, on the one hand, and with the millions of have-nots in the Indo-Pacific sphere, on the other, directed at the arrogant Anglo-Saxon powers, who, as Haushofer put it, "of our own race have expelled us from their midst."[39]

Hans Weigert, writing in 1942 from his American exile, rightly observed that Haushofer and the editors of the *Zeitschrift* "had stubbornly advocated reconciliation and friendship with the Soviets from the beginning, and Hitler's noisy crusade against the archenemy, Bolshevism, made no impression on them."[40] "Germany will have to decide," wrote Erich Obst, an editor in 1925, whether she wants to be "a satellite of the Anglo-Saxon powers and their supercapitalism, which are united with the other European nations against Russia, or will she be an ally of the Pan-Asiatic union against Europe and America?" And he provided the answer: "No nation is closer to Russia than is Germany; only Germany can understand the Russian soul; Germany and Russia have been friends for centuries; their economic structures are complementary; they must hang together."[41]

While Haushofer preached the establishment of a Eurasian Transcontinental Bloc challenging the Anglo-Saxons,[42] Hitler's racial *Weltanschuung* favored a Nordic alliance between Germany and England directed against "Judeo-Bolshevik" Russia. Consequently, the signing of the Nazi-Soviet Pact in August 1939 must have been Haushofer's greatest triumph. "One only needs to read the famous chapter XIV of *Mein Kampf*," Hans Weigert commented boldly in 1942, "to see that Hitler's and Haushofer's ideas of Soviet Russia and of Germany's eastern policy were worlds apart."[43]

The idea of the Transcontinental Bloc seemed in many ways to fit the political concept of the Nazi foreign minister, Joachim von Ribbentrop, whose adviser for a while had been Haushofer's son Albrecht. Until Hitler's attack on the Soviet Union in June 1941, Ribbentrop appeared to have been successful in prevailing on his master with his Quadruple Alliance scheme, which consisted of the Berlin-Rome-Tokyo Axis enlarged by Moscow.[44] Haushofer, for his part, tried to shore up the short-lived Ribbentrop-Molotov Pact with a pamphlet of his own, *The Continental Bloc*, published just before the invasion of Russia. In it he acknowledged that his sources of inspiration, apart from the obligatory tribute to Mackinder, were also the American "protogeopoliticians," such as Brooks Adams and Homer Lea. Both men had visualized the future conflict between the great powers in bipolar terms, predicting the formation of a Eurasian alliwance composed of Germany, Russia, and Japan that would ultimately challenge the Anglo-Saxon powers.[45]

In Haushofer's wishful thinking, Eastern Eurasia and the Western Pacific could become the main theaters in the war if Russia coordinated her actions with the Axis Powers. And if India's enormous potential for self-determination could be mobilized, not by the nonviolent philosophy of Gandhi but by more radical leaders like Jawaharlal Nehru and Subhas Chandra Bose, Haushofer was convinced that this would be decisively important for the disintegration of the colonial world from Egypt to China, and consequently for the outcome of the war.[46]

Consequently, Haushofer welcomed the shift of the continental world axis eastward to the Pacific coast, and southward toward India, as it was announced at the turn of the century by Brooks Adams and Homer Lea, or passionately discussed by Russian geographers and statisticians. These ideas were not entirely new; they had been in circulation for some time. One has to be reminded that during World War I German diplomats and strategists concocted a whole series of the most radical subversive schemes, with at least one of lasting albeit unexpected consequence—the transfer to Russia of Vladimir Ulyanov (Lenin) and his fellow revolutionaries to undermine Russia's participation in the war.[47]

In trying to interpret Haushofer's tendency to embrace similar radical schemes during the 1920s and his views on the Moscow-Berlin partnership, we turn again to Hans Weigert, who captured the essence of the Russo-German "elective affinity" (*Wahlverwandschaft*) rather well.

> The concepts of individual freedom and Western democracy were popular only on the surface of cultural life in Germany. In its depths the German soul remained closely related to the East. . . . The national socialism that the Asiatics Lenin and Stalin had brought about in Russia—it could be understood by those Germans to whom the idea of Prussian Socialism was more than an adroit catchword. No, it was no coincidence that the circle around Haushofer, that exactly those groups to whom he addressed his teachings, saw in Leninism and Stalinism a flame that was their flame, too. Their minds were prepared to turn to the East.[48]

And as for German support for the anticipated revolt of the oppressed against the aged colonial empires, Haushofer already had this to say in 1924: "The struggle for liberation of India and China from foreign domination and foreign capitalist pressure meets with the secret dreams of Central Europe."[49]

The conclusion of the Nazi-Soviet Non-Aggression Pact occasioned a penetrating commentary in London's *The New Statesman*, which pointed out the striking connection between Mackinder, "one of the leading spirits of British Imperialism," and General Haushofer's *Geopolitik*. The path of Hitler's "World Revolution" might well have followed Haushofer's wishful scenario via the Transcontinental Bloc and his "apocalyptic vision of a world-wide rising of the coloured nations of the East against the capitalist rule of the Western Democracies, sponsored and led by the Soviet Union and by Germany . . . which aims at nothing less than the revolutionising of the Colonial World against the capitalist rule . . . and the establishment of a New World Order, in which Berlin would distribute the spheres of influence amongst its partners and satellites and, where necessary, mediate between them."[50] Haushofer, who must have been more flattered than upset by the article (he kept referring to it for the rest of his life), tacitly agreed: "Russia and Germany both lost the war because they fought on opposite sides. It took a long, a much longer time than Sir Halford Mackinder had expected, for the Germans and Russians to find that out."[51]

Hitler's attack on the Soviet Union in June 1941 must have shattered Haushofer's wishful speculations about the feasibility of the Eurasian Transcontinental Bloc in conjunction with the great anticolonial revolution. He was shocked, but publicly he acquiesced.[52] In Moscow, Stalin must have been even more shattered than Haushofer, though he probably never believed in those fantasylike geopolitical combinations, occasionally tossed in the air by Radek (whom he sent to the Gulag to die). According to his daughter, Svetlana, he would have been happier with a lasting German alliance than with the option of being forced by circumstances to conclude one with the Anglo-American imperialists. Even after the war Stalin was in the habit of repeating in front of his daughter "Ech, together with the Germans we would have been invincible!"[53] As a native of Caucasia he knew how to play the Asiatic card. When Japanese Foreign Minister Matsuoka was visiting the Kremlin in April 1941 to negotiate the Non-Aggression Pact between the two countries, Stalin went out of his way to accommodate him, even boasting "You are an Asiatic, so am I."[54]

With the invasion of Russia, Hitler began to be preoccupied more actively with the Eurasian space, but his views remained dominated by his perverse racial vision. Even when he discussed seemingly technical and economic questions the racial attitude always prevailed. His visionary *Lebensraum* in the East was to be protected against the "Central Asian masses" by the "Eastwall" (*Ostwall*).[55] Like previous European conquerors, notably Alexander of Macedonia and Napoleon, Hitler wanted to advance after defeating Russia in the direction of the Persian Gulf and Afghanistan, literally to India's doorstep.[56] To facilitate the logistics of the future Eastern *Lebensraum*, Hitler decided in 1941, after discussing the problem with his technocratic genius, Dr. Fritz Todt, to expand the *Autobahn* network (superhighway) eastward and to start the construction of a giant, three-meter gauge superrailway, running from Berlin as far as Baku. During the summer of 1942, at the height of the German planning euphoria when the Persian Gulf was to be reached across the Caucasus, some railway enthusiasts already saw the superrailway stretched out as far as Vladivostok.[57]

Whereas Hitler's war of racial annihilation against the Soviet Union ruled out further transcontinental plans as devised by Haushofer or Ribbentrop, on the Japanese side there remained throughout the entire war a strong lobby that advocated partnership with the Soviets and kept pressing the Germans to sign an armistice with Moscow to concentrate on the war against the Anglo-Saxon powers. This only further infuriated Hitler. For the time being, however, as long as the Soviets were excluded by the Germans, the Axis Powers decided to divide Eurasia tentatively in two halves along the 70° eastern longitude. According to this secret military convention, signed on 18 January 1942 (strangely reminiscent of the early geopolitical demarcation line negotiated between the Spanish and the Portuguese colonial empires in the Treaty of Tordesillas of 1494, and some more recent schemes),[58] Germany, Italy, and Japan were to coordinate their actions along the Eurasian rimlands. The Japanese preferred to omit any mention of the Soviet Union because they did not want to exclude the possibility of mediating the conclusion of a separate peace between Moscow and Berlin. But in drawing the demarcation line the Japanese delegates prevailed on the Germans and secured the incorporation into their prospective sphere of valuable coal resources in the Kuznetsk basin in Siberia and almost the whole of

British India up to the Indus River. However, they left the oil reserves of the Near and Middle East in German and Italian hands. But this convention was a mere formality as the Germans agreed among themselves that the 70° meridian was not to be considered the definitive political boundary between the "Pan-regions" (see Figure 8.1).

Having had Subhas Chandra Bose in Berlin to mastermind subversive actions and radio propaganda against British India, and two smaller outfits for the Arab Independent and Pan-Turanian movements, the Germans believed that they were in a stronger bargaining position than their Japanese allies. Hitler, for instance, told the Japanese ambassador in January 1942 that he was going to authorize no declaration of independence nor assistance to the freedom movements in India and among the Arabs, let alone on behalf of the vague Pan-Turanian cause, until after German troops crossed the Caucasus. Little did he know that India had already figured as part of the "Greater East Asian Co-Prosperity Sphere" in a number of Japanese geopolitical blueprints concocted by various types of think tank institutes. It should be recalled that Kingoro Hashimoto, one of the ideological fathers of the Greater East Asian Co-Prosperity Sphere and, with a grain of salt, the counterpart of General Haushofer in Japan, conceived a Greater East Asia that was to include India and Afghanistan.[59]

Haushofer's *Liaison Fatale*

A few words must be said about Haushofer's *liaison fatale* with the Nazi movement. Although the direct influence of Haushofer's teachings on the actual foreign policy of the Third Reich were heavily exaggerated, first in wartime Allied propaganda[60] and subsequently in the Soviet Union,[61] it cannot be denied that *Geopolitik* played a very important role in the ideological arsenal of Nazism. It provided a pseudoscientific and thus rational justification for Germany's territorial expansion toward *Weltherrschaft*. Consequently, Hitler and Haushofer could very easily be placed in the same equation. Because of the almost inherent incapacity among Hitler's adversaries to diagnose his racial bias, the view that "history will rate Karl Haushofer, the prophet of German geopolitics, more important than Adolf Hitler," was quite

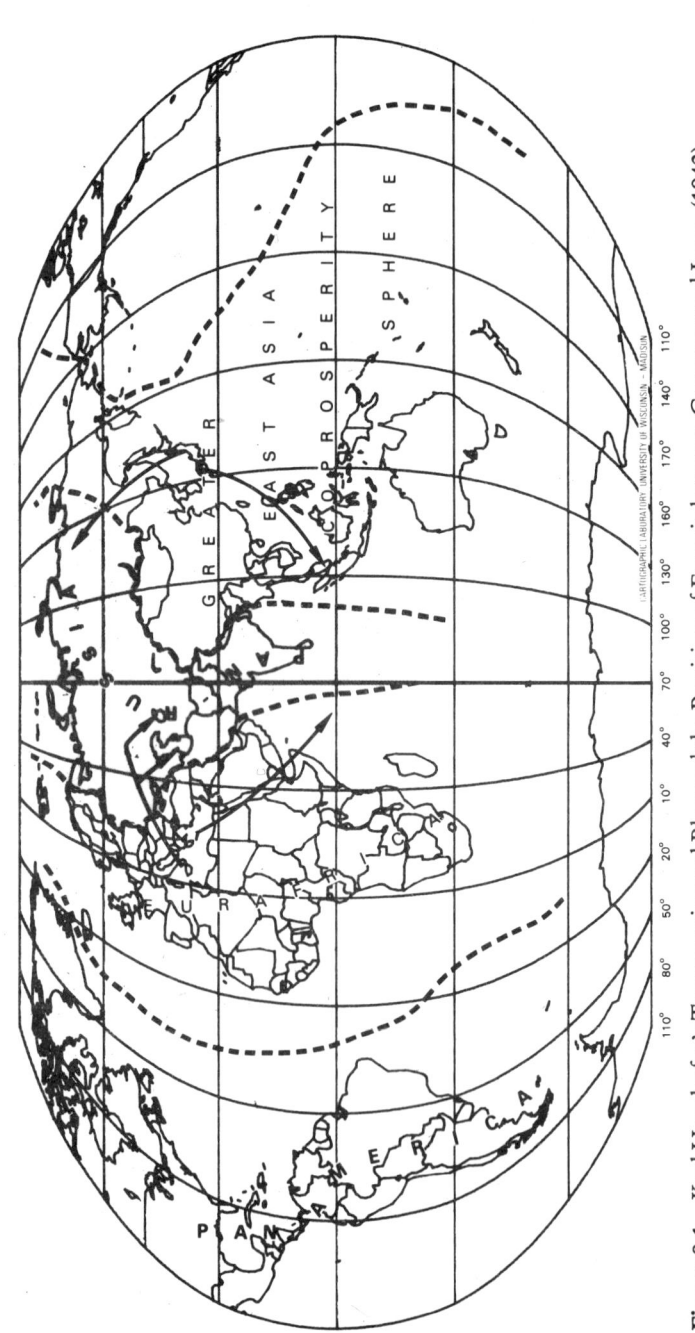

Figure 8.1 Karl Haushofer's Transcontinental Bloc and the Partition of Eurasia between Germany and Japan (1942)

Note: The World According to Haushofer in 1941, prior to Hitler's attack on the Soviet Union. The 70th meridian east of Greenwich, on which this projection is centered, shows the agreed partition between the Japanese and German (including Italian) spheres of influence, stipulated in the Military Convention of January 18, 1942.

Source: © Hauner 1989.

common.⁶² In another example, the more penetrating Strausz-Hupé wants to become in his verdicts on the meaning of German geopolitics, the more he contradicts himself.

> The Nazi war machine is the *instrument* of conquest; *Geopolitik* is the *master plan* designed to tell those who wield the instrument what to conquer and how.... There is no reason to believe that Hitler consulted Haushofer when making his momentous decisions. He did not need to. *Geopolitik* is Nazi foreign policy.... No direct evidence has, so far, come to hand that Hitler has sought or taken Haushofer's advice on matters of practical foreign policy.⁶³

The extraordinarily close association between Haushofer and his pupil and assistant, Rudolf Hess (the future deputy to the *Führer*), in the early years of the Nazi movement,⁶⁴ led many foreign critics to conclude hastily that the Munich geopolitician must have contributed his lion's share in the intellectual tutoring of ex-Corporal Hitler himself, especially when the latter was dictating *Mein Kampf* during his 1924 imprisonment in the Landsberg fortress. It was here, according to Edmund A. Walsh, an American political scientist, that "visiting both Hess and Hitler in their prison, the Herr Doctor began his indoctrination."⁶⁵ "We were told," writes Hans Weigert, tongue in cheek, "that Haushofer and his followers dominated the thinking of Hitler (as if he was Hitler's 'secret weapon'), and that it was Haushofer who directed the German General Staff's plans for world dominion."⁶⁶

And yet, whether this claim was ironic or made in earnest, as Peter Scholler wrote in his balanced analysis after the war, *Geopolitik* per se was never recognized by the majority of German scholars as a proper discipline of geography; they were reluctant to cross the fine line that separated Ratzel's political geography from the practical application of the *Lebensraum* thesis in the realm of foreign policy and, ultimately, military conquest.⁶⁷ It is, therefore, fundamentally wrong to speak of "the thousand scientists behind Hitler," as if *Geopolitik* achieved some kind of a superscience status in the Third Reich.⁶⁸ On the other hand, it is undeniable that Haushofer allowed himself initially to be prostituted by the Nazi state; he accepted his promotion to president of the German Academy (1934–37) by Hitler, which flattered his inflated ego of being recognized as a latecomer among the scholars. Moreover, he failed to protest against the outrageous Nazi transgressions of human rights, allegedly, as he claimed after the war, because he had a Jewish wife. He should have protested and resigned in spite of—or precisely because of—that.

Haushofer's fate was tragic, and he paid the maximum price for his initial indulgence in self-importance while condoning the evil. Deprived of Rudolf Hess's protecting hand after the Führer's deputy fled to England in 1941, Haushofer and his family were no longer *personae gratae* in Nazi Germany. He continued to edit the *Zeitschrift für Geopolitik* for a time as a matter of routine, obediently changing tack to give it a more anti-Bolshevik flavor when it was required.[69] Meanwhile, he jotted down his melancholic reflections on the nature of the Russian-Soviet phenomenon, the forthcoming deluge that seemed inevitable, and his understanding of Mackinder—the distant English enemy whom he admired but never met.[70] The abortive July 1944 attempt on Hitler's life, in which his son Albrecht was directly involved, unleashed a chain of tragic events for Haushofer and his family. Arrest, interrogation, and detention by the Gestapo followed. With the murder of Albrecht[71] by the Nazis in the last days of the war, the *Finis Germaniae*, the fiasco of *Geopolitik*, and personal tragedy, were merged into one for the aged and ailing father. Feebly he tried to justify his conduct under the Nazi regime before the American interrogators in his "Apology of German *Geopolitik*."[72] Before the judges from the Nuremberg Military Tribunal could have changed their minds and had him indicted as a war criminal, Karl Haushofer and his Jewish wife, Martha, committed suicide on 10 March 1946, in a bizarre and sinister ceremony.

> My father broke the seal,
> Ignoring the whiff of evil,
> Allowing the demon to spread in the world.[73]

Thus wrote Albrecht about his father in his *Sonnet of Moabit*, named after the Berlin jail where he was held before his execution.[74] Karl Haushofer's responsibility remains huge and heavy; he set up a deceiving example in the relationship between scholar and state authority, allowing himself to be exploited totally by the Nazi thugs. This is, of course, a moral judgment. But would the politicians' judgment be equally as stern had Haushofer's idea of the Transcontinental Bloc, combined with a widespread anti-colonial uprising in the Indo-Pacific sphere, succeeded? For unless we take a strict deterministic view of history, the post-1945 constellation of power blocs in the world was by no means certain during the earlier stages of the war, at least not until the end of 1942.

Politicians must be pragmatic in dealing with realities of power. They do accept, for instance, the existence of the Soviet Union—not to mention many petty but ghastly dictatorships that have emerged recently—the direct and legitimate successor of Stalin's Russia, burdened with many more unexplained millions of victims than Hitler's Germany was responsible for eliminating during wartime. I have no illusions that Hitler's systematic policy of racial genocide, directed against such minorities as Jews and Gypsies and against people with alleged hereditary or incurable diseases, would have been made palatable to the outside world had he not overreached himself by gambling away several unique opportunities. Had Hitler died right after the Munich Conference of 1938, he would have been celebrated (not only by the Germans) as the greatest German statesman since Bismarck.

As for the assumed causal link between Mackinder and Haushofer, the British geographer must have been highly embarrassed by this association, which he never tried to cultivate. There is no evidence of a meeting, not even a letter exchanged between the two men. It is an irony of history that whereas Mackinder remained ignored in his own country until about 1939, when *The New Statesman* article "discovered" him, his provocative ideas and concepts flourished in Germany and—at least by implication as we have tried to argue—in the Soviet Union. Mackinder himself felt compelled to address this unpleasant issue in 1944.

> I have been criticized in certain quarters as having helped to lay the foundation of Nazi militarism. It has, I am told, been rumoured that I inspired Haushofer, who inspired Hess, who in turn suggested to Hitler while he was writing 'Mein Kampf' certain geo-political ideas which are said to have originated with me. Those are three links in a chain, but of the second and third I know nothing. This, however, I do know from the evidence of his own pen that whatever Haushofer adapted from me he took from an address I gave before the Royal Geographical Society just forty years ago, long before there was any question of a Nazi Party.[75]

In comparing the political behavior and instincts of the two rival geographers, the evolution of Mackinder's ideas seems more interesting. From a pronounced liberal imperialist defending the existence of the British Empire as the best guarantor of human progress,[76] an ardent enemy of the Bolshevik putchists in 1919–20 (but not anti-Russian, not even anti-Soviet),[77] he moved, at the outbreak of World War II, toward a more harmonious international system without world dominion or hegemony by a particular empire or race: "... a balanced globe of human beings. And happy, because balanced and thus free."[78]

Haushofer, on the other hand, moved in the opposite direction.[79] He chose to stay on the Ratzelian path of *Raum und Boden*, in which the acquisition of the *Lebensraum* by the state, depicted as a living organism, remained the essence. In 1928 Haushofer defined *Geopolitik* as determined by what he called *Erdgebundenheit*, that is, dependence of political events on the soil.[80] Finally, one additional aspect may have strongly inspired Haushofer in the interpretation of Mackinder after his return from Japan and his experience in World War I. Though never mentioned explicitly by Haushofer, this imaginary influence would have fallen under what Strausz-Hupé perceptively calls the Wagnerian mentality in German national pathology. Thus, the wishful "Heartland" (*Herzland*) was to be found in much more distant places on the globe than *Mitteleuropa*. It was something that could be endowed with transcendental qualities as the imaginary cradle of the Aryan race, a constant attraction to world conquerors, such as Alexander the Great, Napoleon, and inevitably Hitler, too.

> The impending struggle promised to be titanic; the goal—domination of the Eurasian Heartland—was challengingly remote as the far-off places toward which Wagner's heroes interminably travel.[81]

Notes

1 Parker, *Geography of Russia* (1969), 106–107; Walter Kolarz, *Russia and Her Colonies* (London: Philip & Son, 1952), 68–75. For a more comprehensive account see Walter Laqueur, *Russia and Germany: Century of Conflict* (Boston: Little, Brown, 1965), here p. 41.

2 Karl Haushofer, *Deutsche Kulturpolitik im Indopazifischen Raum* (Hamburg: Hoffmann Campe, 1939), 67–72; Agursky, *Third Rome* (1987), 4.

3 Alfred Rosenberg, *Der Mythus des 20. Jahrhunderts. Eine Wertung der seelischgeistigen Gestaltenkämpfe unserer Zeit* (Munich: Hoheneichen, 1930), 198, 601–605; Weigert, *Generals and Geographers* (1942), 116–17, 135; Klaus Hildebrand, *Vom Reich zum Weltreich: Hitler, NSDAP und koloniale Frage 1919–1945* (Munich: Fink, 1969), 84–85; Hans-Adolf Jacobsen, *Karl Haushofer—Leben und Werk* (Boppard: Harald Boldt, 1979), I:534–35, 639–45.
4 Erich Obst, "Das Raumschicksal des russischen Volkes," In *Bausteine zur Geopolitik*, Karl Haushofer et al. (Berlin: Vowinckel, 1928), 201–202. A surprisingly bold stand against the Nazi racial doctrine was taken by Richard Henning in his article "Geopolitik und Rassenkunde: Eine notwendige Klarstellung," *Zeitschrift für Geopolitik* 13 (1936), 58–64. Against his critics, who attacked him for failing to defend the position that in National-Socialist Germany geopolitics must be interpreted from a racial standpoint, Henning stated unequivocally: "I protest against throwing geopolitics and race studies (*Rassenforschung*) into one pot."
5 On the preponderant influence of German *Orientalistik* on Russian *Vostokovedenie*, see Richard N. Frye's "Oriental Studies in Russia." In *Russia and Asia*, ed. Wayne S. Vucinich (Stanford: Hoover Institute, 1972), 34–36.
6 A. v. Humboldt, *Tsentral'naya Aziya*, vol. 1 (1915).
7 Karl Ritter, *Zemlevedenie Azii*, 5 vols. (St. Petersburg, 1856–79), translated and edited by P. P. Semyonov et al. Until 1895 ten volumes were published. See also Preston E. James, *All Possible Worlds. A History of Geographical Ideas* (New York: Odyssey, 1972), 284–90.
8 F. v. Richthofen, *China, Ergebnisse eigener Reisen und darauf gegründeter Studien*, 5 vols. (Berlin, 1877–1912).
9 Haushofer, *Deutsche Kulturpolitik* (1939), 94.
10 Sven Hedin assisted the German General Staff in its Central Asian schemes with direct advice and his invaluable maps during both world wars. Hitler was a great admirer of Sven Hedin, inviting him to be the keynote speaker at the 1936 Berlin Olympics. During World War II Hedin frequently visited Germany, did propaganda work for the Nazi regime, and was twice received by Hitler (cf. Sven Hedin, *German Diary 1935–1942* [Dublin: Euphorion, 1951]). When Hedin died on 26 November 1952 the London *Times* published an obituary notice by Sir Clement Skrine, at one time the British Consul General at Kashgar. He remembered Hedin as "a bold and most ambitious explorer," who "by temperament was a Nazi to whom exploration was a *Kampf*. . . . It is not surprising that he esposed in turn the causes of Kaiser Wilhelm II and Adolf Hitler" (cf. Charles Allen, *A Mountain in Tibet* [London: Futura, 1983], 11–12, 190–94).
11 Laqueur, *Russia and Germany* (1965), 12, 53.
12 The recent book by Geoffrey Stoakes depicts Rosenberg as someone who was free from Russophobia, admired Russian literature, and showed genuine sympathy for the Russian people (*Hitler and the Quest for World Dominion* [Leamington Spa: Berg Publishers, 1986], 11). Twenty years earlier Walter Laqueur presented Rosenberg as a Russia baiter (*Russia and Germany* [1965], 68–78).
13 Stoakes, *Hitler and the Quest* (1986), 122–35, 209–17. See also Paul Leverkuehn, *Posten auf ewiger Wache. Aus dem abenteurreichen Leben des*

Max von Scheubner-Richter (Essen: Essener Verlagsanstalt, 1938), 18–91, 180–206; Hans-Erich Volkmann, *Die russische Emigration in Deutschland, 1919–29* (Würzburg: Holzner, 1966), 74–84, 90.

14 A. Rosenberg, *Der Zukunftsweg einer deutschen Aussenpolitik* (Munich, 1927), 14, 142–44; *The Memoirs of Alfred Rosenberg*, ed. S. Lang and E. von Schenck (Chicago: Ziff-Davis, 1949), 31–39; Stephan, *Russian Fascists* (1978), 18–30; Heinz Gollwitzer, *Geschichte des weltpolitischen Denkens* (Göttingen: Vandenhoeck & Ruprecht, 1982), II:545.

15 Laqueur, *Russia and Germany* (1965), 79–104, 114–21; Stephan, *Russian Fascists* (1978), 22; A. Rosenberg, *Pest in Russland* (Munich: F. Eher, 1922), 38, 81, 93.

16 Rosenberg, *Der Mythus* (1930), 198, 601–605, 622, 634–35.

17 O. Spengler, *Jahre der Entscheidung* (Munich: Beck, 1933), 58.

18 Wolfgang Pfeiler, "Das Deutschlandbild und die Deutschlandpolitik Josef Stalins," *Deutschland Archiv* 12 (1979), 1258–82.

19 John Erickson, *The Soviet High Command* (New York: St. Martin's, 1962), 152–54; Francis F. Carsten, *The Reichswehr and Politics, 1918–1933* (Berkeley: University of California, 1973), 135. Gustav Hilger and Alfred G. Meyer, *The Imcompatible Allies. A Memoir—History of German-Soviet Relations 1918–1941* (New York: Macmillan, 1953), 188–91, 268, 278; E. Gnedin, a former secretary to Soviet foreign minister, Maxim Litvinov, has confirmed Radek's key role as mediator between the two countries also during the 1930s: *Iz istorii otnosheniy mezhdu SSSR i fashistskoi Germaniey* (New York: Khronika Press, 1977). Alas, Marie-Louise Goldbach, in her monograph, ignores completely the Haushofer-Niedermayer-Radek connection (*Karl Radek und die deutsch-sowjetischen Beziehungen 1918–1923* [Bonn: Verlag Neue Gesellschaft, 1973]).

20 Niedermayer headed the Reichswehr office in Moscow for 11 years until 1932, when the officially appointed German military attaché, General Köstring, replaced him. Niedermayer then resigned from the army and taught military geography (*Wehrgeographie*) at the University of Berlin. During World War II he rejoined the Wehrmacht and was promoted to the rank of major-general; he fought for the establishment of separate military units recruited from Soviet non-Slavic prisoners of war. In 1942 he was appointed commander of the 162nd (Turk) infantry division, which had a truly Central Asian composition: two legions of Turkestanis, and one each of Armenians, Azerbaijanis, and Georgians. Accused of defeatism for showing concern for his soldiers, Niedermayer was arrested and awaiting trial when Germany surrendered. He was then taken to Moscow by the Red Army and was never seen or heard of again. Many years thereafter a witness emerged who reported that Niedermayer may have died of tuberculosis in the prison of Vladimir in 1948. Cf. Franz W. Seidler, "Oskar von Niedermayer im Zweiten Weltkrieg," *Wehrwissenschaftliche Rundschau* 3/20 (1970), 168–74, 193–208.

21 O. v. Niedermayer, *Unter-Der Glutsonne Irans. Kriegserlebnisse der Deutschen Expedition nach Persien und Afghanistan* (Munich, 1925), and *Afghanistan* (Leipzig, 1924). See chapter 5, "Three Elements of Russian Strategy."

22 Jacobsen, *Karl Haushofer* (1979), I:221–22, 259, 334, 546, 635–39, and (1979), II:5, 16–19, 52, 92–94.

23 Through Radek's and Niedermayer's mediation, Haushofer was receiving *Novyi Vostok* and was meeting a string of Soviet visitors coming to Germany. But it is impossible to verify A. J. Pearce's claim that Haushofer at any time became "adviser to Stalin" (cf. introduction to Mackinder's reprint of *Democratic Ideals and Reality* [New York: Norton, 1962], ix, xxii).
24 Weigert, *Generals and Geographers* (1942), 116.
25 Ibid.
26 Bernard Semmel, "Sir Halford Mackinder: Theorist of Imperialism," *Canadian Journal of Economics and Political Science* 24/4 (November 1958), 554–61.
27 K. Haushofer, *Dai-Nihon: Betrachtungen über Gross-Japans Wehrkraft, Weltstellung und Zukunft* (Berlin: Mittler, 1913).
28 Friedrich Ratzel, *Der Lebensraum. Eine biogeographische Studie. Festgabe für Albert Schaeffle* (Tübingen, 1901); Karl Lange, "Der Terminus 'Lebensraum' in Hitler's 'Mein Kampf,'" *Vierteljahreshefte für Zeitgeschichte* 13 (1965), 426–37; Woodruff D. Smith, "Friedrich Ratzel and the Origins of Lebensraum," *German Studies Review* 3 (1980), 51–68.
29 R. Kjellén, *Der Staat als Lebensform* (Leipzig: S. Hirzel, 1917). Rudolf Kjellén, regarded as Ratzel's spiritual disciple, was apparently the first political scientist to apply the term *Geopolitik* as early as 1905 (cf. Josef Matznetter, ed., *Politische Geographie* [Darmstadt: Wissenschaftliche Buchgesellschaft, 1977], 8).
30 Rosenberg, *Der Mythus* (1930), 195, 601–605, 634.
31 Edmund A. Walsh, "The Mystery of Haushofer," *Life* (16 September 1946), 107–21; see also Haushofer's testimony summarized in Jacobsen, *Karl Haushofer* (1979), I:344–45. Dan Diner's postulate that anti-Semitism should be included among the main elements of Haushofer's *Geopolitik* is not convincing (cf. Dan Diner, "Grundbuch der Planeten: Zur Geopolitik Karl Haushofer's," *Vierteljahreshefte für Zeitgeschichte* 32/1 [1984], 1–28). For a more balanced analysis see Peter Scholler, "Wege und Irrwege der politischen Geographie und Geopolitik," *Erdkunde* 11 (1957), 1–20, and Stoakes, *Hitler and the Quest* (1986), 140–70.
32 For more discussion of the complex question dealing with the revival of German colonial ambitions in Africa during the 1930s, the Eurafrica projects among them, see: Hildebrand, *Vom Reich zum Weltreich* (1969); Hauner, *India in Axis Strategy* (1981), 178–81; Derwent Whittlesey, *German Strategy of World Conquest* (New York: Farrar, 1942), 205–15.
33 Jacobsen, *Karl Haushofer* (1979), I:267–72, 278, 456–59.
34 Contained in Haushofer's seminal work on self-determination in which he welcomes the 900-million Southeast Asians as Germany's "fellow-travellers in disaster" against the Western colonial powers: "Südostasiens Wiederaufstieg zur Selbstbestimmung." In *Zur Geopolitik der Selbstbestimmung*, ed. K. Haushofer and J. März (Munich: Rösl, 1923). In this book Mackinder is mentioned for the first time by Haushofer. See also Whittlesey, *German Strategy* (1942), 217; Weigert, *Generals and Geographers* (1942), 167–91. Haushofer's geopolitical ideas about the political emancipation of the Indo-Pacific region were welcomed by some Indian radicals, such as Benoy Kumar Sarkar, a political scientist, and Subhas Chandra Bose, a Bengali nationalist. Bose visited Haushofer in Munich at least twice, in 1924 and 1925. See: Johannes

H. Voigt, *Indien im Zweiten Weltkrieg* (Stuttgart: Deutsche Verlagsanstalt, 1978), 33–34; Hauner, *India in Axis Strategy* (1981), 22–24, 61, 183–84.
35 Haushofer, *Geopolitik der Panideen* (Berlin: Zentral-Verlag, 1931).
36 Strausz-Hupé, *Geopolitics* (1942), 152.
37 Haushofer, *Dai-Nihon* (1913), 262, 271.
38 Haushofer, *Geopolitik des Pazifischen Ozeans* (Berlin: Vowinckel, 1924), 142.
39 Hans W. Weigert, "Asia through Haushofer's Glasses." In *Compass of the World. A Symposium on Political Geography*, ed. H. Weigert and V. Stefansson (New York: Macmillan, 1944), 399; and Weigert, *Generals and Geographers* (1942), 176.
40 Weigert, "Asia" (1944), 403–404.
41 Ibid., 404.
42 Haushofer, "Der Nahe Osten im Vorschatten eurasiatischer Festland politik," *Zeitschrift für Geopolitik* (1939), 781–85. Here Haushofer advocates a creation of a new Eurasian large-space region (*Grossraumordnung*) in concert with an anticolonial uprising of the have-nots. He recalls that similar geopolitical ideas were at one time expressed by Karl Radek, "one clever servant of the Soviets."
43 Weigert, *Generals and Geographers* (1942), 149, 155.
44 Hauner, *India in Axis Strategy* (1981), 183–86; Wolfgang Michalka, *Nationalsozialistische Aussenpolitik* (Frankfurt and Darmstadt: Metzner, 1978), 471–92, and *Ribbentrop und die deutsche Weltpolitik 1933–1940* (Munich: Fink, 1980), 278–97.
45 Haushofer, *Der Kontinentalblock: Mitteleuropa-Eurasien-Japan* (Munich: Zentralverlag der NSDAP, 1941); see also Jacobsen, *Karl Haushofer* (1979), 1:606–34. Homer Lea, author of *The Day of the Saxon* (1912), ended his adventurous career as military adviser to Dr. Sun Yat Sen. He predicted that East Asia would become a battle zone between two alliances: the Sino-British and the Russo-German-Japanese. Brooks Adams (1848–1927) hinted, in *America's Economic Supremacy* (1900), at the emergence of a possible Berlin-Moscow-Peking axis, epitomized by a new railway line, which would rival the Anglo-Saxon alliance.
46 See Haushofer, *Der Kontinentalblock* (1941). On S. C. Bose and the Indian nationalists during World War II, see the relevant passages in Hauner, *India in Axis Strategy* (1981).
47 Fritz Fischer, *Germany's Aims in the First World War* (New York: Norton, 1967), 120–54.
48 Weigert, *Generals and Geographers* (1942), 145.
49 Ibid., 173; see also Haushofer, *Geopolitik* (1924), 132.
50 "Hitler's World Revolution," *The New Statesman and Nation* (26 August 1939), 301–302.
51 *Zeitschrift für Geopolitik* (1939), 777; Charles Kruszewski, "The Pivot of History," *Foreign Affairs* (April 1954), 399.
52 *Zeitschrift für Geopolitik* (1941), 369–70.
53 Svetlana Allilueva, *Only One Year* (New York: Harper & Row, 1969), 392. According to a Soviet intelligence officer, Stalin's favorite partner for the Soviet Union had been Germany, with a possible alliance with Japan, against the United States. See Ismail Akhmedov, *In and Out of Stalin's GRU* (Washington, D.C.: University Publications of America, 1904), 134. See also Pfeiler (1979) in note 18.

54 Stephan, "Asia in the Soviet Conception" (1982), 36 (quotes *Asahi Shimbun* of 28 April 1941). The cunning Stalin was capable of using his Asiatic roots with the opposite effect when it suited his purpose. During the conclusion of the Nazi-Soviet Non-Aggression Pact on 23 August 1939, he apparently boasted in front of the German diplomat, Gustav Hilger, of the lesson that Soviet troops had just dealt the Japanese troops. He added almost sadistically that 20,000 Japanese had been killed on that occasion: "That is the only language these Asiatics understand; after all, I am an Asiatic too, so I ought to know." (Cf. Hilger and Meyer, *Incompatible Allies* [1953], 305).

55 H. R. Trevor-Roper (ed.), *Hitler's Table Talk 1941–44* (London: Weidenfels & Nicolson, 1973), 24, 40.

56 Hauner, *India in Axis Strategy* (1981), 259–73.

57 Anton Joachimsthaler, *Die Breitspurbahn. Das Projekt zur Erschliessung des gross-europäischen Raumes 1942–1945* (Munich: Herbig, 1985), 59–63, 293–96, 370. After Germany's surrender the Soviets put their hands on everything even remotely connected with the broad-gauge transcontinental railway, presumably with the intention of using the German blueprints for their own purposes to upgrade the Trans-Siberian Railway (Ibid., 5).

58 In a remarkable but little known article, "Panegyriens auf Russlands Kulturaufgaben im Osten" ("Panegyric on Russia's Cultural Tasks in the East"), published in *Verhandlungen der Gesellschaft für Erdkunde in Berlin* (1891), 2–5, the German ethnographer, Adolf Bastian, while warmly welcoming Russia's advance in Central Asia, suggests that the future dividing line (*Scheidungslinie*) between West and East has been pushed eastward by the "White Tsar" and should be marked by the meridian connecting Samarkand, Kabul, and Northwest India (roughly identical with 70° east).

59 Hauner, *India in Axis Strategy* (1981), 377–90. A map showing the principal pan-regions is reproduced in D. Whittlesey's article on Haushofer in *Makers of Modern Strategy*, ed. E. M. Earle (Princeton University Press, 1941), 401. (See Figure 8.1.)

60 See notes 31 and 50.

61 See for example, Evgeniy Tarle, "Vostochnoe Prostranstvo i fashistskaya geopolitika." In *Protiv fashistskoi fal'sifikatsii istorii*, F. I. Notovich ed. (Moscow, 1939), 259–79.

62 Colonel H. Beukema, a West Point instructor, as quoted in *Time*, 19 January 1942; see also Parker, *Mackinder* (1982), 180.

63 Strausz-Hupé, *Geopolitics* (1942), 79, 84, 264.

64 Jacobsen, *Karl Haushofer* (1979), I:224–31, 448–63.

65 E. A. Walsh, "Geopolitics and International Morals." In *Compass of the World*, ed. Weigert and Stefansson (1944), 21.

66 Ibid., 396.

67 Scholler, "Wege und Irrwege" (1957), 1–20.

68 Weigert and Stefansson, *Compass of the World* (1944), 396.

69 *Zeitschrift für Geopolitik* 18/7 (1941), 369–70.

70 K. Haushofer, "Nostris ex Ossibus. Gedanken eines Optimisten," unpublished manuscript, written in October 1944 after Haushofer's release from temporary detention in the concentration camp of Dachau. Reproduced in Jacobsen, *Karl Haushofer* (1979), I:634–39.

71 Ursula Laack-Michel, *Albrecht Haushofer und der Nationalsozialismus* (Stuttgart: Klett, 1974).
72 K. Haushofer, "Apologie der deutschen Geopolitik." In Jacobsen, *Karl Haushofer* (1979), I:639–45.
73 E. A. Walsh, *Wahre anstatt falsche Geopolitik für Deutschland* (Frankfurt/M, 1946), and "Die Tragödie Karl Haushofers," *Neue Auslese* 3 (1947), 19.
74 Albrecht Haushofer, *Moabiter Sonette* (Berlin, 1946), 47.
75 As quoted by Parker, *Mackinder* (1982), 176.
76 See Semmel "Sir Halford Mackinder" (1958).
77 See, for example, Mackinder's foreword to the translation of Nikolai N. Mikhailov, *Soviet Geography* (London: Methuen, 1935).
78 Mackinder, "The Round World" (1943), 605.
79 Geoffrey Parker, *Western Political Thought in the Twentieth Century* (London: Croom Helm, 1985), 84.
80 K. Haushofer (ed.), *Bausteine zur Geopolitik* (Berlin: Vowinckel, 1927), 27, 271.
81 Quoted from Strausz-Hupé, *Geopolitics* (1942), 155. The most fascinating portrait of Hitler as the extreme incarnation of the wandering romantic German soul, whom "only Richard Wagner could overcome," has been Hans-Jürgen Syberberg's film *Our Hitler: A Film from Germany* (interview with the author in *Frankfurter Allgemeine Zeitung* of 8 July 1978). Susan Sontag called it "one of the great works of art of the 20th century" (*New York Review of Books*, 21 February 1980). One of the less known and perhaps most extreme cases of a successful Russo-German transcontinental cooperation over the "center of the world" was Moscow's permission and assistance rendered to two SS expeditions to Tibet, traveling via the Soviet Union during the brief Nazi-Soviet honeymoon of 1940 and 1941. Both were led by *SS Sturmbannführer* Dr. Ernst Schäfer, a protégé of Himmler at the time and known for his explorations of Tibet prior to and after the war. See Hedin, *German Diary* (1951), 122, 144, 166–67; Hauner, *India in Axis Strategy* (1981), 161, 166.

9

The Heartland Revisited: Geopolitics in Soviet Perspective

Mackinder—The First Visitor

"Revisiting" the heartland appears to have been a rather popular exercise in the years following World War II, considering the number of critical studies bearing the same, or almost identical, title.[1] Yet, while the theoretical revisiting of the Eurasian heartland was going on, very few observers asked themselves whether Mackinder knew Russia at all. He had, in fact, been there once, almost the very first visitor one might say, but never within the heartland itself; he merely touched Russia's Black Sea coast for less than three weeks, hardly stepping ashore, spending most of his time aboard a British warship anchored in the harbor of Novorossiysk. This was in January 1920 after Lord Curzon, then the Foreign Secretary, had appointed Mackinder the British High Commissioner in Southern Russia to act as liaison with the White Russian forces of General Denikin, who was attempting to wring power from the Bolsheviks. Despite the knighthood he earned for his endeavors, the mission itself, especially as far as its major political aim was concerned, ended in failure.[2]

There was no way the war-wary British government could follow his advice and take immediate and energetic steps to help forge a new anti-Bolshevik alliance out of such an incongruous coalition ridden with deep contradictions. Mackinder's wise recommendations, inspired by his *Democratic Ideals and Reality* (published just a few months earlier in anticipation of the Peace Conference), was that it was "a vital necessity that there should be a tier of independent states between Germany and Russia."[3] True, such *cordon sanitaire* did emerge in Eastern Europe, but it could never play the role of a third power sandwiched between Germany and Russia, both of whom were to recover and remilitarize much faster than Mackinder had dared to speculate between 1918 and 1920.

Thereafter Mackinder was to follow events in Soviet Russia with intense curiosity, although perhaps less intense than that of his German rival, Haushofer. Witness his brief foreword to N. N. Mikhailov's *Soviet Geography* (1935) in which Mackinder displayed his skill for a flowery but misty metaphor; in one sentence he calls the book "remarkable," in the next one, "a political pamphlet of the indirect order . . . charged with political electricity . . . oratorical rather than literary." Mackinder's irony is obvious when he refers to the claim of the Soviets "to be re-making the geography, physical as well as human, of one-seventh of the land on this globe," and when he describes the author as incapable of distinguishing between "fact and prophecy." He concludes that in sketching "the new map of Scythia . . . only the future will tell whether these 'engineers' both of society and environment have underrated the momentum of human values from the past."[4] Almost 50 years later, N. N. Mikhailov, the author in question, recalls how he felt flattered that the Oxford professor, Halford Mackinder, "the patriarch of western geography," had written what he perceived to be a commending foreword to his book.[5] In light of the official Soviet condemnation of Mackinder (about which more will be said), one is somewhat surprised at any seemingly favorable comment in print by a Soviet scholar concerning Mackinder. Does it reflect a vestige of a genuine appreciation? Or is it token evidence of an internal dialogue that went unrecorded inside the Soviet academic community. As such it might represent a more truthful statement about Mackinder's status among Soviet geographers. We shall never know.

The main focus of the Soviet heartland, which we propose to examine through Mackinder's eyes in this and the next chapter, is precisely the shift of the center of gravity eastward in the socio-economic and strategic balance of the Soviet Eurasian Empire.

Before Mackinder, Ratzel had already developed his concept of space as the basis of state power, and he designated North America and Russian Asia as the two major "powerhouses" of the future. But it was Mackinder who succeeded in marrying space and strategic location with the topical dichotomy between land and sea power in a catchy and simple map.[6]

German Geopolitik and the New Soviet *Herzland*

Haushofer, too, wrote a preface to a geopolitical study about the Soviet Union at about the same time. Not only was he more specific than Mackinder, but he was also less ironic and much more sympathetic to Soviet aims. He characterized the Soviet Union as "the world's biggest geopolitical problem," bigger even, in his view, than the problem of the "Yellow Race" in Asia. He admitted that he contemplated Russia like an immense, mysterious, sleeping giant, like a fairy-tale *Golem*, the mechanical man, the robot created in the Central European sagas. "What happened," he asked anxiously, "to the soul of the Russian people, so wonderfully vibrant in its music and language? Has it been captured, overcome by foreign doctrines, or is it only asleep to wake up suddenly and terribly?" Haushofer concluded that he hoped that the book would captivate the minds of those readers receptive to large-space concepts, "by which greatness must be measured."[7] This was not the first compliment Haushofer paid to the Soviets. He regularly read *Novyi Vostok* and described that periodical as "the masterpiece of geopolitical writing."[8]

Did the Bolshevik Revolution change fundamentally the geopolitical role of the heartland within Russian Eurasia? And if so, in what respect? Yuriy Semyonov, a Russian emigré living in Germany, had asked precisely this question in 1925.[9] He observed that although the Bolsheviks had not formulated an explicit geopolitical program, their striving for world revolution, combined with the struggle for self-determination of the Asian peoples, which they helped to unleash, constituted a substitutive geopolitical program in its own right. At the same time, however, Semyonov was convinced that the same historical process to create a cohesive and viable Eurasian Empire, which Tsarist Russia had been trying to accomplish, must be continued under the Soviets.

He also noticed that the old Anglo-Russian antagonism had intensified since the Revolution, and he rightly saw the cause of it in the increased agitation among Asian nationalists allied with the Bolsheviks. British and Bolshevik troops clashed in the course of the Civil War along the entire middle latitude of Central Asia, from Transcaucasia, Persia, and Transcaspia to the Pamirs and Kashgaria. It seemed as if the polarization between the have-nots, incited by the Bolsheviks, and the haves, defended by the British Empire as the status-quo power, was bound to lead to the creation of a Soviet-sponsored "Continental Bloc" across Eurasia that would challenge the British hegemony. The establishment of such a Bloc was, as we noted earlier, the most cherished idea of Karl Haushofer. Summing up, Semyonov saw the essence of the geopolitical change affecting Soviet foreign policy in the decisive shift of the center of gravity from west to east, from the Black Sea to the Pacific Ocean.

A decade later, the same Yuriy Semyonov, together with Oskar von Niedermayer (already known to us), published a study on Soviet Russia's geopolitical problems. Hans Weigert described the work as "a brilliant digest of an immense factual material and a masterpiece of a geopolitical study of modern Russia."[10] Indeed, there was nothing comparable in any language, including Russian, that combined analysis with the latest information about Soviet developments from a geopolitical standpoint. The hitherto standard reference book on Russia's "people, state, and culture" by Ratzel's pupil, Alfred Hettner (1916), looked at the Russian Empire as a hostile power;[11] Semyonov and Niedermayer wrote their book in 1933 presumably under the assumption that Soviet Russia, regardless of whether Germany turned National-Socialist, should be considered as a potential ally of Germany rather than her perennial enemy.

Regarding the distant aim of world revolution with the support of the Asian peoples, Semyonov reckoned that its pursuit was no longer the number one Soviet priority. Instead of exporting revolution abroad, all effort went into the heroic domestic reconstruction under the iron fist of Stalin, thereby obscuring the USSR's true geopolitical aims. Semyonov, however, remained convinced that a radical spatial shift from west to east, resulting partly from the loss of substantial territories in the west and partly from the thirst for certain raw materials found only in the east, was very much part of Stalin's industrialization program. As an example, he cited the emergence during the first five-year plan of the Ural-Kuznetsk industrial combine, a merger of a traditional metallurgical center with a new major coal-producing area (*Kuzbas*) in the middle of Asia, separated by a distance of more than 2,000 km. This radical industrialization of the Eurasian heartland, underlined by the spectacular increase in the number of workers and employees east of the Urals, a number that had more than doubled during the first five-year plan, led Semyonov to a negative conclusion about its cost efficiency. That conclusion is still valid today. Even ignoring the forced labor factor, and assuming that the Soviet Union might have been trying to improve its military position by becoming more autarkic, none of the products manufactured in or raw materials extracted from the heartland could be sold abroad because of the astronomic transport costs.[12]

The Empire's Center of Gravity Is Moving Eastward

A number of Western authors (East, Hopper, Meinig, Mills, Hooson) supported this idea of an eastward spatial shift favoring the industrialization of the heartland,[13] which already had been forecast by the genius of Mendeleev and Mackinder. But these post-1945 authors could not agree on the reason for this shift. Did the establishment of the new Kuzbas Combine and the accelerated industrialization of the Urals represent genuine indicators that a new Soviet heartland was emerging in this vast zone stretching from the Volga to the Baykal, an area endowed with major industrial and raw material capacities as well as the fastest growing working population? Or were all these changes merely an exaggerated Soviet preoccupation with security? Because both interpretations are plausible, the autarkic obsession with self-sufficiency must have won out in the considerations of Stalin and his advisers, underlying his or their geopolitical visions as part of the not too enviable geostrategic predicament created by the two-front war complex. By moving strategic industries from the frontier zones and locating new ones inside what Mackinder would call the "pivot region," to be served by an improved rail infrastructure, Stalin created during the first five-year plan a formidable military-industrial base. It was approximately equidistant from the two main potential theaters of military operations at the western and eastern extremities of his Eurasian Empire (see Figure 10.1).

When Nazi Germany invaded Soviet Russia and occupied most of the old industrial centers in western and southern Russia, the new industrial base created in the heartland of Eurasia sprang into preeminence. Moreover, its contribution to Soviet armaments industry increased further because of the evacuation of more than 1,300 larger industrial plants from the threatened regions. The majority of them were relocated to the safe eastern regions (that is, the heartland), the Urals, Western Siberia, Central Asia, and Kazakhstan. Whereas in 1940 these eastern regions contributed 34 percent to Soviet overall industrial output, by the end of the war the figure must have been well over 50 percent, notwithstanding the inevitable decline in nonmilitary production, food, and energy supplies during the war years.[14]

The point that such an intensive economic development of the Eurasian heartland appeared extremely uneconomical could be plausibly argued from a capitalist perspective of cost efficiency within a peaceful world interested only in the exchange of goods. This, however, did not appear to be Stalin's vision of the future based on growing contradictions between the capitalist and socialist worlds. Events leading to the outbreak of World War II seemed to have supported his economic strategy.

It seems, therefore, plausible that not just one but a multitude of factors must have influenced the shaping of Soviet strategy in Asia. These factors were primarily determined by the critical situation in the Far East, where the Soviet position was weaker than elsewhere, and had a direct bearing on the policy of building up the military-industrial complex in the center of Soviet heartland. As mentioned earlier, this weakness was demonstrated during the Civil War when the Czech Legion seized the entire Trans-Siberian Railway and the Japanese expeditionary force advanced westward almost to Lake Baykal. Not until October 1922 did the Japanese troops reluctantly embark from Vladivostok, the last of the interventionist armies to leave Russian territory.[15]

Moscow's weakness at the easternmost extremity of Eurasia was also reflected in the pragmatic decision to grant a considerable degree of autonomy to the short-lived Far Eastern Republic (1920–22). Although this unusual buffer state, with its own constitution and flag, had been created as a temporary measure within a centralized communist dictatorship, there was always fear in Moscow that it ultimately could be detached. Besides, it established a dangerous precedent for other border regions of the Soviet Union.[16]

The chief Soviet interest in the Far East, apart from the protracted Chinese civil war, was the simmering Sino-Japanese conflict. Whereas, for purposes of revolutionary rhetoric and to keep the pot boiling, the Komintern conducted an activist policy in the Chinese civil war, the Soviet government pursued a pragmatic course vis-à-vis Tokyo, which resulted in the Soviet-Japanese Treaty of January 1925. Whether or not the Soviet-Japanese rapproachement of the mid-1920s was the outcome of Stalin's "appeasement policy in the name of Pan-Asiatism," as has been argued by some,[17] remains a matter of conjecture.

By contrast, the pivotal position of the heartland, which was advantageous for spreading the gospel of revolution throughout Asia (especially in the direction of India via Persia and Afghanistan), as the Second Komintern Congress and the Baku Conference of the Peoples of the Orient proclaimed in 1920, could not be sustained for longer than a few years. Again, as in the case of Japanese-Soviet relations, pragmatic considerations prevailed. Following the Curzon Ultimatum (May 1923), the Soviet government, anxious to resume normal trade relations with Great Britain, halted overt revolutionary subversion in India and along the entire heartland's "soft underbelly."[18]

At this junction, according to one author, "Stalin's conception of foreign policy definitely veered away from Leninism to geopolitics of Haushofer's variety,"[19] and the surmise of the Soviet-German geopolitical connection made sense. This is why, as mentioned earlier, Haushofer's unique Japanese expertise became so attractive to Moscow. This may also explain why Haushofer was urged several times through Niedermayer, then active in Moscow in forging the close cooperation between the *Reichswehr* and the Red Army, to supply the Soviets with his expert analyses of recent Japanese writings.[20] Finally, Haushofer's grand concept of a Eurasian Transcontinental bloc, rallying Germany, Soviet Russia, India, China, and Japan and stretching "from the Rhine to the Amur and Yangtse,"[21] may have caught Stalin's fancy—and if not his, then certainly Karl Radek's. This line of speculation also helps us understand why Haushofer persistently urged Japan, through friends and acquaintances, to terminate her involvement in the "Chinese Incident."[22] If Japan, nevertheless, continued her expansion into China, Haushofer warned, "she will be drowned." The dire consequence would be to encourage the creation of "an unconquerable human bloc of 800 million (then in 1935) Indians and Chinese drawn together. He recommended instead that the Japanese admirals should assert themselves against the generals and withdraw from the Asian Continent to concentrate all their striking power against the Anglo-American and other Western colonial possessions in the Pacific.[23]

This raises the question that if Haushofer, the leading representative of German *Geopolitik*, was so well known and respected in the inner circles of the Soviet leadership, why does the present official Soviet view of geopolitics remain so viciously negative? Why has there been no serious attempt to analyze Mackinder's heartland concept? To answer these difficult questions it is important to establish the correct chronology that will enable us to see the evolving Soviet view of geopolitics in proper perspective. There is little evidence, for instance, of an outright condemnation of *Geopolitik* on the part of Soviet officialdom prior to the German aggression of 1941.

A Heartland Navy?

Although the German-Soviet geopolitical connection has been mentioned several times, one rare case of the Soviets' adapting one of Mackinder's central ideas concerning the defensive function of the heartland has not yet been cited. In the early 1920s two senior Soviet naval officers referred favorably to Mackinder's heartland concept in the pages of *Morskoi Sbornik*. According to one secondary source, the Mackinder paradigm about the control of the rimlands from the Eurasian heartland was used to justify a radical reconstruction of the Red Navy.

Based on Russia's extremely negative experience in applying sea power in her recent wars, the future sea power status of the Soviet Union was to be determined primarily by taking full advantage of its internal communications, either by land or water (that is, via inland seas, canals, and rivers). The Red Navy would achieve greater mobility through numerous small naval craft, which could be transferred relatively quickly from one corner of the Soviet Eurasian Empire to the other, rather than large oceangoing vessels, which would have to be kept in four separate fleets (actually five if the Caspian Flotilla is included) that could not be brought together for a concentrated action. Hence the emphasis during the first five-year plan on building a relatively large quantity of patrol craft, torpedo boats, and small submarines (for example the 600-ton *Shchuka* and the 200-ton *Molodka* class) that could be disassembled and shipped by rail from one coast to the other.[24]

During the same period strategic implications were also evident in the reckless effort based on extensive use of forced labor to improve inland waterways, connecting the Baltic with the North Sea and with the Caspian. The final interlocking with the Black Sea waterways via the Volga-Don Canal was accomplished only in 1952. Still, to attribute all this to a secret reading of Mackinder by Soviet admirals seems rather far-fetched. At the most Mackinder may have constituted but one of many contributing factors in which Russian and foreign experience merged together. For instance, the idea of transporting dismantled naval craft over land did not originate among the Soviets; it had been practiced during World War I by the Germans, who ferried small submarines by rail and rivers from North Sea naval yards to the Adriatic and the Black Sea.

When the Soviet government announced the construction of the White Sea-Baltic-Volga canal network, some prominent emigré writers, like N. V. Ustryalov, emphasized the striking coincidence between the Soviet plans and some parallel geostrategic ideas developed by exiled Eurasianists, the first of whom was P. N. Savitsky. Savitsky had advocated the construction of intersea canals across Russia as the only feasible solution to the terrible geopolitical predicament of Russian Eurasia: the "quadripartition" (*chetvertovannost*) of its sea shores.[25] The other solution, alas impractical, was a miraculous technological revolution that would allow regular navigation in the Arctic Sea and its coastal rivers. This solution has been pursued with great energy by the Soviet regime until today, but the desirable breakthrough has not been achieved.[26]

Ustryalov could not resist citing the obvious paradox that he found in contrasting the practical aims of the five-year plan with the revolutionary ethos back in 1917, when the victorious Bolsheviks had declared that the aims of the new Soviet Russia were to be fundamentally different from those of all previous regimes. By the weight of inescapable historical logic, writes Ustryalov by quoting Savitsky, the Soviet government was compelled to solve Russia's perennial geopolitical task, "the economic self-assertion of the Eurasian Continent-Ocean." Consequently, Stalin's first five-year plan was, from Savitsky's perspective, nothing but a Soviet version of a "historical Eurasianist program."[27] In this context it is worth recalling the guiding idea of the great Russian geographer, V. P. Semyonov-Tyan-Shansky, who visualized the Russian Eurasian Empire precisely in these geopolitical terms as a "Continent-Ocean," stretching from "sea to sea."[28] Finally, it is impossible not to quote Halford Mackinder in this context. In 1904 he spoke of the Russian Eurasian Empire as a symbiosis of a remarkable correlation between natural environment and political organization, unlikely to be altered by any possible social revolution, which could never change her "essential relations to the great geographical limits of her existence."[29]

Marxism and *Aziatchina*

For all its attacks against geopolitics, there has never been a genuine critical Marxist analysis of this phenomenon, which emerged during the era of high imperialism when the world, as Mackinder liked to describe it, happened to be "closed." Curiously enough, the first analytical, and also the last systematic attempt from a Marxist point of view, was undertaken by the young Karl Wittfogel in the autumn of 1928.[30] It was exhaustive, but also one-sided. Wittfogel's *Geopolitics, Geographical Materialism and Marxism* does not discuss Mackinder at all; it deals primarily with German geographers of the nineteenth-century mold, categorized by him as advocates of "geographical materialism." It is a historico-phenomenological essay, mostly in the form of Wittfogel's critical comments on the theme of "nature-conditioned moments" in history (*naturbedingte Momente*). Wittfogel tried to relate geography, with its locational and environmental aspects, to the Marxist world view based on the primacy of production forces in history. For the larger picture, namely, the spatial dimension of the problem—what was, in fact, Mackinder's chief concern—Wittfogel had nothing but contempt, referring to it as a concept that degenerated into "metaphysics to satisfy the requirements of imperialism or into a collection of artificial rules from the realm of foreign policy and strategy."[31] His criticism of Karl Haushofer, though mitigated and not as vicious as his criticism of Kjellén, tells us something of Wittfogel's conceptual confusion regarding Haushofer's unambiguously positive treatment of emancipation movements in Southeast Asia.[32] The young Wittfogel obviously regarded Moscow, that is, the Komintern, as the only legitimate authority to judge what was and was not revolutionary movement in Asia, and he accused Haushofer of flirting with imperialism and of fighting on the wrong side of the barricade. The common denominator of Wittfogel's defense of Marxism is the emphasis on the primacy of social (productive) forces versus natural forces. He was convinced that he detected in this geopolitical phenomenon a dangerous tendency of a new materialism from the political right, which could only serve international imperialism; hence, his warning that the *Geopolitiker* had substituted the geographical determinism of Haushofer for the economic materialism of Marx.[33]

Many years later, in the form of an epilogue written in 1974, Wittfogel refers to his 1929 essay with a mixture of embarrassment and apology. He admits that his essay was not liked in Moscow because of his attempt to develop in it his own interpretation of the "Asiatic Mode of Production," for which he later became famous and which remains today his chief theoretical contribution. This seems rather premature because Wittfogel's theory was not yet fully developed in the 1920s. However, it is possible that the Komintern censors discovered in Wittfogel's footnotes a dangerous deviation indicating that Tsarist Russia must be seen from the "geohistorical" perspective as one of the variants of Oriental despotism.[34]

Oriental despotism has been frequently identified with the phenomenon of *Aziatchina*, which in the specific Russian context carries the pejorative meaning of cultural backwardness inherited from Asia (*nekul'turnost'*). Wittfogel has used *Aziatchina* for a convincing interpretation of Lenin's theoretical, and after the October Revolution also practical, deviations from the original concept of the "Asiatic mode of production" as developed by Marx. Whereas until 1914 Lenin had accepted its relevance for Russian conditions, during World War I he began to avoid it. He gradually returned to it during the last period of his life, realizing that the "Asiatic" disease of Soviet bureaucracy was almost incurable.[35]

Because the presumed territorial realm of *Aziatchina* encapsulates our Central Asian heartland, it is important to realize that this phenomenon does possess a wide range of meanings, including not only explicitly negative ones, as cited above, but also positive ones. Particularly in the sphere that might be classified as cultural anthropology or cultural sociology, one encounters a wide variety of symbioses, ambivalence as well as discord, underlying the old dichotomy between West and East, with which Russian intelligentsia constantly grappled.

The idea of a friendly coexistence between the Russian and Asian (Muslim) subjects of the Eurasian Empire is the leading article of faith in the work of the remarkable Crimean Tatar educator, Ismail Bey Gaspraly, alias Gasprinski (1851–1914).[36] By contrast, *Aziatchina* in the eyes of the "Red Tatar," Sultan Galiev, is a kind of Socialist Pan-Turanism, with Soviet Muslims not only enjoying full autonomy within Soviet Eurasia, but also acting as the ideological avant-guard for a communist takeover of Muslim Asia as a whole.[37] At the opposite end of the scale is Vladimir Solovyov's nightmare of Pan-Mongolism, only partially mitigated by the aspirations of the *Vostochniki*; looking farther afield, we can contrast the ambivalent appeal of Alexander Blok's "Scythianism" (*skifstvo*) with the optimistic message of the exiled Eurasianists.[38]

Soviet Definition of *Geopolitika*

Today it is still difficult to establish the authentic evolution of Soviet views on geopolitics because the country had gone through so many ideological reversals since World War I. Unless one can complement the official views with reliable evidence of the intense private debate that must have occurred within Soviet academia during the 1920s and 1930s, the definition of geopolitics, as formulated in the different editions of the *Great Soviet Encyclopedia*, cannot be accepted as valid.

In any case, a comparison of the three editions of the *Bol'shaya Sovetskaya Entsiklopedia* (*BSE*: 1929, 1952, 1971) could be quite revealing for our understanding of the changes in the official Soviet attitude to geopolitics. The 1971 edition defines *Geopolitika* (geopolicy) as "a bourgeois, reactionary conception ... that employs misinterpreted data of physical and economic geography, to substantiate and to carry out through propaganda the aggressive policies of imperialist states." The original 1929 encyclopedia remains by and large neutral, factual, and informative, besides having an entry for *Geopolitika* that is three times as long. The 1971 edition treats geopolitics as the source of all evils directed against the Soviet state: geopolitics is founded on the idea of primacy as far as physical and geographical conditions are concerned, and these play a decisive role in human society; geopolitics, furthermore, supports racial inequality, thereby becoming guilty of social Darwinism and Malthusianism. The climax of criticism is reached when "geopolicy" is defined as the official doctrine of German Fascism under Karl Haushofer and, after World War II, as an instrument of militarism and revanchism in West Germany. Finally, assisted by U.S. imperialism, geopolicy, as the encyclopedia maintains, is also directed against socialist countries and national liberation movements.[39]

The formula in the 1971 *BSE*, carried over from the 1952 edition, can be considered as the nadir (or zenith, depending on how we look at it) of official Soviet views on geopolicy. Because these views could hardly become worse, there was only room for improvement. Opinion has become more balanced though still critical. An interesting example is the entry of "Geopolitical Theories of War" in the 1976 edition of the *Soviet Military Encyclopedia (SVE)*. The writer of the entry appears to have made at least a modest attempt to read Mackinder. He is familiar with the heartland concept (*serdtse zemli*), but does not reveal that Mackinder located it within the confines of the Russian Empire. As for the academic validity of geopolitical theories, the author regards them as absolutely unfounded. Although he cannot deny the influence of environment on the life of society and on the character of military operations, he persists that "the internal and external policies of the bourgeois state, the question of war and peace, are determined not by the geographic environment, but by the deep-rooted class interests of state-monopoly capitalism." "The source of wars in our epoch," he declares, "was and remains imperialism."[40] Although the *SVE* notes the importance of the "Geographic Factor in War," the main stress is on the technological progress with which man, particularly when he is inspired with the right kind of progressive ideas, can overcome the natural obstacles created by the physical environment and regarded as hitherto impassable. This boundless optimism, however, is clearly exaggerated when referring to the experience of World War II, whence "large-scale operations took place during all seasons regardless of climatic conditions."[41]

It was not enough, however, to treat geopolitical determinism as an anathema; it was necessary to offer a positive alternative, namely, how the new Soviet Man (*Sovetskiy chelovek*), in spite of the harsh Eurasian climate, was able to transform nature according to the commandments of the greatest living disciple of the (Marxist-Leninist) classics—Stalin. The ambitious five-year plans of rapid industrialization required strong ideological inducements to stir Soviet youth to take up the demanding task of building socialism, regardless of the hardships caused by adverse geographical conditions. This heroic approach produced a successful propaganda image, exemplified in the forced exploration of the Arctic or in the proverbial youth brigade leader building a new Siberian town "faraway from Moscow."[42] However, this almost contemptuous attitude toward environmental factors not only further aggravated the perennial difficulties of Soviet agriculture, but also created additional, almost insoluble, problems for the new industries and the transport system. What was completely ignored here was that in these circumstances the environmental factor itself becomes an economic factor.[43]

Demography and the New Soviet Man

What did it matter to the ruthless Stalin and his associates if they could, during the interwar period, combine heroic appeals with forced labor of the Gulag system at a time when human resources of young laborers seemed almost inexhaustible? Between 1926 and 1939, according to the official censuses, Soviet population increased from 147 to 170 million; the 1938 birth rate was an enviable 3.83 percent. Although the Ukraine, West Siberia, and Kazakhstan lost much of their rural, nomadic population, these losses were offset by massive migration into the northern regions, the Urals, and beyond, which accounted for substantial increases in urban, predominantly Slavic, populations. Thus, between 1926 and 1939, the population of Karelia and the Murmansk region jumped by 458 percent, East Siberia by 284 percent, the Far East by 229 percent, Kazakhstan by 229 percent, Central Siberia by 212 percent, and Turkmenistan by 204 percent.[44]

It seemed as if Soviet Russia, despite the territorial and human losses following World War I and the Civil War, had reinvigorated her vitality to regain the momentum of the rapid population growth of the Tsarist period. Then Mendeleev had predicted that the Russian Empire, with its center of gravity moving irresistibly eastward, would account for 283 million inhabitants by 1950, almost 600 million by the year 2000, and up to 1,280 million by 2052, provided that the net annual rate of increase could be maintained at 1.5 percent.[45] Moreover, as a result of the territorial annexations between 1939 and 1940, the total population rose to 196 million and could not have been far short of 200 million when Nazi Germany invaded in June 1941.

All these population statistics are, of course, deceptive if the official increments are not measured against the enormous human losses due to unnatural deaths, wars, famine, forced collectivization, and political purges. About 20 million people, perhaps as many as 25 million, mostly males, died between 1924 and 1940; approximately 15 million were lost between 1914 and 1924, according to the sober estimates of Iosif Dyadkin, a dissident Soviet demographer, and Murray Feshbach, a leading U.S. expert on Soviet population. The Great Patriotic War, as the bloody struggle against Nazi Germany is known, accounted for about 30 million more deaths: 20 million deaths, which is the semiofficial Soviet total casualty figure, may have occurred in actual fighting; the remaining 10 million died from deprivation and the Gulag.[46]

With political purges reaching their peak at the end of the 1930s, all theoretical discussion within Soviet academia was silenced. The only voices heard were those that supported Stalin's plans for the transformation of nature. Geography as science ceased to be involved in objective discussions on the relationship between man and nature, between social conditions of man and the physical environment. This dichotomy had been solved once and for all by the "Wise Leader." A truly absurd yet tragic state of affairs was reached in 1938. Stalin ruled that it was no longer permissible to mention the influence of physical environment on society;[47] paradoxically, he sanctioned the pseudoscience of "Lysenkoism," which ordained that man's hereditary features were decisively influenced by environmental changes, not by genes.[48] Stalin declared the victory of the Soviet Man engaged in the heroic struggle to transform the laws of nature, and all traces of geographical determinism among individual scientists had to be eradicated. Soviet geographers fled in panic from public responsibility, leaving "human engineering" to Stalin. It was only ten years after the dictator's death in 1953 that Soviet geographers slowly began to abandon their adamant "anti-determinist" line.[49]

Lenin, Bukharin, and Geopolitics

Even if the Soviet Union had never experienced Stalinism, the principal constraint on the free discussion of geopolitics by geographers would have remained the ghost of Lenin. The fact that the founder of the Soviet state said nothing about the subject in his voluminous utterances, collected in 55 volumes, is a sufficient brake even for the boldest among critical Soviet geographers. Had Lenin, however, stumbled across Mackinder's heartland lecture of 1904 in the course of his reading on imperialism, as suggested earlier, the encounter might have been intellectually beneficial. There is the example of Lenin's absorption of *On War*, written by the Prussian General Carl von Clausewitz. Lenin's accidental omission meant, that unlike the study of "classical bourgeois military science," there was no divine sanction allowing Soviet geographers and political scientists to study geopolitics.[50]

Lenin himself had a very practical view of geography. Through his friend, the economic geographer, Nikolai N. Baransky (1881–1963), Lenin became interested in using geographical knowledge for the economic and social transformation of Russia (for example, GOELRO, the electrification plan). Being an economic determinist, he was strongly opposed to suggestions that the natural environment, in spite of the fact that it is also an economic factor, could in any way control man's destiny.[51] There is no evidence that he ever showed any interest in geopolitics, though as a pragmatic statesman he had to reckon with it during the years of revolutionary upheavals and Civil War.

The realities of power struggle and Russia's own military predicament after the successful Bolshevik coup forced Lenin to adopt unorthodox tactics that can be interpreted from a geopolitical standpoint. His earlier acceptance of the German offer to transfer him from Switzerland to Russia and his adherence to the humiliating terms of the Brest-Litovsk Peace Treaty[52] are evidence that Lenin was unscrupulously betting on a German Revolution as the ultimate goal. From Lenin's perspective this was the inescapable conclusion of Marxist logic: the Russian Revolution, taking place in a much less capitalistically developed society, should serve as a catalyst for the more advanced German Revolution, whose success would create the decisive breakthrough for a worldwide revolutionary transformation.

Meanwhile, the critical situation inside Russia forced Lenin to reckon with certain, one might say brutal, realities to maintain power. He used non-Russian nationalities, such as Latvian riflemen, Bashkir cavalry, and especially German and Austro-Hungarian prisoners of war posing as "internationalists," who outnumbered the Russian element in the Red Army during the early months of the Civil War. He needed them, as one author put it cynically, "to kill the large number of Russians who would have to be removed if he was to achieve success."[53] However, when the Red Army failed to capture Warsaw and the long-expected German Revolution did not materialize, Lenin's revolutionary genius was flexible enough to make a fundamental departure from Marx by shifting the focus away from Western Europe to Asia (that is, "Ex Oriente Lux"). Lenin knew how to gain the maximum advantage from spreading the slogan of national self-determination; but the geopolitical realities of preserving the territorial power base of the former Tsarist Eurasian Empire, still stretching "from sea to sea," were gradually forcing Lenin to behave like a Great Russian imperialist, whom he strongly detested, as his earlier writings testify. With regard to the borderlands that had just been promised national self-determination, this meant a fleeting period of official independence followed by annexation into the allegedly multinational Union of Soviet Socialist Republics. True, there were some short cuts to this scenario taken against Lenin's explicit wishes. On his deathbed he had a row with Stalin and Dzerzhinski because the cunning Georgian and Pole had been overcome with revolutionary zeal during the pacification of the independent republics in the Caucasus and had bypassed the first stage, which called for a brief show of *de jure* independence.[54]

Even the power struggle between Stalin and Trotsky after

Lenin's death could be seen as essentially a geopolitical contest: whether the building of socialism should be confined exclusively to the former territories of the Russian Empire or whether it should be internationalized by exporting the revolution abroad. It must be added, however, that Stalin's defensive doctrine of capitalist encirclement rested on the belief that war between the two camps was inevitable. His policy in this respect was highly paradoxical. On the one hand he was rearming on such a scale that when war broke out in 1939 the Soviet Union had more tanks, artillery, and military aircraft than all the other great powers put together; on the other hand, Stalin also tried by diplomatic means, especially under the guise of collective security and disarmament proposals, to prevent the formation of an anti-Soviet crusade until the Soviet Union, free of the two-front war trauma, enjoyed the optimal advantage and could throw its armed forces into the fray as the *Tertius Gaudens*. This ideal scenario, of course, did not stop Stalin from exploiting the USSR's geopolitical position for arranging short-term pacts of nonaggression with both Germany and Japan and indulging in a series of calculated aggressions and annexations along its Eurasian rimlands.

Saul Cohen, in his comprehensive treatment of Soviet territorial annexations since 1939, has, nevertheless, discounted the possibility that Soviet foreign policy could have been inspired by the "organic frontier" theory, as developed by Ratzel and propounded by German geopoliticians. On the other hand, Cohen does admit that behind the strategic issues of Soviet border security are transparent nationalistic and historic claims.[55] The so-called Brezhnev Doctrine, used to justify the Soviet invasions of Czechoslovakia in 1968 and Afghanistan in 1979, could be cited as the more recent manifestation of the unmentionable Soviet geopolitical credo, enforced by the fearful experience of World War II. "Our soldiers, who sacrificed their lives also for your freedom," Brezhnev lectured the subdued Czechoslovak leaders in the Kremlin on 26 August 1968, "had reached the river Elbe in the last war: And that is and will remain our Soviet border."[56] What other epithet than geopolitical does Brezhnev's statement deserve?

Although Lenin did not pay as much attention to environmental factors as he did to factors of material production and political struggle, he must have believed, perhaps subconsciously and despite the terrible losses caused by the war and revolution, in the unstoppable Russian population boom, though he never referred to Mendeleev's important book of 1906. (One can forgive his ignorance of Mackinder, but how could a Russian ignore Mendeleev?) This optimistic belief is doubtless reflected in one of his often-quoted and self-deceiving forecasts: "In the last analysis, the outcome of the struggle will be determined by the fact that Russia, India, China, etc., account for the overwhelming majority of the population of the globe. ... In this sense, the complete victory of socialism is fully and absolutely assured."[57] In this instance it is not quite clear whether Lenin considered population an economic or a natural factor; consequently, he could be charged in theory with inconsistancy vis-à-vis his Marxist beliefs. In light of what has already been noted, one could imagine a certain ex-German general, named Karl Haushofer, signing such a statement as his own declaration of faith—perhaps with a slight reservation about socialism. Almost 50 years later, however, a dissident Soviet author, Andrei Amalrik, rectified Lenin's delusive statement by elaborating a more realistic vision. It was based not on the wishful solidarity between the ever-increasing masses of have-nots, but on what were essentially geopolitical differences between China and Soviet Eurasia, in light of the recent border clashes that could easily degenerate into a racial war.[58]

Among the Soviet Marxists who could offer a more sophisticated criticism of geopolitics in the 1930s, one could think of at least two: Karl Radek and Nikolai Bukharin. After Hitler's seizure of power in Germany, Radek and Bukharin, while fundamentally in favor of German partnership, used their pens to mobilize Western liberal opinion against the specter of an emerging imperialist, Berlin-Rome-Tokyo axis,[59] which Moscow feared would be directed primarily against the USSR. Bukharin's lively article "Imperialism and Communism," published in the United States in July 1936,[60] is worth reading even today, notwithstanding the tragic irony illustrated in the fate of Bukharin, who was arrested six months later and subsequently executed as an "imperialist spy." In this article, Bukharin reveals his acquaintance with Haushofer's *Zeitschrift für Geopolitik* and other works of political geographers; he also pays tribute to the pioneering work of the nineteenth-century British social historian, Henry Thomas Buckle, whose *History of Civilization in England*, as we have already emphasized, was an immensely popular book among the Russian intelligentsia.

He was probably more widely read than Karl Marx, because of his emphasis on "natural laws" determining man's environment, and because of the obvious implications for the growth and expansion of the Russian Empire.[61]

With regard to the contemporary realities of international politics, Bukharin was trying to contrast the predatory world of imperialism with the peaceful character of the Soviet state, which in his description resembles a charming kindergarten. He denies vehemently that the "U.S.S.R. will ever pursue an aggressive policy . . . or fight for the expansion of socialism."[62] In case the innocent Westerner has doubts, Bukharin has a ready answer: Because such a war, according to the teachings of the Marxist-Leninist classics, could be fought only in the interest of finance capital, which, as everyone should know, had been abolished in the Soviet Union. Theories that claim to be based on certain "geophysical laws," predicting that Russia would always fight Germany and Japan, are "pieces of geopolitical sophistry in circulation," writes Bukharin. "War may break out . . . war may be forced upon us," he concedes, because "contiguity of frontiers and territory certainly have an influence here, but not directly, and the war guilt will lie not with 'the land' but with Japanese imperialism."[63]

Wittfogel's and Bukharin's contemporary criticisms of geopolitics are probably the only two outstanding pieces written on this topic, the former from the standpoint of a Marxist scholar, the latter from the pen of a skillful Soviet propagandist. What came after, with the notable exception of a recent monograph by a Polish author, Anna Wolff-Powęska,[64] did not exceed the level of black and white propaganda.[65] This is particularly true of the writings by Yuriy Nikolaevich Semyonov (not to be confused with another Yuriy Semyonov mentioned earlier), who started a series of articles in 1948 on the alleged love affair between American and West German geopoliticians. These articles were published in the East German periodical *Neue Welt*.[66] In his notorious *The Fascist Geopolicy in the Service of American Imperialism*, Semyonov describes Mackinder's heartland theory as a camouflage for Hitler's plans to attack the USSR: Germany's frontiers were to be pushed eastward to reach the Eurasian heartland. Semyonov denies flatly that Haushofer ever wanted friendship between Germany and the Soviet Union.[67] *The Critique of German Geopolitik* by a German Democratic Republic author, Konrad Heyden, is written in a similar vein. There is, of course, absolutely no mention of the intimate geopolitical connection between Germany and the Soviet Union during the 1920s, let alone between 1939 and 1941. Heyden is particularly concerned with refuting geographical determinism as a pseudoscientific and reactionary concept. "The geographical environment provides the necessary and stable condition for material life," explains Heyden, "but it is *not the main factor* [Heyden's emphasis] of social development, nor is it the only condition enabling material life in society . . . the main factor being the mode of production of goods."[68] Looking back at the rich and diversified scale of opinions concerned with the various aspects of Russia's Eurasian legacy (and with its geopolitical implications) and the much more complex nature of Russo-German relations, Semyonov and Heyden's point of view hardly deserves further comment.

Notes

1 Hans W. Weigert, "Heartland Revisited." In *New Compass of the World. A Symposium on Political Geography*, ed. H. W. Weigert, V. Stefansson, and R. E. Harrison (New York: Macmillan, 1949), 80–90; Owen Lattimore, "A New Center of Gravity in the World." Chapter 1 in *Pivot of Asia* (q.v.); Geoffrey Parker, "Heartland Revisited: New Perspectives after World War II." Chapter 8 in *Western Geopolitical Thought in the Twentieth Century* (London: Croom Helm, 1985), 120–39.
2 See chapter 6, "Who Commands the Heartland?" Blouet, *Mackinder* (1987), 172–77; Parker, *Mackinder* (1982), 47–49, 169–72. On Lord Curzon's talent as geographer, see A. S. Goudie, "George Nathaniel Curzon—superior geographer," *Geographical Journal* 146 (1980), 203–209. Mackinder's report on the situation in Southern Russia to the Foreign Office, dated 21 January 1920, has been published in *Documents on British Foreign Policy 1919–39*, 1st series, vol. iii (London: HMSO, 1949), 768–87.
3 Mackinder, *Democratic Ideals* (1919), 205.
4 Nikolai N. Mikhaylov, *Soviet Geography. The New Industrial and Economic Distributions of the USSR*. Forword by Sir Halford Mackinder (London: Methuen, 1935).
5 N. N. Mikhailov reminiscing on the Soviet geographer N. N. Baransky, in *Zemlya i Lyudi* (Moscow: Mysl', 1981), 202–203.
6 Patrick O'Sullivan, *Geopolitics* (New York: St. Martin's, 1986), 26.
7 Introduction on Soviet geopolitics by Karl Haushofer in Oskar von Niedermayer and Juri Semjonow, *Sowjet-Russland. Eine geopolitische Problemstellung* (Berlin: Vowinckel, 1934), 9–11.
8 Haushofer, *Bausteine* (1928), 42.

9 Georg Semenoff, "Das geopolitische Problem der russischen Revolution," *Zeitschrift für Geopolitik* 8/ii (1925), 548–59.
10 Niedermayer and Semjonow, *Sowjet Russland* (1934); Weigert, *Generals and Geographers* (1942), 265. Outside the German language sphere the important Niedermayer-Semjonow book remained virtually unknown. To my knowledge no Anglo-American author has even referred to it.
11 Alfred Hettner, *Russland: Eine geographische Betrachtung von Volk, Staat und Kultur* (Leipzig-Berlin: Teubner, 1916). The second and third editions of Hettner's *Russia*, both published in 1916, were adjusted to the fact that Russia and Germany had become enemies—unlike the first edition of 1905 (*Das europäische Russland: Eine Studie zur Geographie des Menschen*), which was twice translated into Russian.
12 Niedermayer and Semjonow, *Sowjet Russland* (1934), 128–47.
13 See Figure 10.1 and chapter 10.
14 W. Gordon East, "How Strong Is the Heartland?" *Foreign Affairs* (October 1950), 87–88.
15 John M. Maki, *Japanese Militarism. Its Cause and Cure* (New York: Knopf, 1945), 201–209; E. E. N. Causton, *Militarism and Foreign Policy in Japan* (London: Allen & Unwin, 1936), 124–30; O. Tanin and E. Yogan, *Voenno-fashistskoe dvizhenie v Yaponii*, introduction by Karl Radek (Moscow, 1933).
16 Ivan Ya. Korostovets, *Rossiya na Dal'nem Vostoke* (Pekin: Vostochnoie Prosveshchenie, 1922); M. A. Persits, *Dal'nevostochnaya Respublika i Kitai* (Moscow: Izdatel'stvo Vostochnoi literatury, 1962); Walther Heissig, *Das gelbe Vorfeld* (Berlin: Vowinckel, 1941); Lars-Erik Nyman, *Great Britain and Chinese, Russian and Japanese Interests in Sinkiang, 1918–1934* (Lund: Ph.D. Dissertation, 1977), 49–51.
17 Boris Nicolaevsky, "Russia, Japan, and the Pan-Asiatic Movement to 1925," *Far Eastern Quarterly* (May 1949), 259–95. See also: Erich Obst, "Sowjetrussische Aussenpolitik," *Zeitschrift für Geopolitik* (January 1925); K. Fuse, *Soviet Policy in the Orient* (Peking: 1927; reprint by Westport Hyperion Press, 1978). One must not forget that in 1916 Russia signed a secret alliance with Japan, which provided for the partition of China. See Harish Kapur, *Soviet Russia and Asia, 1917–1927. A Study of Soviet Policy toward Turkey, Iran and Afghanistan* (Geneva, 1966), 37.
18 Kapur, *Soviet Russia* (1966), 46–52; Louis Fischer, *The Soviets in World Affairs* (Princeton: Princeton University Press, 1951), I:435–49. See chapter 5.
19 Nicolaevsky, "Russia, Japan" (1949), 295.
20 See Jacobsen, *Haushofer* (1979), II:4–5, 16–19, 52, 92–94. Nevertheless, it is misleading to describe Haushofer as "one-time adviser to Stalin," as A. J. Pearce has done in the introduction to the reprint of Mackinder's *Democratic Ideals and Reality* (New York: Norton, 1962), ix, xxii.
21 Haushofer, *Geopolitik des Pazifischen Ozeans* (1924), 142; and in *Zeitschrift für Geopolitik* (1924), 961. See also the positive comments on Haushofer's book, *Japan und die Japaner* (1923), in Tanin and Yogan, *Voenno-fashistskoe* (1933), 37–42.
22 Weigert, *Generals and Geographers* (1942), 167–91.
23 Ibid., 190.

24 Compiled from: V. Zof, "Mezhdunarodnoe polozhenie i zadachi morskoi oborony SSSR," *Morskoi Sbornik* 5 (1925), 3–26; A. V. Dombrovsky, "Kakoi RSFSR nuzhen flot?" *Morskoi Sbornik* 3 (1922), 79–85. See also: William F. Pauly, "The Writings of Halford Mackinder Applied to the Evolution of Soviet Naval Power," *The Pennsylvania Geographer* 12/4 (December 1974), 3–7; Jurg Meister, *Soviet Warships of the Second World War* (London: Macdonald & Jane's, 1977).
25 N. V. Ustryalov, *Nashe Vremya* (Shanghai, 1934), 186–88, on P. N. Savitsky's article "Glavy z ocherka geografii Rossii" (chapters from a Sketch of Russia's Geography). More on Savitsky in chapters 4 and 7 above.
26 Ernest C. Ropes, "The Soviet Arctic and the Future." In *Compass*, ed. Weigert and Stefansson (1944), 348–63.
27 As in note 25.
28 See in chapter 7, "Empire from Sea to Sea."
29 See in chapter 6, "Who Commands the Heartland?"
30 Karl A. Wittfogel, "Geopolitik, geographischer Materialismus und Marxismus," *Unter dem Banner des Marxismus* 3/1 (1929), 17–51, 3/4 (1929), 485–522, 698–735.
31 Ibid., vol. 3/4 (1929), 500.
32 Cf. K. Haushofer, *Zur Geopolitik der Selbstbestimmung. Südostasiens Wiederaufstieg zur Selbstbestimmung* (Munich-Leipzig: Rosl, 1923).
33 Wittfogel, "Geopolitik," 3/1 (1929), 17–25.
34 K. Wittfogel in *Politische Geographie*, ed. Josef Matznetter (Darmstadt: Wissenschaftliche Buchgesellschaft, 1977), 230–31.
35 K. Wittfogel, *Oriental Despotism. A Comparative Study of Total Power* (New York: Vintage Book, 1981), 378–400. See also in chapter 4, "Yellow Russia."
36 Ismail Bey Gasprinski, *Russkoe Musul'manstvo* (Simferopol: Spiro, 1881).
37 See Bennigsen and Wimbush, *Muslim National Communism* (1980). See in chapter 5, "The Historic Perspective of Central Asia."
38 This rather confusing and colorful scale of opinions is well described in Kristof, *Russian Image* (1968), 376–79, and *Nation in Space* (1969), 96–100. See also chapters 2 and 4.
39 *BSE*, vol. 6 (1971), 935; *BSE*, vol. 15 (1929), 389–91. See also Peter Scholler, "Wege und Irrwege der politischen Geographie und Geopolitik." In *Politische Geographie*, ed. Matznetter (1977), 262–66.
40 *SVE*, vol. 2 (1976), 521–22.
41 Ibid., 515–16.
42 *Daleko ot Moskvy* (1949), by Vasiliy N. Azhaev (1915–68), a popular novel that glorified the construction of an oil pipeline in the Siberian taiga.
43 Parker, *Geography of Russia* (1969), 376–77.
44 Ibid., 340–43; Niedermayer and Semjonow, *Sowjet Russland* (1934), 132; V. P. Semyonov-Tyan-Shansky, "Russia: Territory and Population. A Perspective on the 1926 Census," *Geographical Review* 18 (1928), 616–40.
45 Mendeleev, *K poznaniyu Rossii* (1906), 12. See in chapter 7, "The Empire from Sea to Sea."
46 Iosif Dyadkin, *Evaluation of Unnatural Deaths in the Population of the USSR, 1927–58* (cf. summary under the title, "Revising Stalin's Legacy," *Wall Street Journal*, 23 July 1980); Murray Feshbach, *The Soviet Union: Population Trends*

and Dilemmas (Washington, DC: Population Reference Bureau, 1982), 6–7. See also Roy Medvedev in *Argumenty i fakty*, no. 5 (1989), 4 February 1989.
47   Massimo Quaini, *Geography and Marxism* (Totowa, NJ: Barnes &Noble, 1982), 150–54.
48   On. T. D. Lysenko see in chapter 7, "A Conspiracy of Silence?"
49   L. N. Kudryasheva (ed.), *Soviet Geography Today. Aspects of Theory* (Moscow: Progress, 1981), 201–41; Parker, *Geography of Russia* (1969), 377.
50   See in chapter 7, "A Conspiracy of Silence?" Peter Vigor, "The Soviet View of Geopolitics." In *On Geopolitics: Classical and Nuclear*, ed. Ciro E. Zoppo and Charles Zorgbibe (Dordrecht: Martinus Nijhoff, 1985), 132.
51   N. N. Baransky, *Selected Works in Geography* (Moscow: Progress, 1981); Preston E. James, *All Possible Worlds. A History of Geographical Ideas* (New York: Odyssey Press, 1972), 281–304.
52   See chapter 5. For an almost racist treatment of the Bolshevik betrayal of Mother Russia, see A. Solzhenitsyn's *Lenin in Zurich* (New York: Bartam, 1976).
53   O'Sullivan, *Geopolitics* (1986), 28–29.
54   Lenin, *O druzhbe* (1961), 333–37.
55   Saul B. Cohen, *Geography and Politics in a World Divided* (New York: Oxford University Press, 1973), 191–236.
56   Zdeněk Mlynář, *Mráz přichází z Kremlu* (Cologne: Index, 1978), 306–307; English edition, *Night Frost in Prague* (London: Hurst, 1980).
57   V. I. Lenin, "Better Fewer, but Better," *Pravda*, 4 March 1923. See in chapter 2, "Long Live Free Asia."
58   Amalrik, *1984* (1969).
59   See Radek's introduction to Tanin and Yogan, *Voenno-fashistskoe* (1933), English edition (1934), 12–22; see also in chapter 8, "A German Lawrence among the Bolsheviks."
60   Nikolai Bukharin, "Imperialism and Communism," *Foreign Affairs* (July 1936), 563–77.
61   See in chapter 7, "A Conspiracy of Silence?" According to James, *All Possible Worlds* (1972), 295, Buckle apparently exercised greater influence on Soviet geographers than did Marx. This is very plausible, though hard to prove through written evidence. See also V. A. Anuchin, *Teoreticheskie problemy geografii* (Moscow: Gosizdat geograficheskoi literatury, 1960), 44, 51, 78.
62   Bukharin, "Imperialism" (1936), 571.
63   Ibid., 572–73.
64   Anna Wolff-Powęska, *Doktryna Geopolityki w Niemczech* (Poznan: Institut Zachodni, 1979). The book stresses Poland's national interest vis-à-vis its German neighbor and is absolutely free of any compulsive references to the classics of Marxism-Leninism.
65   Alas, this is very much the case with Evgeniy Tarle's article, "Vostochnoe prostranstvo i fashistskaya geopolitika," published in *Protiv fashistskoi fal'sifikatsii istorii*, ed. F. I. Notovich (Moscow: Izdatelstvo Akademii nauk, 1939), 259–79. This propaganda tract is a good illustration of how a talented Russian historian like Tarle (1874–1955) could degrade himself during the Stalinist purges.
66   Yuriy N. Semyonov, "Die geopolitische Begründung des amerikanischen Imperialismus," *Neue Welt* 12 (1948), 55–64, "Die Geopolitik als ideologische

Waffe des USA-Imperialismus," *Neue Welt* 2 (1953), 203–18, and "Die Geopolitik im Dienste der westdeutschen Revanchpolitiker," *Neue Welt* 12 (1954), 1606–14.

67 Yuriy N. Semyonov, *Die faschistische Geopolitik im Dienste des amerikanischen Imperialismus* (Berlin: Dietz, 1955), 122, 151–53 (translated from a Russian edition published in Moscow in 1952).

68 Konrad Heyden, *Kritik der deutschen Geopolitik* (Berlin: Dietz, 1958), 72–73, Russian edition printed in 1960.

10

Geopolitics and the Soviet Eurasian Empire Today

Environmental Determinism—Still Undetermined

Neither the search of Russian prerevolutionary geopolitical thinking nor the investigation into the early Soviet era has given us decisive clues to answer satisfactorily the question of why Mackinder's heartland concept, as outlined in 1904, was utterly ignored by the Russians. And if their Soviet successors showed some marginal knowledge of Mackinder, it was not original but derivative. A partial answer, which in our view helps unveil the missing link, must be sought in the Russo-German geopolitical connection of the 1920s and the controversial role played by Karl Haushofer and his colleagues.

A more plausible reason for ignoring Mackinder could have been the Russian understanding of "geopolicy" (*geopolitika*). To them it involved not spatial relations but rather the impact of environmental factors, because they have been constantly challenged by the Empire's obvious structural imbalances and the enormous climatic varieties of Eurasia. What is this specific Russian geopolicy? Mendeleev and Semyonov-Tyan-Shansky are just two representatives of the pinnacle of Russian geopolitical thinking of spatial processes generated within the Russian Eurasian Empire prior to Revolution. But it is important to recognize that they were not responding to any specific Western conceptual challenges, such as those exemplified in Mackinder's heartland concept.

Thus, the specific Russian approach to the Western notion of geopolitics, as it should be clear by now, was mostly absorbed in the exhausting discussion about environmental determinism, which, during the Stalinist era, took the absurd twist of denying the environmental factor any economic function whatsoever. The broader, spatial dimension of geopolitics, which was the main concern of Western geographers of the imperialist age (like Mackinder), was very much muted and discouraged in Russia.[1]

W. H. Parker is right when he warns against the pitfalls of a reverse trend, exemplified in "a modern tendency to minimize the environmental factor ... which leads to a serious error of judgement."[2] We have already witnessed a complete *volte-face* in the development of Russian geography. From the uncritical acceptance of natural factors as dominant forces influencing human societies (for example, the impact of H. T. Buckle's theory) by the nineteenth-century Russian worshippers of materialism, it shifted to the utter condemnation of environmental determinism during the days of Stalin (the official cult of Lysenkoism notwithstanding). At that point the triumph of the Soviet Man over nature was to be demonstrated through the giant construction schemes in remote and hostile environments.

But we should bear in mind one useful lesson. Although Man may develop, to some extent, the inhospitable and vast interior with the aid of modern technology and the ruthless application of noneconomic means of coercion (Russian euphemism for the use of violence through the Gulag system in fostering the economic development of Siberia), the undisputed fact remains that such development is definitely more costly in both economic and human terms.[3] This, in turn, must adversely affect the chances for successful commercial competition with other nations located in more favorable geographic conditions and applying less coercive economic methods of production and transportation. Taking all this into account, it is difficult to disagree with Parker's truism that the success of the Soviet economic heartland "is not assured."[4] Shipment of heavy goods by sea, though slower, is much cheaper than is any form of land transport.[5]

If we were not living in a real world of international tensions and conflicts, the logical implication of this observation would long ago have led to the fundamental correction of Mackinder's theory, in a sense abolishing the entire heartland concept that is, after all, a geostrategic construct. But neither the Russians nor the Soviets could act this way in the world of *Realpolitik*. Instead of opening the Eurasian heartland, region by region, to the optimal commercial and ethno-cultural contacts, allowing for the expansion of cross-border traffic by economic forces, Moscow has so far persisted in the autarkic control of the economic development of its borderlands from its ideological and administrative center. However, a surrender to the rationalism of the economic argument, which is implied in the new *perestroika* course, might entail a return to the prerevolutionary days when industrial development was dangerously concentrated in the margins and within easier reach of the great seaports. Second, such a development could also undermine Moscow's strategic control over the west-east axis of communication, which is best exemplified by the economic and military significance of the Trans-Siberian Railway, a vastly extended umbilical cord connecting the two largest Soviet military and naval complexes.[6]

It remains to be seen whether the Soviet Eurasian Empire of the 1990s, under Gorbachev's leadership, will be capable of recognizing its own limits on the geostrategic level. Will the emphasis on intensive rather than extensive economic programs lead to a fundamental *volte-face* in the Empire's autarkic reliance on its own faraway resources and costly transportation?

The Empire's Moving Center of Gravity and the Soviet People

In addition to the broader ramifications of environmental determinism, there was a relatively narrow sphere where the relationship between state power and territory was discussed in Russia in spatial terms. But this was almost exclusively an inward-looking discussion focused on the quest for a new center of gravity. This was to be located at the geographical center of a self-contained, autarkic Russian Eurasian Empire. To borrow from a contemporary geopolitical event in Latin America, it was a quest for a Russian Brasilia. On the surface this was usually understood, or more frequently misunderstood, as implying the transfer of the capital city farther east of the Volga, in the Urals, or even beyond in what appeared to be the genuine geometrical center of Russian Eurasia. Such propositions were bound to arouse violent protests among the guardians of the Russian Idea, who continued to believe that the center of Russian Orthodoxy could not be moved outside the holy triangle of Moscow, Kiev, and the old Novgorod. This truly Russian equivalent of the heartland debate has been confounded many times by the emotional issue of *Aziatchina* in its multiple forms, including the very intense subconscious racial fear of the yellow peril.

Although the Eurasianist ideology itself had been rejected by the Soviet establishment for political reasons, even the most orthodox interpreters of Soviet ideology could not deny the obvious geopolitical realities of the Eurasian space within which their own state was located. They faced the dilemma of how to define Soviet history and geography in its entirety by using non-geopolitical terms, because the territory their historical and geographical textbooks usually treat is *de facto* Russian/Soviet Eurasia. Thus, concessions have been made to allow the usage of Eurasia (which implies a different geographic center of contemplation) by Soviet geologists and climatologists, but not by political scientists or historians.

Although in fact the Soviet Eurasian Empire existed territorially prior to 1917, its inhabitants, the "Soviet people," apparently did not. Reading Soviet history textbooks one often has the feeling that 150 million homogeneous and loyal Soviet people emerged suddenly in October 1917 and filled the vacuum. In describing the territorial expansion of Tsarist Russia, postrevolutionary Soviet Marxist historians, as Ladis Kristof has remarked, really had no choice but to decide between two contrasting interpretations. They could either justify the expansion on the grounds of certain "historical progressiveness" of Tsarism, which, of course, is basically a neo-imperialist argument dressed in a patriotic garb with red lining. Almost all officially approved Soviet interpretations, following the fall of the Pokrovsky School in 1927, adhered to this option. The alternative view was to admit the influence, at least to some extent, of geographical determinism affecting the course of Russian/Soviet history, as the great Russian historians of the prerevolutionary period had emphasized without exception. Although from the historian's point of view many more factors contribute to the formation of an expansionist policy, and others complicate its execution, Kristof's comment is a fair one.[7]

The theories of historical materialism, either in the form of a crude materialistic interpretation of history (Buckle) or in a seemingly global concept based on class struggle (Marxism as interpreted by Pokrovsky and Wittfogel, for instance), did easily influence the minds of political geographers. Lenin's unwitting geopolitical landscape must have consisted of a roster of working-class bastions concentrated in the large industrial centers. People living outside of and faraway from these neo-medieval fortresses of material progress did not really matter; they did not participate in the making of history. Therefore, one should not assume, as Saul Cohen rightly underlines, that economics and class are the only or even the essential basis for linking a people with territory. A growing awareness among geographers and other social scientists is approaching a consensus that "race, religion and culture are more important operational forces in the politics of space at all geographical scales, than is economics."[8] Moreover, before long social scientists in the socialist countries will reach a consensus that class struggle, the alpha and omega of nineteenth-century Marxian socialism, is out of date and that cultural struggle instead is the major common denominator of domestic and international strife. Consequently, rather than in terms of Marxist-Leninist class struggle, conflicts between nations will be seen as developing around issues of religion, race, ethnicity, politics, and history—not of resources. This observation goes beyond the Mackinderian concept because although he provided such a penetrating model for geostrategic spatial relationships, he was not interested in the people as such who inhabited his heartland.

The advent of modern telecommunications and the revolution in transportation did not open particular spaces like Central Asia to a radical transformation of spatially conditioned socio-cultural values. In a majority of cases there was a tendency of cultural groups to cling to neighborhoods, cities, rural areas, and regions, despite the radical uprooting brought about by forced deportation and liquidation of the native elites (for example, the Crimean Tatars under Stalin). One can only speculate about the future, but it seems highly unlikely that the new industrial revolution in the making, based on information and data technology, is going to alter this experience radically. In fact, a conservative backlash in response to forced modernization, like the ones we witnessed in Iran and subsequently in Afghanistan, is more likely.

Excursion I: Prokhanovshtina—An Example of New Soviet Geopolitics or an Anachronism?

In spite of the fact that no Soviet historian or geographer has explicitly endorsed geographical determinism to date, it is often implied in disguised form in their texts. Journalists and novelists feel less inhibited by the orthodox canon of the Marxist-Leninist doctrine. One astonishing example of recent Soviet geopolitical writing is Alexander Prokhanov, whom the Moscow intelligentsia sarcastically call "our Soviet Kipling." Prokhanov has not only used the geopolitical approach implicitly in his articles and novels, but also has explicitly declared—as published in the Soviet press even before *glasnost*—that he regarded his books as types of "geopolitical or military-political novels."[9] It was not surprising that two of his four books, which received wide publicity through extensive serialization in leading Soviet youth magazines, were concerned with the Soviet counterinsurgency war in Afghanistan.[10]

In *Notes on Armor* (1985), for instance, Prokhanov has cleverly woven together several threads, the Oriental exotica (camels, mountains and deserts, the inimitable smell of the bazaar, mysterious veiled women, etc.) with the blend of Russian patriotism and Soviet internationalism, over which he has imposed his geopolitical and imperial vision:

> I have the feeling that Afghanistan has cleaved and split our time in two. It has left behind us the bountiful life, guaranteed personal and social well-being, and guaranteed peace. And it has brought ominous days and years, days and years associated with intense danger, struggle, defense and personal sacrifice . . . for the sake of the state's common ideas. . . . Our peacetime army, that forty years ago shattered the enemy in a terrible war, won the victory, gained experience in mighty battles, and now has maintained world equilibrium for forty years through its titanic military efforts . . . had not shed blood. . . . Until Afghanistan. . . .
>
> The formula that justifies our temporary military presence in Afghanistan is the performance of our international allied mission and the defense of our southern borders. . . . Several times in the prewar years Soviet servicemen had to unsheath their weapons on foreign territory. In Mongolia, on the River Khalkhin Gol, we clashed with the Samurai. . . . Our graves lie on Mongolian soil. . . . Our volunteer flyers, tankmen, riflemen fought in Spain against Franco, they fought against Hitler. . . . In Spain, at Guadalajara and Madrid, we also fought for Brest, for Kiev

and for the Volga.... We are not utopians, nor are we crazy. We are those who yesterday crossed a flaming Europe and Asia. Those who today hold the enemy in check in the compartments of submarines, out on long patrol. Those who sit in the hot interiors of armored personnel carriers. Those who are performing our State's centuries-old task.... Today's 'theatres of military action,'[11] merge instantaneously. The enemy is preparing to strike against the Fatherland simultaneously from all corners of the world. From Europe... from the Mediterranean and from the Persian Gulf, from the Indian Ocean, Diego Garcia and over the North Pole.... Our defense is global. It passes over the poles and over the Equator, through the skies and across the bottom of the ocean. ... A different vision emerges. Of the world as a whole. Of the people as a whole. Of the Homeland as a whole.[12]

In an unusual testimony published in Moscow's *Literaturnaya Gazeta* of 6 November 1985, Prokhanov reiterated why he considered the war in Afghanistan to be the radical cleavage for the post-World War II Soviet generation to which he belonged and revealed why he decided to experiment with the new geopolitical genre in his literary work:

As a writer I am more and more captivated by the situation of global contradictions, by the global mechanism of military rivalry, by the problem of defending the human race from itself. All this has not yet been fully understood ... either by the strategists—the HQ staff officers, or by the most prominent politicians and philosophers.... All these problems go with one edge deep somewhere into the Earth's magma, into the natural resources ... with the other edge into human psychology, into the complex connected with the idea of struggle, of hate, of rivalry, of overcoming, of freedom and conscience, with the historical legacy of weapons. Here, I repeat, there are many extensive and interesting spring-boards which one would like to master, to fill with people and collisions.[13]

What does this extraordinary eclecticism mean? Prokhanov's talk of fighting for the preservation of "space equilibrium," "the idea of life-struggle," sounds like an anachronistic revival of the standard German repository of Ratzelian and Nietzscheian terms of *Lebensraum* and *Lebenskampf*. But there is more in Prokhanov than this hopefully accidental, coincidence with the German geopolitical vocabulary of the Nazi era. His wide-ranging challenge has not yet been taken up by the Soviet *literati*.

Prokhanov has been subjected to severe literary criticism and accused of being both a fast and mediocre writer, especially by those who fear the emergence of a new military genre in Soviet prose under the disguise of pseudomodernity.[14] However, "the nightingale of the general staff" seems to have survived all attacks thanks to tacit support from the top military brass, particularly from the Soviet Army's Main Political Directorate. His work fits the requirements of military-patriotic education (*voenno-patrioticheskoe vospitanie*), a comprehensive system of collective lectures, songs, and other rituals, which accompanies the Soviet citizen-soldier from cradle to grave and reinforces the unique Soviet values of patriotism, heroism, discipline, loyalty, and obedience.[15]

Apart from the traditional military patriotic themes, assuming a true Slavophile posture in his more recent prose devoted to Afghanistan,[16] Prokhanov displays his strong Kiplingesque quality in imitating the attraction to the exotic lands of the Orient. The fact that he sees the Soviet presence in the world as a global one ("Our defense is global; it passes over the poles and over the Equator"), whether it is in Cambodia, Mozambique, Nicaragua,[17] or, above all, in Afghanistan, makes him the most geopolitical (by his own account) contemporary Soviet author, with global neocolonialist overtones. He portrays the Soviet representatives of "international assistance," in their wishful self-projection as compassionate elder brothers, as the generous ambassadors of Soviet modernization, patronizing the underdeveloped Orientals who are grateful to receive the fruits of Soviet communism at such generous terms and in such large doses.

In comparing Prokhanov and one of the previous apostles of Russian Manifest Destiny in Asia, that is, Colonel Venyukov, Prokhanov carefully avoids the racial theme that might throw unfavorable light on his Russian heroes exploring the exotic Orient. However, he does use the yellow peril theme skillfully as a product of Western propaganda and anti-Soviet schemes, which cannot subvert a true Soviet man. Thus, in one of his more recent stories on Afghanistan, a captured Soviet soldier refuses to accept crude overtures from a British agent that they should work and fight together, "against this Asia, against this yellow world which threatens you Russians. And against the blacks, the coloreds, which threaten us."[18] As a point of curiosity, there is a recent renewal of interest inside the Soviet Union in the exotic poems of Nikolai Gumilyov (1886–1921), a famous Russian poet executed by the Bolsheviks. Some of his work (for example, *The African Notebook*) is now being reprinted in the Soviet Union, which suggests a residual interest in "tropical" subjects, no doubt stimulated by recent Soviet imperial ventures overseas that still have official support, in spite, or perhaps because, of *glasnost*.[19]

However, the problematic artistic or exotic quality of Prokhanov's work is not at issue here; it is the ideological and geopolitical implications emanating from his work. He should not be underestimated. This particular challenge has not yet been taken up by any of his numerous critics. Prokhanov has been speaking for the embittered veterans from Afghanistan (known as *Afgantsy*), who have become a more conspicuous factor in Soviet domestic politics.[20] In the weekly television program "I serve the Soviet Union," Prokhanov accused "a certain section of our intelligentsia for falsely painting the military as the internal opposition" against the reform inside the country. With him appeared General Dmitriy Yazov, the defense minister, who lamented a lack of discipline among contemporary Soviet recruits and charged the writers as responsible for failing to instill clear patriotic values in young people, inspiring them with a sense of the superiority of communism over capitalism.[21]

What will, however, be the fate of Prokhanovism after the withdrawal of troops from Afghanistan? Since the spring of 1988 the prevalent themes in the Soviet media have become cutting the losses and reaching a political settlement in Afghanistan—not victory, as Prokhanov had preached until then. After the Kremlin leadership announced its determination to withdraw troops from Afghanistan, Prokhanov put on the image of self-searching introspection. In *Literaturnaya Gazeta* of 17 February 1988, he suggested two major reasons socialism failed in Afghanistan: first, the weakness of the indigenous Afghan communists, who were politically immature and ridden by internal feuds; second, Moscow's own erroneous projections in underestimating the strength of Islamic tribal resistance and in overestimating the readiness of communist-controlled Afghanistan to merge with the socialist world camp. In a later interview Prokhanov declared that he saw his duty as writing "about the tragedy and heroism of the 40th Army," which could never win the war because of its insufficient strength—just over 100,000 men. He categorically refused to see the withdrawal from Afghanistan as a military defeat and advised people to refrain from excessive jubilation over the troops' return.[22]

Although there is no available evidence, it is conceivable that, under certain circumstances, Prokhanovism, being a kind of a lyrical variant of the Brezhnev Doctrine, could be viewed by the conservative elements opposing Gorbachev's *perestroika* as one of their potential assets. It is by no means certain that the withdrawal of Soviet troops from Afghanistan will pass without causing frictions between the "patriots" and the "reformists." In particular, the discontented officer corps, which is threatened by massive demobilization as part of Gorbachev's troop reduction program, might become the spearhead of an opposition bloc comprising the bulk of the inert bureaucracy, Afghan veterans, and various xenophobic, anti-Semitic, and overtly racist, patriotic associations like the *Pamyat* groups.[23]

Excursion II: The Heartland Debate after Mackinder's Death

As for the validity of Mackinder's thesis and the reverberations of the Heartland Debate in the Soviet context, since the late 1970s the Central Asian heartland has again been in a state of flux. The most visible signs of the crisis are ideological and political: with the upsurge of Islamic fundamentalism waves of political unrest passed through the region. One might almost say that all subsequent events in this region, like the revolution in Iran, the Soviet invasion of Afghanistan and the widespread resistance against it, and the Gulf War between Iraq and Iran, followed from it. The border between the Soviet Muslim republics and Iran and Afghanistan is no longer hermetically closed. "Subversive" Islamic literature, cassette recordings, and radio programs do travel across and affect Soviet Muslims. Though it may be premature to try to quantify this influence, all indicators show that it will continue to grow.

At the same time it is important to realize that profound structural changes have been underway for some time inside the Soviet Eurasian Empire. These changes are exemplified by the steady eastward shift of the center of gravity in the search for more energy and mineral resources. These have been located in the northern segment of Mackinder's pivot area. The northern portion of Western Siberia, however, which today contains the bulk of exploitable Soviet hydrocarbons, is an extraordinarily inhospitable place with a very poor infrastructure, though this has been partially improved by the recent expansion of pipelines, new railways, and roads. Moreover, it lacks manpower. The nearest reservoir of surplus labor is Soviet Turkestan, which the young Muslims refuse to quit mainly for cultural reasons. They fear that, cut from their sunny home, they might easily become Russified and alienated from their Islamic roots. Rather than go far north to earn some extra rubles in the permafrost taiga, they prefer to face unemployment at home.

The process of continued spatial polarization within an empire that had never been properly integrated through market forces has been exacerbated recently by the untractable forces of *perestroika*. Taking all these factors together, one finds more than enough arguments to justify resuming the Heartland Debate.

Such a debate took place in the 1950s, but in a different geopolitical context and for different reasons. It was then recognized that the Cold War brought the bipolar world of two antagonistic global systems to an impasse; this was underlined by the mutual frustration surrounding the Korean War. A few thought that it was the late Mackinder who should have carried the major share of blame for the U.S. policy of containment, which set up a chain of alliances along the rimland of Eurasia (NATO, CENTO, SEATO) against the combined Russo-Chinese land fortress. But rather than Mackinder's, these were the implementations of another geopolitical theory, one advocated by the late Nicholas Spykman, which challenged and reversed the basic postulates of the 1904 heartland thesis.[24]

The most significant event during this phase of the Cold War was the quasi-absorption of China into the Soviet Eurasian bloc after 1949. The geopolitical interpretation of this new global power configuration strongly resembled one of Mackinder's prophesies of 1904 and one variant of Haushofer's "Transcontinental Bloc" of the interwar vintage. In both cases, however, the extended Soviet Eurasian bloc did not include two important "marginal crescents," the western zone of Germany and the entire Japanese archipelago; nor was the control of the heartland exercised from the right center (Haushofer would certainly have preferred a German-controlled center). Stalin also failed to secure the important warm water outlets into the Mediterranean and the Persian Gulf through the Turkish Straits and across the Iranian plateau.

The harsh facts by which the combined Soviet Eurasian military potential was measured in those days consisted of the following: not only had Stalin's Russia expanded its control over Eastern and Southern Europe after crushing Germany in 1945, but the Red Army had also smashed the largest concentration of Japanese ground forces in Manchuria in August 1945. Since then, Moscow's influence constantly overflowed the rims of the Soviet heartland into the adjacent parts of Eurasia. In September 1944 the nominally independent People's Republic of Tannu Tuva on the Soviet-Mongolian border was "granted" admission to the Soviet family of nations; in 1945 China was compelled to renounce its titular rights in Outer Mongolia, thus making the Mongolian People's Republic more a Soviet preserve than before; Port Arthur, the former principal warm water naval base of the Russian Pacific Fleet that had been lost to Japan in 1905, returned to direct Soviet control; and the Soviets continued to control the East Turkestan Republic, established by them in 1944 in Sinkiang. As a final point, all these territorial gains were achieved before the USSR acquired nuclear weapons.

The pursuit of further Soviet ambitions was linked with the fate of *generalissimus* Stalin, whose death in early March 1953 signaled a major domestic and international watershed. The inevitable Sino-Soviet split that followed the dictator's demise and the advent of nuclear weapons constituted the turning points in the geopolitical interpretation of the contemporary world and provided the necessary incentives for the resumption of the Heartland Debate.

In 1950, three years after Mackinder's death, W. Gordon East, British Geographer, published his critique of the master's famous triplet of 1919 ("Who rules East Europe commands the Heartland; Who rules the Heartland commands the World-Island [that is, Eurasia plus Africa]; Who rules the World-Island commands the World"). He argued that the second dictum, implying that the control of the heartland by the ruler of East Europe, namely Russia, would automatically lead to command over the whole of Eurasia and the adjacent African Continent, had lost its validity in the light of the new technological progress. Because "geography changes as rapidly as ideas and technology change," East argued that "our whole conception of mobility and accessibility, considerations to which Mackinder attached prime importance, have been revolutionized by the internal combustion engine and the airplane; no less, too, have science and technology . . . and the advent of a new offensive weapon, the atom bomb." The aggregate of all this, East continued, invalidates Mackinder's premise in spite of Russia's growing territorial expansion and increased military strength, because "the Western powers, armed with a superiority in atom bombs and in long-range aircraft, now possess a means of depriving an enemy of economic and military assets on a greatly enlarged scale."[25]

With the benefit of hindsight we can also enlarge the category of technological progress by the missile dimension of transcontinental, nuclear-tipped rockets, which in the late 1950s began to shape decisively the military balance between the two superpowers. The new phenomenon of the nuclear deterrent based on these absolute weapons seemed to abolish, in a more radical way than the advent of the long-distance bomber, the chief geostrategic advantage of the heartland's inaccessibility to sea powers (as Mackinder had postulated in 1904). Yet even the availability of multiple thousands of these ultimate weapons in the superpowers' arsenals does not make a nuclear holocaust a foregone conclusion. So far, a precarious nuclear balance has survived a number of crises, with paradoxical effect: the possession of these ultimate weapons by the USSR and the United States has had a neutralizing impact on the chances that a nuclear first strike might lead to anything but mutual suicide. Consequently, regardless of the advances in nuclear and missile technology, regional conflicts affecting the Eurasian heartland directly (but the remote American continent or Western Europe only indirectly) will continue to be governed by the geostrategic dicta of the prenuclear era—notwithstanding the important impact of modern transport technology in overcoming the geographic obstacles of the heartland.

In the spring of 1955 Richard Hartshorne, a distinguished American geographer from the University of Wisconsin at Madison, in an unpublished conference paper, characterized Mackinder's heartland as a "dead center of the world." In spite of bordering on all four major areas of world population, it remained largely underpopulated, had relatively little productive power and no modern means of land transportation, was inaccessible for most of the year by sea, and still presented great natural obstacles to the movement of land forces.[26] Hartshorne did not like the idea of a single Eurasian heartland as put forward by Mackinder in its three principal modifications, and he suggested sensibly that Eastern Europe and the Central Asia pivot area be treated as separate entities. He thought that there was too great a contradiction between the optimal geometric center of the heartland and what he calls the real base of power, which, of course, was concentrated in the rimland or, in Mackinder's parlance, the "marginal crescent."[27] Hartshorne, however, has an untarnished vision of the victorious heartland power, firmly controlling the nearly empty areas in the center and accumulating enormous strength to push toward the coastal margins of Eurasia, from which its naval forces could dominate the world ocean.

But Hartshorne also found Mackinder's optimism regarding the rapid and intensive development of Siberia greatly exaggerated. From the perspective of the last ten years, however, it is the Mackinder of 1904 rather than the Hartshorne of 1955 who proved right. Siberia, not the incongruent Central Europe, is becoming the powerhouse of the heartland, having almost 90 percent of all mineral and energy resources available to the Soviet economy and the highest proportional share of capital investment allotted in the current five-year plan. This is more than mere potential. The largest operational Soviet oilfield (Samotlor) is located in Western Siberia; by the end of 1972 three out of the world's six greatest water dams, as measured by electricity power capacity, were located in the Asian part of the Soviet heartland (Krasnoyarsk on the Yenisei River, Bratsk on the Angara River, and Nurek on the Vakhsh River in Tajikistan, the last one having the world's highest dam).[28] Modern technology has also helped overcome a number of mountain barriers lying between Central Asia and the Indian Ocean, as part of the gradual improvement in transportation since 1955.

The most perceptive analysis of all three stages in the development of Mackinder's thesis (1904, 1919, 1943) was offered in 1955 by Arthur Hall.[29] While admitting that Mackinder's thesis in its several presentations had been generally correct, Hall nevertheless suggested several major errors of judgment on Mackinder's part. First, the area chosen by Mackinder as the most important seat of power had, in fact, not played a pivotal role in world history during a very long period of time. Second, Mackinder overlooked most seriously, in 1904 and even in 1919, not only the existence of another heartland, which Hall calls "Anglo-America," but also that this heartland had taken as important a place in planetary affairs as the one in Eurasia.[30] Like Hartshorne, Hall believed that Eastern Europe, included in Mackinder's heartland in 1919, proved more important than the pivot area of Central Asia.[31] On the whole Hall foresaw a steady increase in the power of the Soviet heartland in the near future, but he warned that the "current eminent state of the area was not foreordained nor is it frozen by geography."[32]

Thus, several Western authors estimated the prospects of the Soviet heartland being transformed into a pivotal area of the future. Donald Meinig, for instance, paradoxically characterized the Soviet Union as a continental rimland power in the process of assimilating most of the Eurasian heartland.[33] But to make the heartland a truly pivotal area, Meinig suggested that the Moscow-Urals-Ukraine triangle, which was in his view still the functional center of gravity, would have to expand eastward to Siberia and southward into Central Asia. Meinig also recognized that to unlock the military and commercial potential of this "nuclear region," more than internal development was required.[34] The logical extension of these designs would be the weaving together of a rail, motorway, pipeline, and air network across the frontiers and the development of regional and national reciprocity between the heartland and rimland. This kind of economic penetration had already given a strategic underpinning to the political extension of the heartland to Sinkiang and Outer Mongolia, and Meinig predicted that "similar designs upon Afghanistan are apparently underway."[35] He concluded that "Once an efficient overland transport system became available, Russia was in a position with enormous potential advantages, for she could place herself in direct functional contact with the entire rimland." Consequently, in 1956 Meinig believed that the trend of Soviet policy was reversed and that the Soviets were pursuing a radical reorientation of Eurasia's rimland toward the Soviet interior in the centripetal sense and away from the seaports and ocean commerce. He warned that this trend constituted the most significant danger to the Western world.[36]

Eight years later, when the Western world seemed to have forgotten about the Heartland Debate, a slim book, entitled *A New Soviet Heartland*, was published in America.[37] Its author, David Hooson, used powerful economic arguments for predicting the establishment of a giant Volga-Baykal zone, which was to become the future industrial heartland of the entire Soviet Eurasian Empire. Hooson included the Middle Volga area because at the time more Soviet oil was being produced from the new wells located between the Volga and the Urals than from the old wells of Baku. Although Hooson took notice of the rupture in Sino-Soviet relations, he still believed that the Soviet Union had to focus its expansion eastward for economic rather than strategic reasons. Furthermore, he believed that Russification of Soviet Central Asia was inevitable due to urbanization and immigration from the Russian mainland (as highlighted during the virgin land campaign in Northern Kazakhstan) and was skeptical about the capacity of the native population to resist Russification and gradual assimilation.

Why Should the Heartland Debate Be Resumed?

There has been no substantial contribution to the Heartland Debate since Hooson's perceptive monograph—notwithstanding W. H. Parker's remarkable biography of Mackinder (1982), which provides a detailed summary of pro and con views on the validity of the heartland thesis. A rich crop of works on geostrategic themes has appeared in the 1980s due to the wars in Afghanistan and in the Persian Gulf, but these studies, important as they are in their own sphere of competence, have not been concerned with the structural changes inside Soviet Eurasia; they have focused mainly on the U.S.-Soviet superpower rivalry.[38]

The last 20 years have brought four significant changes, most of them predicted in various degrees by Mackinder as early as 1904. These changes should provide enough reason to resume the Heartland Debate. The human factor, though often neglected and never elaborated on by Mackinder in detail,[39] deserves to be mentioned first. It is not enough to quote recent demographic statistics regarding the high birth rates of the Soviet Muslims. Taken in conjunction with the assumed impact of the radical Islamic ideology from the other side of the border, it creates the impression that these two elements alone could form an explosive mixture that would blow the Soviet Empire to pieces. The centrifugal forces of national emancipation, unleashed by *perestroika* in the borderlands, have not yet produced a united platform under the common denominator *finis imperii*. Bearing in mind the vast geographical, historical, and ethno-cultural differences, it is hard to imagine how they could.

If certain young Muslims in Soviet Central Asia are said to be influenced by Islamic fundamentalism in conjunction with the war in Afghanistan,[40] then the grievances of the Azeri Turks in Transcaucasia are first determined by the age-old enmity with the Armenians, rather than by their concern with the Russian overlords in Moscow or by the pronouncements of the late Ayatollah Khomeini. As for the dramatic, but so far nonviolent, nationalist revival in the three Baltic republics, it is inspired, above all, by the strong memory of the brief period of independent statehood between the two world wars. Combining mass agitation in the streets through the Popular Fronts with the legislative work of the republics' existing Supreme Soviets, Estonia, Latvia, and Lithuania have been trying since November 1988 to pass legislation that would, short of cession, proclaim national sovereignty and the replacement of Russian by their respective national languages. Until now the Moscow Politburo has shown extreme reluctance to give its approval but has neither outlawed the new legislation nor prosecuted the culprits.

As long as the nationalistic agitation in the Baltics does not reach the boiling point (as in the Caucasus), Gorbachev and his colleagues will be extremely reluctant to apply force because they want to avoid new bloodshed. This, by contrast, occurred in the three Caucasian republics where ethnic massacres had taken place and people were killed by troops during 1988 and early 1989. In vain, it seems, did the Russian poet, Evgenii Evtushenko, warn the public that the Caucasus could become a Soviet Northern Ireland.[41]

There is also an important geostrategic dimension to the whole question of national sovereignty in the Soviet borderlands that should not be taken lightly. Full independence for Lithuania, for instance, would completely cut off the artificial Russian-speaking enclave of the Kaliningrad region (ex-Königsberg), which was created in 1945 from parts of former Eastern Prussia and attached directly to the Russian Federation (RSFR). Since Kaliningrad is also a major ice-free naval base for the Soviet Navy, it is difficult to imagine that Moscow would compromise on this sensitive issue.

Even if the nationalist upsurge in the borderlands can, at least in theory, be contained, it will be much more difficult to reduce the present demographic upswing in Soviet Central Asia. While the Muslim population will roughly double every 30 years, its European counterparts, mainly the Slavs of Soviet Eurasia, will become progressively older and begin their negative growth. This demographic discrepancy is already reflected in the composition of civilian and military manpower: every third Red Army recruit is of Muslim background, and the phenomenon is derisively referred to by the Russian intelligentsia as the "yellowing of the Red Army" (*Ozheltenie Krasnoi Armii*).[42] In the eyes of many Great Russians the scores of Muslim draftees are not a desirable addition to the artificially neutral category of Soviet people, of which the socialist family of nations is allegedly composed. The Soviet people, in accordance with Lenin's wishes, should have stopped noticing by now any surviving racial and cultural differences among themselves. In real life the Slavs see the Soviet Muslims as a potential threat, along with the awesome millions of yellow Asians, subconsciously regarded as descendants of the Mongol invaders.

On the other hand, there is substantial optimism regarding further dramatic improvement in Sino-Soviet relations, foreshadowed by Foreign Minister Eduard Shevardnadze's and President Mikhail Gorbachev's visits to Peking in 1988 and 1989. The preceding Sino-Soviet split, which started in 1960, marked the most important geostrategic change in Asia in the last quarter century. In the mid-1960s Moscow planners were preparing "preventive" nuclear strikes against China's major missile test center at Lop Nor (reportedly considered by Khrushchev in 1964, and very definitively during the summer of 1969, according to Henry Kissinger).[43] During the 1960s and 1970s approximately one-third of the entire Soviet military power was swung round to confront Chairman Mao's yellow peril. Billions of rubles were invested in new airfields, barracks, strategic roads, and railways, of which the Baykal-Amur Mainline (BAM) has achieved some notoriety.

To minimize the possibility of fighting a two-front war, one against the Chinese in the Far East, the other against NATO in Europe, the Kremlin used every opportunity to exploit the climate of detente. By spreading the message of "Yellow Peril" among the Americans and West Europeans, they hoped to gain their psychological and, if possible, diplomatic support. To divert Chinese attention from the Manchurian border, the Soviets also tried to exploit the Indian factor and the presence of Muslim minorities in Sinkiang, who could easily be incited against Peking.[44]

Throughout the 1960s and 1970s the Russian dissident writers, such as Andrei Amalrik and Alexander Solzhenitsyn, expressed similar fears over the alleged Chinese population pressure, as did the Slavophiles in the nineteenth century.[45] In his challenging letter of September 1973, known as the appeal "To the Soviet Leaders," Russia's greatest contemporary writer opted for the ideological legacy of Dostoevsky, Solovyov, and Blok. Solzhenitsyn warned that the forthcoming Sino-Soviet war would cost 60 million Russian lives and last a minimum of 10 to 15 years. He urged the masters of the Kremlin to give up "ideology" and seek physical and spiritual salvation, not in the conquest of foreign territories, but in the colonization of Russia's own "North-East" along the Arctic shore (see Figure 10.1 at the end of this chapter). Solzhenitsyn's clarion call may have evoked the colonization trend of the historic Republic of the Great Novgorod, but his intention was more prosaic: to provide Russia with a new military frontier, endowed with solid Russian stock, against the anticipated Chinese penetration. As a geopolitical idea it could not be taken seriously.[46]

The importance of the second factor, exemplified in the irresistible eastward shift of Soviet Eurasia's center of gravity, has already been emphasized. Today, 90 percent of all Soviet mineral and energy resources lie east of the Urals. Moreover, current Soviet efforts to turn Western Siberia, with its oil and gas reserves, into a real powerhouse of the Empire, the giant BAM construction site in eastern Siberia, the gas oil fields in Western Siberia, the mining complex of Yakutiya, and the irrigation projects in Central Asia are all major economic activities in this part of the world. The most ambitious project of all, namely, the colossal scheme of diverting Siberian river water into the arid steppes and deserts of Turkestan, seemed to have been shelved yet again. However, the catastrophic decline of Lake Aral's water levels due to senseless irrigation, which destroyed the natural environment for several thousand square miles round the lake, has led to a reopening of the discussion.[47]

This economic factor has exercised its continuous influence on Russian Asia since the beginning of the century. Because of its long-term impact it was present in the Heartland Debate of the 1950s and 1960s. In 1943 Mackinder reiterated his earlier belief that "upon and beneath the Heartland there is a store of rich soil for cultivation and of ores and fuels for extraction, the equal—or thereabouts—of all that lies upon and beneath the United States and the Canadian Dominion."⁴⁸ Today this economic factor has even greater potential significance judging from the steady eastward shift of extractive industries.

The third factor of change is predominantly military and strategic in character. It is, above all, connected with the phenomenal rearmament of the Soviet Far East, which has turned during the last two decades into a second major Theater of Military Operations (after the European TVD). During those years the size of the ground forces in the Far East first doubled and then tripled; within the same period the Soviet Pacific Fleet became the largest of the four fleets maintained by the Red Navy.⁴⁹

At this critical junction a fourth factor must be added, one that affected the very "heart" of the Eurasian heartland: the implications of the recent Soviet occupation and military campaign in Afghanistan. After more than eight years of war, the Kremlin leader, Gorbachev, announced his determination to begin troop withdrawals in May 1988 and complete them by February 1989. The pullout of troops from Afghanistan has provided a useful watershed to review the long-term impact of the Soviet presence in the entire region.⁵⁰

By narrowing our focus on the heartland of Russian Eurasia, it is easier to sum up its strategic function, which consisted of the task of buttressing the vulnerable single west-east lifeline connecting the two main potential theaters of war, one in the West against the European enemies and the other in the Far East against the "Yellow Peril." (The second historic function of Central Asia for Russia's grand strategy consisted of the exploitation of the Indo-Persian corridor for diversionary activities against the British Empire. This function lost its significance in 1947 after the British had left the Indian subcontinent.) This century-old, west-east axis has recently been put under mounting pressure from a new axis of spatial polarization, running in the north-south direction right across Central Asia. At the northern pole of the new fulcrum lies the main area of extractive industries, but it is barren of population and exposed to a ferocious climate. At the opposite end of the fulcrum lies ancient Turkestan. It is endowed with an agreeable climate and a relatively huge surplus of young labor, but it suffers from a critical shortage of water and from an uneven distribution of its industrial and agricultural resources.

During the last three decades the southern tier of Soviet Central Asia, protruding into the neighboring regions contiguous with the Indian ocean, has witnessed a major Soviet economic and political penetration. This resulted in an improved transport infrastructure, built to establish better economic and political links throughout the region. But since the end of the 1970s, much to Moscow's distress, this "soft underbelly" (to apply the often-quoted Churchillian term) of the Soviet Eurasian Empire has become the most unstable region in the world. The war in Afghanistan carried with it the dangerous potential for further political escalation, which could have easily confronted the Soviet military with neighboring Iran and Pakistan. Moreover, this region has also been surrounded by the highest concentration of separatist movements in the world.

It would be premature, however, to confuse potentialities with realities. Although the Soviets, judging by their past record of systematic subversion in this region and elsewhere, might have been tempted to exploit the regional unrest, they also had ample reasons to behave more cautiously so that their military activism did not backfire in their own Muslim republics. The last thing Moscow wished to encourage, then as well as now, was self-determination in its borderlands seething with discontent, a by-product of *perestroika*.

It is, nevertheless, at this vulnerable crossroad of the two axes of spatial polarization that Mackinder's heartland concept will have to undergo its decisive test to rectify its preconceived fixation on the pivot of Eurasia. Mackinder selected his "Pivot Area" because it was the natural center of the largest landmass on Earth and inaccessible to the application of sea power (see Figure 10.1). Today, however, there is not a single spot on our globe that could not be attacked by air power and nuclear missiles.

But this is only one aspect of the problem; as a superpower the Soviet Union must have the capacity to reach out from the Eurasian heartland to the rimland. In our specific context this means the capability of deploying its forces without hindrance in the ice-free waters of the Indian Ocean.[51]

After 1943 it became obvious that the rise of the new superpower in Eurasia was the unavoidable consequence of the war, just as Mackinder had predicted in 1904, or, as in his third and final modification of the heartland concept when he characterized the Soviet Eurasian Empire as "the greatest natural fortress on earth."[52]

In 1919 Mackinder sent out strong warnings that Germany could one day become that power, either by allying herself with Russia or by subjugating her. This scenario, as we know, had failed only narrowly.[53]

As for Mackinder's legacy, it can be interpreted in numerous ways. On the one hand, it cannot be denied that the heartland concept contributed to the temptation to resume the German *Drang nach Osten* in the direction of the Russian *Lebensraum*, rather than along the *Bagdadbahn* toward the Middle East, as was the case during World War I. Nor can it be ignored that the heartland concept substantially influenced the postwar U.S. policy of containing Moscow's expansionist appetite along the Eurasian rimland. On the other hand, one must also recognize in Mackinder the defender of the status quo of 1919, not only exclusively in favor of the Anglo-Americans, but also very much in support of the small Central European nations. He firmly believed that the victorious powers should contain the imperialist ambitions of Germany and Russia. However unbalanced and unfair the international arrangement of 1919 appeared at the time, we can see now, with the benefit of hindsight, that it was more humane for the smaller nations, such as the Czechs,[54] than the options preached by the Soviets, German Nazis, Italian Fascists, or the Imperial Japanese. There may be perfectly valid warnings against the abuse of the heartland theory and countless Marxist-Leninist denunciations of it, but as long as the Soviet Eurasian Empire stretches from "sea to sea," they do not seem to affect the concept itself.[55]

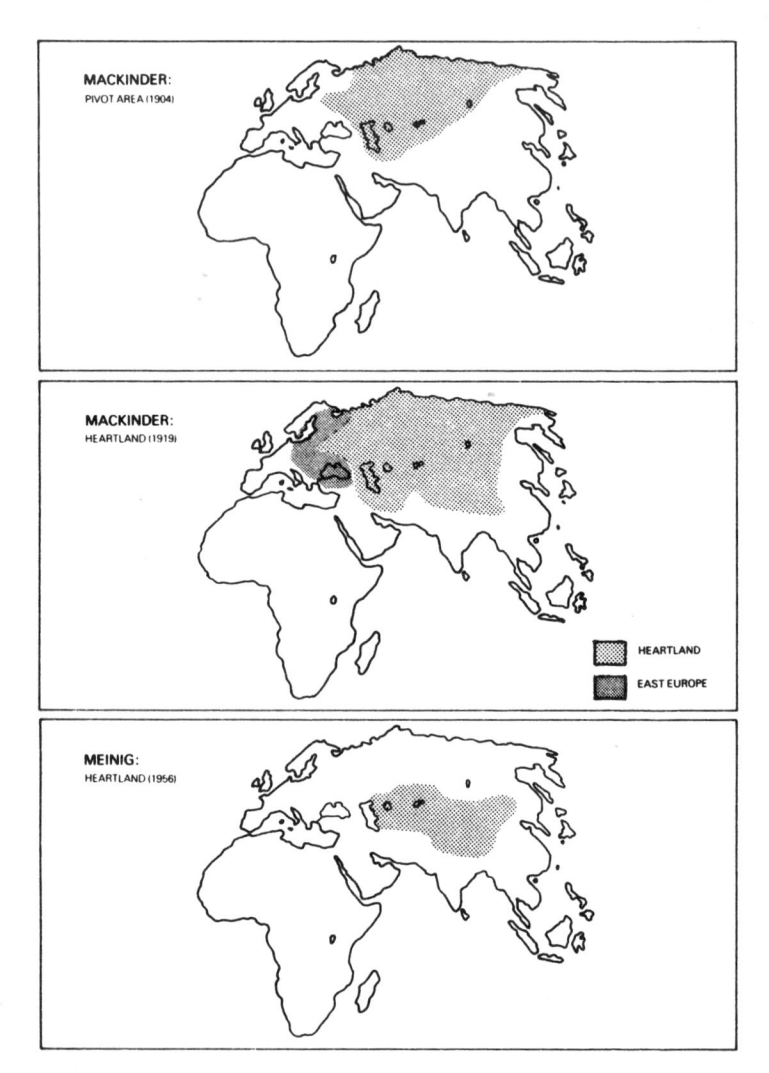

Figure 10.1 Variations on the Heartland Theme

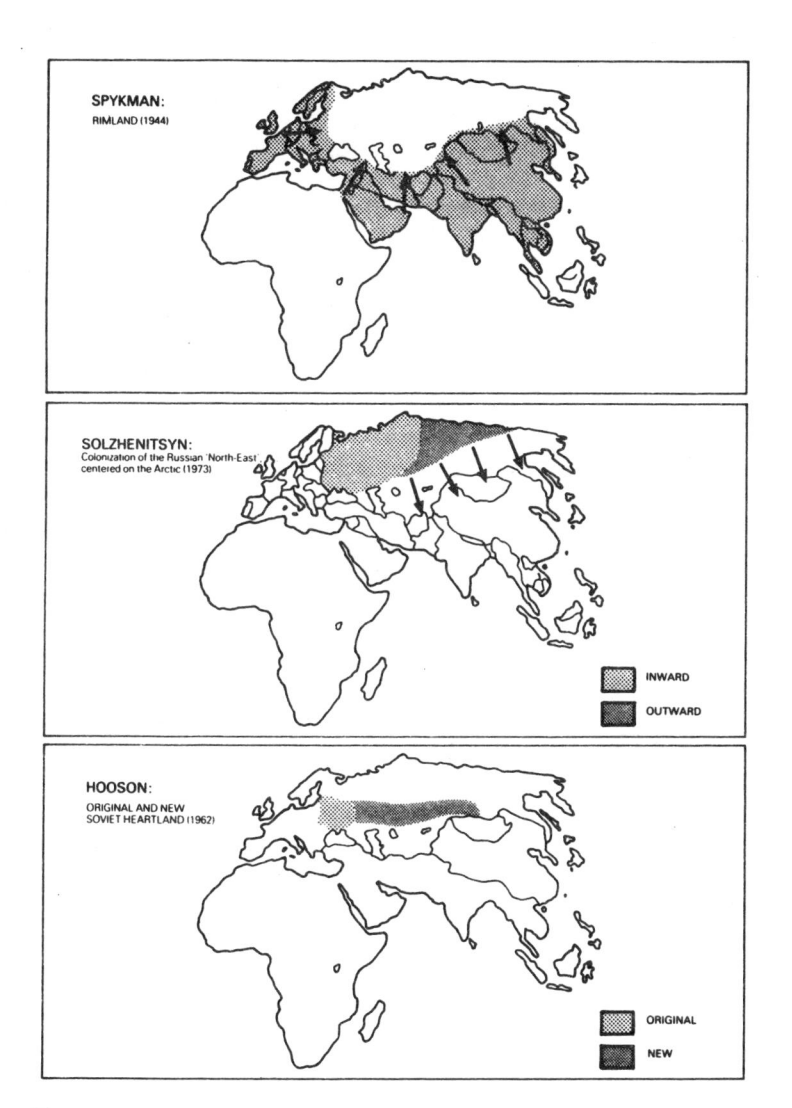

Figure 10.1 *(cont.)* Variations on the Heartland Theme

Notes

1. See, for example, Anatoly Isachenko, "Determinism and Indeterminism in the Work of Foreign Geographers." In *Soviet Geography*, ed. Kudryasheva (1981), 201–41.
2. Parker, *Historical Geography* (1969), 367–80.
3. Using data from Robert Conquest's *The Great Terror* (London: Macmillan, 1968), 530–35, Geoffrey Jukes concludes that the proportion of prisoners to free citizens in Siberia and the Far East in 1939 must have been more than one to two; see G. Jukes, *The Soviet Union and Asia* (Sydney: Angus & Robertson, 1973), 50.
4. Parker, *Historical Geography* (1969), 377. See also the more elaborate conclusions by Leslie Dienes in his recent monograph, *Soviet Asia* (1987), 267–79, and the theoretical observations in his article, "Regional Planning and the Development of Soviet Asia," in *Soviet Geography* (May 1987), 287–314. Similar conclusions are expressed by the panel of geographers, led by the late Theodore Shabad, discussing the prospects of Soviet economy in its geographical context in the year 2000: *Soviet Geography* (June 1987), 388–425.
5. Parker, *Historical Geography* (1969), 378. Note 25 in chapter 7.
6. Milan Hauner, "Soviet Eurasian Empire and the Indo-Persian Corridor," *Problems of Communism* (January-February 1987), 32–33.
7. Kristof, *Nation in Space* (1969), 68–69.
8. Saul B. Cohen, "Theory and Traditional Political Geography." In *Pluralism and Political Geography*, ed. Nurit Kliot and Stanley Waterman (London: Croom Helm, 1983), 21.
9. Alexander Prokhanov, "A Monologue about the Times and about Myself," *Literaturnaya Gazeta* of 6 November 1985.
10. Cf. Aleksander Prokhanov's "geopolitical" novels dealing with the Soviet occupation of Afghanistan: *Derevo v tsentre Kabula* (The Tree in the Center of Kabul), *Zapiski na brone* (Notes on Armor). *Radio Liberty Bulletin* 81/85, "The Defence Genre: The Literature of Tomorrow?" 15 March 1985; *Literaturnaya Gazeta*, Nos. 35, 38, 45 (1985).
11. "Theater of Military Action" is a widely used Soviet military term, *teatr voennykh deistvyi* (TVD).
12. "*Zapiski na brone,*" *Literaturnaya Gazeta* of 28 August 1985; *The Current Digest of the Soviet Press* of 20 November 1985.
13. See note 9.
14. Sergei Yurenin, "The Vulnerability of Armor: Aleksandr Prokhanov under Fire from Literary Critics," *Radio Liberty* 207/886, 26 May 1986; Vitautas Matulyavichyus, "Romany na konveiere," *Neva* 10 (1987), 158–64.
15. See Prokhanov's passionate defense in "Nashe vremya goryachee," *Krasnaya zvezda* of 6 March 1987. Interesting observations on "Prokhanovism" and the connection with the Soviet military establishment are found in *Storm over the Hindukush* (Images and Realities of the Soviet War in Afghanistan), a monograph by Norman M. Naimark from the Russian Research Center at Harvard, unpublished, 1989.
16. A. Prokhanov: "Svetlei lazuri," *Oktyabr'* 9 (1986), 3–55; "Risunki batalistka," *Moskva* 9 (1986), 33–155, and 10 (1986), 11–106.

17 See extracts from Prokhanov's own writings in note 10. Allusions to Prokhanov's earlier "geopolitical" (or "military-political") novels: *V ostrovakh okhotnik* (A Hunter in the Islands), *Afrikanist* (The Africanist), *I vot prikhodit veter* (And Now Comes the Wind), located in Cambodia, Mozambique, and Nicaragua, respectively.
18 See "Risunki batalistka," 61–62 (as in note 16).
19 Nikolai Gumilyov, "Afrikanskiy dnevnik," *Ogonëk* 14 (April 1987), 3. His son, Lev N. Gumilyov (*1920), gained notoriety in the 1960s and 1970s for his attacks against interethnic marriages, particularly between Slavic Russians and Muslim Central Asians, which he implied would lead to physical and moral degeneration of both groups. Russian nationalists in exile around the *Veche* group picked up this theme and spread it in *samizdat* channels. Despite his racist views, Lev Gumilyov has remained a respected professor of ethnography at the Leningrad University and continues to publish some of the best Soviet texts on early Turkic communities in Central Asia (cf. *Soviet Nationalities Survey*, U.S. Dept. of State, 12 [1986]). See in chapter 2, "The Russian Idea Today."
20 A. Prokhanov, "Tak ponimayu," *Literaturnaya Rossiya* of 3 April 1987: 3. See also Bill Keller, "Soviet Afghanistan Veterans Call for End of Neglect and for Honor," *The New York Times* of 23 November 1987.
21 See Bill Keller, "Soviet Official Says Press Harms Army," *The New York Times* of 21 January 1988.
22 A. Prokhanov in *Literaturnaya Gazeta* of 17 February 1988; German Belousov et al., *Afghanistan in Our Lives* (Moscow: Novosti, 1989), 20–24.
23 On *Pamyat* see a long article by the banned Soviet geneticist, Valeriy Soifer, "Rettet Russland! Schlagt die Juden!" *Der Spiegel* 34 (1987), 100–103; see also Felicity Barringer in *The New York Times* of 24 May 1987, and Dominique Dohombres in *Le Monde* of 24 June 1987.
24 Spykman argued that the control of the rimland rather than Mackinder's heartland was the key to Eurasian and ultimately to global dominance. See in chapter 6, "Who Commands the Heartland?" For an example of a systematic critique of the heartland theory during the Cold War, stressing the vulnerability of Soviet Eurasia, see Robert E. Walters, *Sea Power and the Nuclear Fallacy: A Reevaluation of Global Strategy* (New York: Holmes & Meier, 1975).
25 W. Gordon East, "How Strong Is the Heartland?" *Foreign Affairs* (October 1950), 78–86. On Leopold Amery's prophesy of the coming of air power made in 1904, see in chapter 6, "Importance of Railroads."
26 Richard Hartshorne, "Analysis of Mackinder's Heartland Concept," unpublished conference paper dated 13 April 1955. I am grateful to Professor Hartshorne for allowing me to read his paper.
27 Ibid., 8–9. However, Parker, *Mackinder* (1982), 220, argues (rightly in my view) that it is not necessary to administer or rule the heartland from its "geometric center." The essential thing is to control it, which can be done from the "marginal crescent," either from Moscow, Berlin, Pekin, or Tokyo. See in chapter 6, "Land Power versus Sea Power."
28 For details see Dienes, *Soviet Asia* (1987), 44–55. Information on power dams as given by the end of 1973 in *Encyclopedia Britannica*, vol. 5:443.

29 Arthur R. Hall, "Mackinder and the Course of Events," *Annals of the Association of American Geographers* 45 (1955), 109–26.
30 Ibid., 121, 125.
31 Ibid., 114–15.
32 Ibid., 121, 126.
33 Donald W. Meinig, "Heartland and Rimland in Eurasian History," *Western Political Quarterly* 9 (1956), 553–69; see also Dennis R. Mills, "The USSR—A Re-appraisal of Mackinder's Heartland Concept," *Scottish Geographical Magazine* 72 (December 1956), 144–53.
34 The term *Nuclear region* can be applied in more than one sense because the Central Asian heartland also comprises the two largest testing complexes for space exploration and ballistic missiles in Eurasia: Lop Nor in Chinese Sinkiang and the dual city Tyuratam-Baikonur (see Thomas Y. Canby, "Are the Soviets Ahead in Space?" *The National Geographic* [October 1986], 420–58).
35 Meinig, "Heartland and Rimland" (1956), 566–67.
36 Ibid., 568.
37 David J. M. Hooson, *A New Soviet Heartland?* (Princeton: Van Nostrand, 1964).
38 For example, Colin S. Gray: *The Geopolitics of the Nuclear Era* (New York: Crane & Russak, 1977); "Keeping the Soviets Landlocked: Geostrategy for a Maritime America," *The National Interest* (Summer 1986), 24–36; *The Geopolitics of Super Power* (Lexington: University Press of Kentucky, 1988); and *On Geopolitics: Classical and Nuclear*, ed. Ciro E. Zoppo and Charles Zorgbibe (Dordrecht: Martinus Nijhoff, 1985); Zbigniew Brzezinski, *Game Plan* (Boston: The Atlantic Monthly Press, 1986).
39 For Mackinder, people are always "manpower" available to fill in the vacuum of an empty space and extract natural resources. It is surprising, to say the least, that Mackinder, who was capable of presenting such penetrating analyses of the level of spatial relationships between great powers, was really not interested, in the broader anthropological sense of the definition as understood today, in people who inhabited the heartland.
40 Argued in particular by Alexandre Bennigsen in "Mullahs, Mujahidin and Soviet Muslims," *Problems of Communism* (November-December 1984), 28–44, and his commentary to "The Confessions of a Soviet Muslim Rebel," *Orbis* (Summer 1988), 432–36.
41 See Murray Feshbach, "The Soviet Union Population Trends and Dilemmas," *Population Bulletin* 37/3 (August 1982), 29; Edmund Brunner, *Soviet Demographic Trends and the Ethnic Composition of Draft Age Males, 1980–1995* (February 1981), Rand Note, N–1654 NA.
42 Alexandre Bennigsen and Marie Broxup, *The Islamic Threat to the Soviet State* (London: Croom Helm, 1983), 133.
43 Haselkorn, *Soviet Security Strategy* (1978), 6; Henry Kissinger, *The White House Years* (Boston: Little, Brown, 1979), 183–86.
44 Roy Medvedev, *China and the Superpowers* (Oxford: Basil Blackwell, 1986), 33, 54; V. Louis, *Chinese Empire* (1979); Harrison Salisbury, *Coming War* (1969).
45 See in chapter 2, *Russian Ideology and Asia*; note 27 above; Amalrik, *1984* (1969), 43.

46 See chapter 2, notes 52 and 53. For Medvedev's dissenting reply to Solzhenitsyn's idea of a new *Lebensraum* for the Russians in the Arctic northeast, see *Der Spiegel* 37 (1974), 98–105; Medvedev, *China* (1986), 52–53; Andrei Samokhin, *Kitaiskiy krug Rossii* (Frankfurt: Possev, 1981).
47 Philip P. Micklin, "The Status of the Soviet Union's North-South Water Transfer Projects before Their Abandonment in 1985–86," *Soviet Geography* (May 1986), 287–329. However, following Gorbachev's visit to Tashkent in April 1988, it was agreed to conduct a new feasibility study on the Siberian river project (cf. Martin Walker in *The Manchester Guardian Weekly* of 24 April 1988).
48 Mackinder, *Round World* (1943), 603–604.
49 See in chapter 5, "Dual Strategy in the Indo-Persian Corridor."
50 My colleagues and I have tried to answer these question in *Afghanistan and the Soviet Union: Collision & Transformation*, ed. R. L. Canfield and M. Hauner (Boulder: Westview, 1989).
51 See in chapter 5, "A Breakout to the Indian Ocean?"
52 Mackinder, "The Round World" (1943), 601.
53 Blouet, *Mackinder* (1987), 204.
54 Mackinder, *Democratic Ideals* (1919), 206.
55 Parker, *Mackinder* (1982), 245. On pp. 231–47, Parker offers the most comprehensive survey of pros and cons vis-à-vis Mackinder's heartland thesis, subdivided into some twenty arguments, the most relevant of which have been taken up here.

11

In Place of Conclusions: What is Asia to Gorbachev's Russia?

How can one offer any conclusive thoughts on Soviet Eurasia when its society is undergoing such a phenomenal transformation? At the time of my writing the Soviet Union offers an amazing picture of change, which even the boldest observers would not have predicted only a year ago. What are the most dramatic changes and their short- and long-term implications for the USSR's future? Has our routine perception of the Soviet Eurasian Empire been upset by the recent developments? Are we capable of taking a fresh look? Can we distinguish between the image of Soviet foreign policy and its substance? The former has been changing rapidly, but has the latter changed?

When Moscow announced in February 1988 that it would begin troop withdrawals from Afghanistan, the West watched with suspicion for the promise to be broken. It was not. On 15 February 1989 the last Soviet military unit was pulled out from Afghanistan. It did not make much sense, many experts concluded, to treat the Soviets with skepsis any more. This uncritical enthusiasm has easily silenced those in the media who continued to ask who bore the chief responsibility for the death of more than 1 million Afghans and for the over 5 million refugees who fled to Pakistan and Iran. This is just one of many paradoxes confronting today's Moscow watchers.

Where Is the Soviet Eurasian Empire Moving under Gorbachev?

How successful will the Soviets be as empire builders (or rather empire defenders) after the debacle in Afghanistan? Will the Empire withstand the mounting centrifugal forces of borderland nationalism and the demographic pressure of its rapidly growing Muslim population? How will Sino-Soviet relations be shaped in the next decade? What will happen to the Empire if the Great Russians can no longer claim that they are its dominant plurality core? Will it survive into the twenty-first century and, if so, under what form? Will it lose not only its borderlands with the non-Russian majorities but also its Asian half—which has never been organically integrated with the European metropolis except by military-autarkic means—because of the growing structural imbalances and increasing polarization?

Only six months to a year ago the Soviet Union could still be primarily characterized, both geopolitically and ideologically, as "a fortress state governed by fear and exclusion of alternative ideas."[1] This description does not quite fit the image the Soviet Union projects today. It remains, geopolitically speaking, the largest land fortress on Earth, but as for the circulation of alternative ideas, a new attitude seems to have emerged in the Soviet Union.

In spite of numerous taboos that still prevail (such as discussions in the media of private lives of Soviet leaders, the legacy of Lenin, the Brezhnev Doctrine, etc.), some correspondents writing from Moscow have the impression that "at the moment, the freedom of expression, the freedom of speech and press, is practically total."[2]

It seems as if the wind of *glasnost* has finally penetrated the thick walls of the Kremlin. There, the leaders are beginning to realize that the process of decolonization, which after World War II had put an end to the European overseas empires, has at last reached the Soviet Eurasian Empire as well.

In the sphere of international relations, there have been two major developments within the last six months that also carried with them deep domestic implications: (1) The withdrawal of Soviet troops from Afghanistan; (2) Gorbachev's two announcements (7 December 1988 and 18 January 1989) to initiate unilateral cuts in the country's huge military budget and its armed forces. The former is to be reduced by 14.2 percent (the entire military budget was estimated to be in the region of 130–140 billion rubles in 1987, that is, at least 17 percent of the GNP), and the latter by 12 percent (thereby reducing the military manpower by 500,000 men and some 10,000 tanks by the end of 1990.[3] Specifically, the three major TVDs are to be reduced as follows: in the West by 240,000 men, in the Far East by 200,000, and in the South by 60,000. The total strength of Soviet armed forces will then be reduced, according to Defense Minister General Dmitriy Yazov, from (the present?) 4,258,000 down to 3,760,000 men by the end of 1990.[4]

Although it is too early to provide a definitive judgment on the wide-ranging domestic and international implications of the Soviet military retreat from Afghanistan, where more dramatic developments are certain to occur, the geopolitical function of Central Asia within the Soviet Eurasian Empire will remain determined for the time by its supportive role. It will continue to function as a buttress supporting the west-east lifeline connecting the Russian metropolis via Siberia with the Chinese frontier and the Pacific shoreline. This supportive function, nevertheless, will increase in importance with the steady eastward shift of the USSR's economic and demographic centers of gravity beyond the Urals.

The third major development, which the leading Soviet journalist, Aleksandr Bovin, predicted would be the most important event in 1989, includes the anticipated changes in Sino-Soviet relations resulting from Foreign Minister Eduard Shevardnadze and President Mikhail Gorbachev's visits to Peking.[5]

Taken together, these three major developments will put Gorbachev's predilection for the Common European House to a severe test. In spite of the concessions made recently to Eastern Europe (Hungary and Poland) and to the non-Russian Union republics in the borderlands of the Empire (Estonia, Latvia, Lithuania), the Gorbachev leadership knows that it must not cross the fine line behind which there is the ominous notion of national self-determination coupled with secession. "Since there is nothing in the character or tradition of the Russian state to suggest that it could ever accept imperial decline gracefully,"[6] we should not be surprised to see the Politburo clamp down again as it has already done on three occasions in the Caucasus.

No one knows what the Kremlin is prepared to tolerate in its Eastern European glacis and in its own borderlands. In the Baltic states a fragile balance between the *raison d'Etat* of the Soviet superstate and the *raison d'être* of the local nationalist forces (tilting steadily in favor of the latter) has been preserved, albeit with difficulties. The three Caucasian republics have experienced a much rougher confrontation, having their capitals occupied by military force and experiencing violent clashes, with dead and injured on both sides. This extraordinary surge of the long overdue nationalist unrest sweeping the union republics is bound to encourage Gorbachev's political opponents. They might accuse him that *glasnost* is leading to anarchy and betrayal of true Marxism-Leninism.

How much more repression is necessary to bring Gorbachev down? Gorbachev and his allies were caught at the beginning of 1989 in the crossfire of nationalist manifestations, many of them violent (Caucasus), without a workable nationalities policy.

Do the Forces of Nationalism Represent the Main Threat to the Empire's Coherence?

Is nationalism the Empire's liability or asset? Most authors believe that the multinational character of the Soviet Eurasian Empire constitutes a serious liability threatening to break up the Empire, especially if 50 million Ukrainians and 50 million Soviet Muslims can mobilize their energies for the sake of national autonomy. The Ukrainians are crucial for the European half, the Muslims for the Central Asian heartland.

The price of preserving the Empire for so many decades against the worldwide trend of decolonization might cost the Great Russians dearly. Even a limited decolonization might ignite violent processes leading to the partition of the Eurasian Empire on the grounds of communal, territorial, ethnocultural, and historically based disputes. This would probably kill the present hopes for the institution of civil and political rights in the borderland republics as well as in the Russian metropolis.[7]

Jerry Hough could be alone in defending the bold view that "the multinational nature of the Soviet Union is a real plus for Gorbachev." He ignores the combination of 50 + 50 million Ukrainians and Muslims and maintains that the individual nationalities, such as the 1.5 million Estonians, are too small to pose a serious threat.[8]

This is a Russo-centrist view. What if the non-Russian nationalities simply refuse to play second fiddle? Will it come to a violent backlash? Will a "New Russian Right" emerge, as the only real alternative to Gorbachev's *perestroika*, to save the integrity of the Empire and resurrect the "Russian Idea?"

What new kind of commonwealth is going to emerge and replace the USSR? Three options seem to be in the offing. The first and most optimistic is a new confederation, indeed, a sort of a commonwealth, for which the compact territory with the existing communication network seems to be speaking. But such a development will almost certainly increase the imbalances between the decaying center and the autonomous regional economies in the peripheries. They will try to become "Finlandized" like the rest of Eastern Europe, thereby confirming the failure of the economic *perestroika* in the Russian colonial metropolis. This could only lead to a Great Russian reaction, a nationalist and military coup attempting desperately to hold together the disintegrating Empire. An apocalyptic scenario for such a backlash, whereby the "Russian New Right," with all its wretched fascist past and hatred of the "Judeo-Masonic Conspiracy," will wrest power in the Kremlin from the discredited Gorbachevites, is dramatically portrayed in Alexander Yanov's recent book, *The Russian Challenge and the Year 2000*.[9] The popular editor of *Ogonëk*, Vitalyi Korotich, predicts that in the event *glasnost*'s fails "I will be destroyed, and we will be left a hungry, stupid, terrible country with a big army—a very dangerous country."[10] Finally, there is a middle course, with Moscow simply trying to muddle through from one crisis to another, but avoiding the final showdown, as the Habsburg and Ottoman empires accomplished until World War I. Indeed, the very term "Ottomanization" has been suggested for this wishful scenario by one of the most perceptive observers of the East European scene.[11]

In the previous chapter we argued on theoretical grounds why the historic Heartland Debate should be resumed today. In view of recent dramatic developments inside the USSR threatening to bring about the Empire's breakup, it might be useful to point out these centrifugal trends as well as conceptual devises designed to prevent disintegration, such as provided by the theoreticians of New Thinking.

With regard to *Prokhanovshtina*, it seems to have turned itself into an anachronism. Its chief protagonist has tried to retreat gracefully. Is Prokhanov now applying his talents on the internal front to prevent the outbreak of civil war? One thing is certain: the pullout of Soviet troops from Afghanistan appeared also to be the withdrawal of Prokhanovism as a botched imperial genre from Soviet literature, at least for the time being.

As for geopolitics itself, it no longer seems to be a bad word. The "New Thinking" approach in current Soviet foreign policy puts a great emphasis on de-ideologization; it becomes implicitly geopolitical. There is no more talk of international class struggle, of the traditional tripartite division of the world (socialist, capitalist, and the developing countries, potentially moving toward the socialist camp); instead, political pragmatism seems to be the leading principle. At the closed *MID* conference (Ministry of Foreign Affairs) in July 1988, the geopolitical approach clearly prevailed over the ideological one. During the discussion on priorities of USSR foreign policy, First Deputy Foreign Minister Anatolii Kovalyov spoke of *three* principal directions (*napravleniya*) of Soviet foreign policy: American, European, and the Asia-Pacific. As for the latter, Kovalyov favored the view implying that the Soviet Union, on the strength of its unique "geostrategic position," could serve as a kind of "bridge between Europe and the APR" (Asia-Pacific Region).[12]

Unconsciously perhaps, the new thinkers in Soviet foreign policy have adopted Karl Haushofer's geopolitical model of Russia's Eurasian "land-bridge," which the readers will recognize. Haushofer's scheme consisted of three major geopolitical regions: Western Europe under German hegemony, the Pacific region under Japanese, and the Soviet Eurasian Empire serving as a bridge between the two.[13]

Gorbachev himself referred to "Eurasia" on at least three occasions: (1) in his book *Perestroika*; (2) in his speech in Murmansk (1 October 1987); and (3) in October 1988 in his welcoming message sent to foreign guests attending the Asia-Pacific Region conference in Vladivostok. In this message he explicitly stressed that "the Soviet Union was a Eurasian state . . . to serve as a hopeful bridge bringing together two great continents."[14]

The spectacular achievements of Gorbachev's new foreign policy cannot overshadow the manifestations of internal frictions and crises his Empire is facing. Most observers, however, are attracted by the noisier and more visible scenes of crisis. They do not have the patience to look for the signs of long-term pressures and tensions, to listen for the distant tremors that, in contrast to an instant earthquake, are not immediately audible or visible.

How, for instance, does Gorbachev's predilection for the Common European House fit into the larger picture of the Eurasian Empire, in which three-quarters of the territory and almost 80 million of its subjects are to be found in Asia? In addition, as already mentioned, almost 90 percent of the USSR's mineral and energy resources are today found east of the Urals. While Gorbachev's heart may be attracted to "our common European heritage," his mind must realize that the structural shift is proceeding exactly in the opposite direction.

Today's ethnodemographic indicators suggest that the ethnic structure of the present Soviet Eurasian Empire will change dramatically within less than 100 years. Ethnic Russians, who had already lost their majority in 1984, will begin their negative growth by 1995. In roughly ten years, every second child born in the USSR will be of a Muslim mother. The European subjects, especially the Great Russians, on the other hand, will experience a serious demographic depression and the possibility of an eventual depopulation. By the year 2080 the USSR, if it still exists in its present form, will be predominantly a Turko-Muslim country.[15]

On the surface Gorbachev obviously faces more immediate problems; he does not dare to think ahead and aloud about the deep structural problems confronting his Empire from a spatial perspective. His short- and mid-term suggestions embracing the Asian space, as contained in his Vladivostok (1986) and Krasnoyarsk (1988) speeches, appear largely rhetorical. Had he been more genuine, he would have reached out to repair decades of neglect and misguided decisions that have aggravated beyond repair the maintenance of the Empire's equilibrium.

Paradoxically, the most concentrated attempt to balance the Empire's western and eastern extremities was carried out during the 1960s and 1970s for a reason that the advocates of *perestroika* now treat with contempt. In the name of imperial security and for the sake of preserving the Empire's autarkic structure, a colossal military buildup of the Far Eastern TVD took place. It was the most spectacular military *perestroika* and has not yet been properly analyzed in Soviet literature. In anticipation of a fictitious invasion to be led by a new Genghis Khan waving a rival red flag, dozens of new Soviet Army divisions were deployed, and an entirely new military infrastructure was hastily established thousands of miles from mother Russia. It was a frightening rebirth of the "Yellow Peril" hysteria, which turned the slogan of proletarian internationalism into a farce. With the completion of the main (*glavnyi*) Far Eastern TVD in 1978, and a smaller one in Central Asia (Southern TVD) in 1984 at the peak of the military campaign in Afghanistan, about two-fifths of the Soviet ground forces manpower and equipment were deployed east of the Urals. The Soviet Pacific Fleet also received massive reinforcements to become the largest among the four separate fleets of the Soviet Navy.[16] This hypermilitarization of Soviet Asia during the preceding two decades must be considered one of the heaviest burdens inherited by Gorbachev's *perestroika* from the Brezhnev era.

Yet, the giant military buildup hardly stimulated the development of nonmilitary economies. In fact future prospects of an economic takeoff in the Soviet Far East are still hampered today largely because of the prevailing parasitic presence of the military element in one of the most militarized zones in the world. In sharp contrast the Pacific region in its immediate vicinity has been enjoying an unprecedented economic boom, which is now beyond the reach of Soviet consumers.[17]

Three significant trends seem to be characteristic for Soviet Asia as forerunners of deeper structural changes yet to come:

1 There is new interest in genuine regionalism, especially in Soviet Muslim Central Asia, emphasizing ethnocultural roots rather than economic links with Moscow. A unified Central Asia would have nearly the population of the Ukraine and more than six times its territory—a potential threat to the centralistic control exercised by Moscow.[18]
2 Regionalism, however, is not only the aim of non-Russian nationalists striving to achieve greater cultural, political, and economic autonomy from the center. It could become the target of Great Russians themselves. An excellent case in point is the program for an autonomous Western and Eastern Siberia, passed on 25 December 1988 by the Democratic Union of Novosibirsk, one of the most dynamic "informal" groups (*neformaly*) established thanks to *glasnost*. Inspired by the

tradition of prerevolutionary movements for Siberian autonomy, the Democratic Union requested in its program the end of Siberia's semicolonial status, which had turned the rich province into a mere raw material appendage of the metropolis, ruined its independent farmers by the imposition of the kolkhoz system, and destroyed its ecology by the ruthless exploitation of its immense natural resources.[19] One must also remember the short-lived existence of the anti-Bolshevik government in Omsk (1918–19) and the semi-independent Far Eastern Republic (1920–22), both of which will serve as inspiration to Siberian autonomists.[20]

3   Inspired by the four special economic zones established by China in the early 1980s, Moscow would like to create similar free economic trade zones in the Far East, dubbed "Far Eastern Singapore," to attract foreign capital. The average Russian is hostile to the idea of letting in Asiatic guest-workers and entrepreneurs. "We would rather let the land go to waste than allow foreigners in," was the leitmotiv of the vast majority of TV viewers who sent letters to a recent panel discussion on the subject "The Asian-Pacific Region: Problems and Prospects for Development."[21] The specter of "Yellow Peril" comes inevitably to mind. In ten years China will have between 240 and 260 million unemployed, mostly young and illiterate peasants, who may become restless. (This figure is higher than the entire adult working population the USSR will have in the year 2000.) Chinese authorities recently admitted that they had been unsuccessful in implementing rigorous birth control measures. China's labor force is growing by an estimated 10 million a year, outstripping the country's capacity to create new jobs.[22] Where will they go if Soviet Siberia and the Far East are declared off-limits for Asians?

Geopolitically speaking, Gorbachev's Eurasian Empire is undergoing a critical structural transformation at this moment, resulting from the socioeconomic and ethnocultural tensions between the center and periphery and along the west-east and north-east axes of its spatial polarization. Whereas the Americans have been more successful (under much more favorable geographic, climatic, and, above all, political conditions) during the last 100 years in integrating their empire from shore to shore and avoiding the dichotomy between the center and periphery; by contrast, the Russians achieved their aim almost exclusively by military means. Their Eurasian Empire of today, stretching from "sea to sea," is a living anachronism of a bygone imperial mission and of an outlived autarkic concept of economic and social organization. Even inside the Empire louder voices are asking how a third-rate economic power can afford a superpower military machine. Is it the fate of Russia to remain a sort of Upper Volta with nuclear bombs? Rather than to preserve the semblance of imperial unity across the Eurasian landmass, *perestroika*, if applied ruthlessly, will be the harbinger of its inevitable breakup.

This melancholic perspective brings us back to Mackinder's original dictum of 1904. He visualized the Russian Eurasian Empire as an almost perfect symbiosis between natural environment and political organization, unlikely to be changed by "any possible social revolution," which itself could never alter her "essential relations to the great geographical limits of her existence."[23] The kind of social revolution Mackinder anticipated flared up briefly in 1905, and then definitely in 1917. Whatever changes and sacrifices Lenin and Stalin's radical social engineering brought on the Eurasian landmass and its population, the preservation of the Empire "from sea to sea," within "the great geographical limits of her existence" had, by and large, followed Mackinder's dictum as formulated at the zenith of the modern imperialist era.

Gorbachev's *perestroika* is a different kind of social revolution. It could become the first reform program to challenge, in its geopolitical implications, Mackinder's famous but no less anachronistic dictum. Will Moscow's reform movement create a system of novel political organizations inside Soviet Eurasia, allowing elected organs of representative democracy and a free market economy, which will no longer correlate with the traditional imperial geographic environment? While "the great geographical limits" of the Empire's existence are permanent in nature, their geopolitical significance and function can be modified by the human element organized in a political fashion. If the political system becomes less imperialistically minded, the natural environment surrounding it will be seen with different eyes. This will make the breakup of the Empire inevitable. What will emerge in its place is by no means certain. And if the Empire goes, so will the heartland theory in the Mackinder mold. But until that cherished moment comes, with its vast repercussions for the rest of the world, we have no choice but to continue the Heartland Debate.

Notes

1. See T. B. Millar, *The East-West Strategic Balance* (London: George Allen & Unwin, 1983), 15. See also Colin S. Gray's latest, *The Geopolitics of Super Power* (Lexington: University of Kentucky Press, 1988).
2. Daniel Vernet in *Le Monde* of 10 March 1989.
3. According to a NATO-CIA study, published in March 1989, quoted by the AFP, 15 March 1989.
4. *Krasnaya Zvezda* of 13 April 1989.
5. A. Bovin in *Komsomolskaya Pravda*, 31 December 1988.
6. Kennedy, *The Rise and Fall* (1987), 514.
7. Dominic Lieven, *Gorbachev and the Nationalities* (London: Centre for Security and Conflict Studies, 1988), 31.
8. *Los Angeles Times* of 31 March 1989.
9. Alexander Yanov, *The Russian Challenge and the Year 2000* (Oxford: B. Blackwell, 1987). See also the special edition of RFE/RL *Research Bulletin*, 19 December 1988, entitled *Russian Nationalism Today*, with articles by John B. Dunlop, Darrell P. Hammer, Andrei Sinyavsky, Ronald Grigor Suny, and Alexander Yanov.
10. See Stanley W. Cloud in *Time* magazine of 10 April 1989.
11. Timothy Garton Ash, "The Empire in Decay," *The New York Review of Books*, 29 September 1988.
12. See *Mezhdunarodnaya zhizn*, no. 9 (1988), 36–39.
13. See in chapter 8, "German Geopolitik . . ."
14. *Vestnik Ministerstva inostrannykh del SSSR*, no. 20 (1 November 1988), 54.
15. M. S. Bernstam, "The Demography of Soviet Ethnic Groups in World Perspective." In *Last Empire*, ed. Robert Conquest (1986), 314–20, 348–49.
16. See in chapter 5, "Dual Strategy in the Indo-Persian Corridor." See also Edward N. Luttwak, "The Transformation of Soviet Grand Strategy and the Security of North-East Asia," paper presented at the International Security Council's conference in Tokyo, 13–15 April 1986.
17. The term "parasitic" for that particular phenomenon was coined by Leslie Dienes in "Economic and Strategic Position of the Soviet Far East," *Soviet Economy*, nos. 1–2 (1985), 146–76.
18. *Pravda* and *Pravda Vostoka* of 24 February 1989; see also James Critchlow, "A Panacea for Nationality Problems?" RL/*Report on the USSR*, 1/16 (1989).
19. Aleksei Manannikov, "Novosibirskie neformaly: Prizyv k bor'be za avtonomiyu Sibiri," *Radio Svoboda*, RL/PC 3/89, 9 January 1989.
20. See the papers of the 20th National Convention of the American Association for the Advancement of Slavic Studies, Honolulu, Hawaii, 18–21 November 1988, panel "Siberia in War and Civil War."
21. M. Hauner, "Does the Soviet Far East Have a Future?" RL/*Report on the USSR*, 1/9 (1989).
22. Xhinhua, 2 March 1989; Reuter from Peking, 6 March 1989.
23. See in chapter 6, "Who Commands the Heartland?"

Index

(The major themes, such as Russian/Soviet attitudes to Asia or the various aspects of the geopolitical debate on the subject of Eurasia's heartland, are detailed in the Contents.)

Abu Fazl-i-Allami 75
Adams, Brooks 98, 175–6
Aden 116, 120
Adriatic Sea 23
Afghanistan 7, 27, 29, 52, 75, 78–83, 86–8, 90, 94–6, 99–123, 170, 178–9, 197, 208, 220–5, 230–2, 235–6, 244–6, 249
Afgantsy 224–5
Africa 139, 172, 227
Aga Khan 89
Agursky, Mikhail 150
Alaska 5
Alexander I, Tsar 76
Alexander II, Tsar 44
Alexander III, Tsar 57
Alexander the Great 24–5, 46, 59, 74–5, 155, 178, 184
Altai 156, 161
Altshuler-Lezhnev, Isaiah 31–2
Amery, Leopold 145, 241
Amalrik, Andrei 35, 209, 234
Amanullah, King 78, 87, 90, 92
Amu Darya 74, 78, 97, 112, 114, 144
Amur 13, 52, 70, 74, 82, 197
Andropov, Yurii V. 30
Angara 229
Anglo-Afghan Wars 87, 90, 101
Anglo-Boer War 4, 83, 104
Anglo-Russian Rivalry 44–6, 49, 52–4, 70–1, 75–115 *passim*, 159, 194
Anglo-Russian Entente 83, 100, 106
Anglo-Russian Conflict (Yuzhakov) 52
Annenkov, General M. N. 99
Anti-Semitism 55, 167–9, 172
Antichrist (Solovyov) 54
Arabs 59, 72
Aral Sea 74, 234
Arctics/Arctic Ocean 12, 74, 140, 157, 160–1, 199, 204, 234
Armenia 27, 30, 232
Arseniev, V. K. 164

Aryans 23, 43, 51, 54, 167, 184
Ashkhabad 53, 103
Asia-Pacific Region 1, 9, 10, 249, 252
Asiatic Mode of Production 34, 201
Astara 109
Astrabad 76, 79–81
Atatürk, Kemal 94
Atlantic Ocean 8, 11, 69, 151, 155
Aufbau (Reconstruction) 167
Austria-Hungary 86, 88, 127, 207
Autarky 8, 218, 253
Axis Powers 95–6, 107, 175–8
Azerbaijan 30, 86, 101, 106, 113, 168
Aziatchina 2, 15, 55, 59, 200–2, 219
Azov 97

Babur 74
Badmaev, P. A. 57, 59
Baer, Karl 41
Bafq 109, 112
Baghdad 86
Baghdadbahn, see under Railways
Baku 27, 89, 92, 178, 197, 231
Bakunin, M. A. 50–1
Balkans 41, 49, 55, 79, 100, 107, 151, 155
Balkan War 24
Baltics 12, 13, 22, 26–7, 30, 32, 41, 57, 70, 87, 97, 101, 122, 167–8, 199, 232, 246
Baluchistan 75, 101, 103, 106, 115
Bandar Abbas 103–4, 109, 112, 114, 120
Bandar Khomeini (Bandar Shahpur) 109, 111
Bandar Shah 109, 111
Barakatullah, Maulavi 93
Baransky, N. N. 206
Barthold, V. V. 15, 59–60
Bashkirs 91, 207
Basmachi 91–2, 94
Basra 144
Bastian, Adolf 189
Baykal 9, 74, 82, 156, 195–6, 231

Baykal-Amur Mainline (BAM), see under Railways
Belov, Vasiliy 32
Belyi, Andrei 55
Bengal 94
Berdyaev, Nicolas 25, 28
Berlin Congress 81
Berlin-Baghdad Axis 56
Bessarabia 87
Bismarck, Prince Otto von 183
Black Hundreds 169
Black Sea 12, 13, 22, 57, 70, 72, 97, 100, 120, 191, 194, 199
Blok, Alexander 55, 202, 234
Blokh, J. S. 51
Bolan Pass 101
Bolsheviks 5, 26–8, 54–5, 59–60, 77–8, 87–8, 91–5, 148, 150, 165, 167–8, 174, 184, 191, 193–4, 199–200, 206–7
Bombay 103
Bose, Subhas Chandra 96, 176, 179, 187
Bosphorus 81, 84, 89, 97, 100
Bovin, Alexander 246
Brasilia 218
Bratsk 229
Bravin, Nicolai 87
Brezhnev, L. N. (and Doctrine) 29, 208, 225, 245
Brest-Litovsk, Peace of 26, 55, 87–9, 207, 221
British India (see under India)
Bromlei, Y. V. 30
Brunnhofer, Hermann 57–8, 64, 103, 149
Buckle, Henry T. 147, 209, 214, 217, 220
Buddhism 58, 140
Bukhara 39, 75, 80–1, 86, 89–92
Bukharin, Nicolai 93, 209–10
Bulganin, Nikolai 113
Buriats 57
Burma 96
Byzantium 24–5, 150

Cairo 72
Calais 75
Calcutta 84
Cam Ranh Bay 116
Cambodia 223
Canada 12, 155, 161, 235
Carrère d'Encausse, Hélène 62
Carthage 155
Casablanca 85

Caspian Sea 44, 70, 72, 76, 86, 144, 160, 199
Castlereagh, Lord Robert Stewart 12
Casus Belli Clause of 1907 95, 100
Catherine II, Empress 166
Catholicism 22
Cawnpore Conspiracy 95
Caucasus 4, 5, 11, 22, 26, 30, 32, 39, 40, 43–4, 79, 85, 91, 93, 116, 122, 156, 168, 177–8, 207, 232, 246–7
Central Asia 9, 22, 30, 32, 40–6, 49–54, 61, 69–131, 157, 166–7, 173, 194, 196, 220, 225, 229–30, 234–6, 246–7, 251
Central Asian Question 70, 74–115 passim
Central Asian Society 105
Chah Bahar 103–4, 109
Chaman 101, 110
Chattopadhyaya, V. N. 93
Chernyaev, General Mikhail G. 45
Chikhachëv, Admiral Nikolai 79
Chimkent 45
China 4, 7, 10, 14, 27–8, 39, 46, 50–9, 70, 95, 97–8, 99, 120–3, 139–40, 144–5, 151, 161, 167, 172–6, 197, 209, 226–7, 233–5, 246, 252
Chitral 77–8
Chokaiev, Mustafa 90
Christianity 22–3, 140, 150
Churchill, Sir Winston 12, 115, 236
Clarendon, Earl George W. F. 45
Claudius Bombarnac (J. Verne) 98
Clausewitz, Carl von 148, 206
Cohen, Saul B. 16, 131, 208, 220
Committee of Imperial Defence 100, 106
Common European Home 10–12, 250
Communism 3, 23, 25
Constantine, Emperor 24
Constantinople 22–4, 42, 53, 81, 84, 137, 150–1
Continent-Ocean (Savitsky) 200
Cossacks 5, 21, 39, 43–4, 52, 73–4, 76, 90, 97, 135
Crimean War 38, 44, 79
Critique of German Geopolitik (Heyden) 210–11
Curzon, Lord George Nathaniel 46, 77, 83–4, 94, 99, 103–4, 142, 191, 211
Curzon Ultimatum 197
Cyprus 72
Czech Legion 87, 196
Czechoslovakia 208, 237

Index

Daewoo 112
Dahlak Islands 116
Dai Nihon (Haushofer) 170, 174
Dalai Lama 50
Damascus 85
Danilevsky, N. Y. 23–4, 60, 150, 158, 169
Danube 58
Daoud, President Muhammad 110
Dardanelles 141
Dar-ul-Islam 74
Dar-ul-Harb 74
Darwin, Charles (and Darwinism) 52, 203
Delhi 84
Democratic Ideals and Reality 141, 171, 191
Denikin, General A. I. 142, 191
Derevenshchiki 32
Dersu Uzala (Arseniev, Kurosawa) 164
Diego Garcia 222
Dienes, Leslie 16–17, 240
Dokuchaev, V. V. 158
Dostoevsky, F. M. 1, 3, 12, 23–5, 49, 54, 98, 112, 234
Dover 75
Drang nach Osten 7, 41, 55–6, 101, 142, 166, 172, 237
Duhamel, General A. O. 79, 84
Durand Line 90
Dushanbe 144
Dvizhenie (Stremlenie) na Vostok 7, 38, 42
Dyadkin, Iosif 205
Dzerzhinski, Felix 207
Dzhugashvili Iosif (*see under* Stalin)
Dzhungarian Gate 144

East, W. Gordon 195, 227–8
Eastern Question 24, 158
Egypt 72, 75, 85, 120, 176
Ekaterinburg (Sverdlov) 156
Elbe 58, 208
Elphinstone, Mountstuart 76
Engels, Friedrich 41
Enver Pasha 86, 89–91
Enzeli 92
Erdkunde Asiens (Ritter) 42, 167
Esenin, Sergei 55
Estonia 232, 246–7
Ethiopia 121
Etnos (Ethnos Theory) 30
Euphrates 58

Eurasianists 15, 60–5, 150, 157–60, 199–202
Europe: Central 172, 176, 237; Eastern 7, 123, 159–60, 173, 192, 227–30
Europe and Mankind (Trubetskoy) 60, 65
Evtushenko, Evgenii 29, 232
Exodus to the East 60, 64

Fadeev, General R. A. 158
Far East 10, 13, 14, 22, 42, 51, 54, 61, 79, 82–4, 98, 100, 104, 115, 120, 136, 158, 166, 172, 196, 205, 235, 246, 251
Far Eastern Republic 196, 252
Far Eastern Singapore 252
Fascism 11, 31, 203; Russian 164, 169
Fascist Geopolicy in the Service of American Imperialism (Semyonov Y. N.) 210
Feshbach, Murray 205
Finland 26–7, 87, 107, 140
Fischer, Fritz 85
France 9
"From Sea to Sea" (*Ot morya do morya*) 13, 69, 121, 135, 155, 200, 207, 237, 253
Frunze, M. V. 91
Fyodorov, N. F. 53–4, 149

Galicia 27
Galiev, Sultan 91, 94, 202
Gandhi, Mahatma 176
Ganges 58, 84
Gardanne, General 76
Gaspraly, Ismail Bey (Gasprinski) 202
Gaule, Charles de 11
Genghis Khan 28, 59, 74, 78, 251
Geographical Pivot in History (Mackinder) 137–46, 148–51
Geographical Society, Royal of Britain 137, 145, 149, 183
Geographical Society, Imperial Russian 41, 153, 166
Geopolitics, Geopolitical Materialism and Marxism (Wittfogel) 200–1
Geopolitik 2, 165–90, 198
Geopolitik des Pazifischen Ozeans (Haushofer) 170, 174
Geopolitika 3, 202–4, 216–18
Georgia 40
Germans, of Russia 32, 41, 165–70
Germany: Communists 169–70; Imperialism 26, 166, 210, 249;

Kulturmission in Russia 166; Strategy 85–9, 95–6, 101, 105–6, 140, 141–2, 159, 161, 165–90, 237; Revolution 207; Social Democrats 27; Participation in the Great Game 85, 101
Geyer, Dietrich 6–7
Gilan, Soviet Republic of 92, 113
Gilgit 78
Glazunov, Ilya 32
Gobi Desert 98, 161
Gobineau, Count Joseph-Arthur de 150
Goek Tepe 1, 99, 112
GOELRO 206
Gorbachev, M. S. 1, 7, 9–14, 17, 30, 115, 118–22, 151, 218, 232–3, 235, 245–97, 249–53
Gorchakov, Prince A. M. 44–5, 49
Gorgan 109
Gorshkov, Admiral Sergei 97
Gosplan 153
Gray, Colin 137
Great Game 41, 44–5, 75, 79, 85, 101
Great Patriotic War 6, 11, 28
Great Soviet Encyclopedia 202–3
Greater Central Asia 73, 83, 100, 122, 124
Greater East Asia Co-Prosperity Sphere 58, 179
Greece/Greek 25, 72, 155
Greenwich Meridian 158
Grigorev, V. V. 41–2
Gulag 177, 204–5, 217, 240
Gulf War 112, 115, 225
Gumilyov, L. N. (son) 30–6, 241
Gumilyov, Nikolai (father) 224

Habibullah, Amir of Afghanistan 170
Habsburg 248
Hajigak 110
Hall, Arthur R. 229–30
Hamburg-Basra Axis 101
Harrison, R. E. 72
Hartshorne, Richard 228–9
Hashimoto, Kingoro 179
Haushofer, Albrecht (son) 175, 182–3
Haushofer, Karl (father) 2, 3, 61, 150, 165–90, 192–4, 197–8, 201, 203, 209–10, 216, 226, 249
Haushofer, Martha (wife) 182
Hayratan 112, 144
Heartland, the Debate 2, 9, 14
Hedin, Dr. Sven 46, 86, 167, 185

Hegel, G. W. F. 166, 174
Helmerson, P.
Helmund 84, 140
Henning, Richard 185
Hentig, Werner Otto von 86, 89, 170
Herat 76, 78–81, 99, 110, 125
Herder, J. G. 166
Herzen, Alexander 23, 151
Hess, Rudolf 181–2
Hettner, Alfred 194, 212
Heyden, Konrad 210–11
Himalayas 57, 110, 145
Hindu Kush 45, 77–8, 80, 97, 110, 114, 144, 161
Hinduism 23, 140
Hitler, Adolf 3, 11, 75–6, 87, 107, 168, 172–7, 181, 184, 209, 267; India 178–9; and attack on the Soviet Union 3, 11, 82, 95–6, 175, 177–8, 196, 205, 210, 221; Racial Genocide 183
Hooson, David J. M. 195, 230–1, 239
Hough, Jerry 247
Humboldt, Alexander von 73, 167
Hungary 246

Idel (*see also* Volga) 17, 74
Imperialism 6, 200–1; and informal empires 6–7, 29; Russian/Soviet 112–23; *see also* "From Sea to Sea"; Western 27
India 10, 12, 17, 46, 52–3, 56, 74–5, 140, 161, 234; British 27–8, 40–5, 50, 58, 61, 75–115 *passim* 119, 137, 141, 150, 168–9, 173, 176, 178–9, 197, 209, 235; India Command 72, 78, 95–6, 106; Sepoy Mutiny 38, 50, 85
India as the Main Factor in the Central Asian Question (Snesarev) 75
Indian National Army (INA) 96
Indian Ocean 9, 12, 17, 72–3, 77–9, 81, 95, 97, 101, 103, 107, 110, 114, 116, 118–23, 155, 222, 229, 236
India Office 80–1, 89–90, 95–6
Indo-Pacific Space 172–4
Indo-Persian Corridor 74, 78, 97, 101, 105, 108, 113, 115, 119, 121–2, 136, 235
Indus 43, 45, 76, 90, 179
Inner Asia 73
Iran (*see also* under Persia) 7, 53, 72, 99, 113–14, 118, 119, 220, 225, 227, 236, 245

Iraq 225
Irtysh 74, 80, 86
Islam 22-3, 49, 140, 158, 224-6, 232
Islamabad 110
Islam Qala 110
Italy 173, 178, 237

Jacobson, Nikolai O. 60
Jadids 90
Japan 7, 10, 39, 50-1, 54, 58, 82-3, 96, 100, 105, 119, 123, 136-9, 155, 170-5, 184, 196, 197-8, 210, 226-7, 237, 249; Secret Military Convention with Germany 178-80
Japheth, Tribe of 38-9, 70
Jaxartes (*see* Syr Darya) 140
Jerusalem 46
Jews 32, 168-9
Jihad 85-6
Judaism 23, 140
Julfa 101-3

Kabul 78-81, 86-7, 110, 114
Kailas, Mount 46
Kaliningrad (ex-Königsberg) 232
Kandahar 76, 78-80, 99, 101, 110
Kanitz, Count von 86
Kansu 57
Kapp-Luttwitz Putsch 168
Karachi 90, 110, 120
Karakhan L. M. 170
Karakoram 110, 114
Karakoram Highway 110, 145
Karelia 204-5
Karpych, V. 40-1
Kashgar 73-5, 80, 110, 145, 194
Kaufman, General von 80
Kazakhstan-Kazakhs 40, 196, 204-5, 231
Kennan, George 141
Kennedy, Paul 9
Kerman 103, 109-10, 112
Khalkhin Gol 221
Khanaqin 103
Kharbin 31, 158
Khilafat Movement 94
Khiva 39, 75, 80-1, 86, 89-92
Khojak Tunnel 101
Khojend 45
Khomeini, Ayatollah 232
Khomyakov, A. S. 22-3
Khorasan 73, 101-3, 136
Khorezm 73, 92

Khrulev, General Stepan 79
Khrushchev, N. S. 29, 61-2, 113, 233
Khyber Pass 101
Kiev 219, 221
Kim (Kipling) 85
Kipling, Rudyard 85, 221, 223
Kirghizia 73
Kirmanshah 103
Kissinger, Dr. Henry 233
Kitchener, General Sir Herbert 104, 106
Kjellén, Rudolf 150, 172, 201
Klyuchevsky, V. O. 39, 70
Kokand 39, 80, 90
Kolchak, Admiral 90
Kolyma 169
Komintern (Communist or Third International) 27-8, 35, 60, 78, 92-6, 169-70, 197, 201
Köppen, P. 41
Korea 54, 58
Korean War 226
Korotich, Vitalyi 248
Kovalyov, Anatolii 249
Kozhevnikov, V. A. 54
Kozhinov, Vadim 34
Kozlov 152-4
Krasnovodsk Bay 80
Krasnoyarsk 229, 250
Kristof, Ladis 148-9, 219-20
Kropotkin, Prince Peter 54, 149
Kuban 21
Kurdistan 103, 113, 115
Kuropatkin, General A. N. 51, 79, 83
Kushka Fortress 78, 99, 101, 114
Kuznetsk Basin (Kuzbas) 178, 195
Kwantung Army 83

Lahore 84, 85
Lamansky, Vladimir I. 158
Lanchow 57, 144
Landsberg Fortress 181
Lansdowne, Marquess Henry K. of 105, 130
Laqueur, Walter 167
Lattimore, Owen 141
Latvia/Latvian 168, 207, 232, 246
Lea, Homer 175-6, 188
Lebanon 72
Lebensraum 7, 61, 151, 172, 174, 177, 181, 184, 222, 237
Lena and "Lenaland" 140, 158, 160-1

Lenin, V. I. 5, 13, 16, 25–9, 40, 62, 85, 87, 90, 93, 96, 148, 150, 176, 201, 206–9, 233, 245, 253
Leontev, Konstantin 22–3, 58
Leroy-Beaulie, Paul 98
Lesseps, Ferdinand 103, 112
Lithuania 232, 246
Literaturnaya Gazeta 222–4
Litvinov, Maxim 149
Lop Nor 233
Ludendorff, General Erich 168
Lütke, F. F. 41
Lysenko, T. D. and Lysenkoism 148, 205–6, 217

Maak, R. 41
Mackinder, Sir Halford 2, 6, 98, 115, 122, 135–50, 156–62, 165, 171–3, 175, 177, 182–4, 191–3, 195, 198–200, 203, 209–10, 216–17, 220, 225–37, 253
Maghreb 72
Mahan, Admiral Alfred T. 136–7
Maimana 81
Maisky, Ivan 149
Malozemoff, Andrew 56
Malthus, T. R. (and Malthusianism) 52, 152, 203
Manannikov, Alexei 254
Manchuria 6, 31, 57, 83, 94, 104–5, 136–7, 158, 227, 233
Mao Tse-tung 232
Marco Polo 46
Martens, F. F. 49–51
Marx, Karl 23, 40–1, 201, 210
Marxism 25, 28, 60, 148, 200–1, 219–21, 237, 247
Matsuoka, Yosuke 177
Ma-waran-Nahr 73
May, Karl 124
Mediterranean 72, 100, 151, 155–6, 173, 222, 227
Mein Kampf (see also under Hitler A.) 172, 175, 181, 183
Meinig, Donald W. 195, 230, 238
Mendeleev D. I. 152–7, 195, 205, 208
Mensheviks 6
Mercator, Gerardus 71
Merv 81, 99, 101
Meshed 81, 103, 109
Meshketian Turks 32
Mesopotamia 105
Metternich, Klemens Wenzel von 12
Middle East Command 72

Mikhailov, N. N. 192
Mills, Dennis R. 195, 242
Milyukov, P. N. 39
Mississippi 3
Mitteleuropa (see also under Europe Central) 172, 184
Molotov, V. M. 7
Moltke Jr., General Helmuth von 85
Mongolia 7, 50, 57, 59, 72–3, 83, 94, 101, 143, 168, 221, 227, 230
Mongols 15, 21, 24, 43, 50, 59, 140, 233
Monroe Doctrine 155
Morskoi Sbornik 198
Moscow 25, 219
Mozambique 223
Mujahidin 118
Munich Conference of 1938 183
Muhajirs 93
Muravyov, N. N. 41
Murmansk 12, 249
Muscovy 12, 15, 69–70, 74
Muslims 9, 29, 40, 43, 85, 95, 202, 225–6, 231, 233, 236, 250–1

Nadir Shah 74
Napoleon 11, 46, 75–6, 79, 178, 184
Narodniki 52
National Bolshevism (see also under Ustryalov, N. V.) 31–4, 36
NATO 11, 226, 233
Navalism 136–7
Nation Socialism (Nazism) 166–70
Nazi-Soviet Non-Aggression Pact 3, 7, 107, 175–7, 209
Nehru, Jawaharlal 176
Nepal 145
Neva 58
Nevelskoy, Admiral G. I. 13, 41
New Political Thinking 123
New Statesman 177, 183
Nicaragua 223
Nicholas I, Tsar 14
Nicholas II, Tsar 56, 106
Niedermayer, Oskar von 86–7, 89, 170, 174, 186, 194, 197
Nietzsche, Friedrich 46, 222
Nikolaevsk 14, 156
Nikolaevsky, Boris 150, 212
Nile 58
Nordic Bloc 172, 175
North Sea Canal 199
North-West Frontier 86, 89, 95–6, 99–101

Index

Novgorod 74, 219, 234
Novorossiysk 191
Novosibirsk 251
Novyi Vostok 187, 193
Nurek 229
Nuremberg, Military Tribunal 182

Obshchnost (Community) 29
Ob 86, 140, 153
Obst, Erich 166, 175, 185
Omsk 89, 153–4, 252
Oppenheim, Max von 85
Orenburg 74, 80, 86, 88–90
Orientalistik 167
Oriental Despotism 201
Orlov, Ataman 76
Osipov, Vladimir 32, 36
Osh 144
Ottomans 22, 44, 72, 79, 158, 248
Ovid, Publius Ovidius Naso 171
Oxus (*see also under* Amu Darya) 43, 45, 80–1, 140

Pacific Fleet 82, 116, 227, 235, 251
Pacific Ocean 8, 9, 12, 13, 14, 23, 57, 69, 71, 74, 83, 120, 135–6, 150–1, 155–8, 166–7, 194, 198, 246, 249
Pakistan 110, 118, 236, 244
Pamir 14, 45, 53–4, 75, 77–8, 80–1, 97, 144, 194
Pamyat 225
Panjdeh Incident 82, 99
Pan-Asiatic 173, 175, 197
Pan-Germanism 23
Pan-Islamist 85, 94
Panmongolism (Solovyov) 54–5
Pan-Mongolism 54–6, 202
Pan-Slavism 23–4, 38, 49, 58, 150–1, 158
Pan-Turanian 86, 89–91, 94, 179, 202
Pashtuns/Pashtunistan 90, 115
Paul I, Tsar 76, 79
Perestroika 7, 10–14, 17, 30, 115, 218, 231, 236, 249, 251, 253
Peking 144
Parker, W. H. 161, 217, 231
Persia (*see also under* Iran) 6, 27, 39, 40, 76, 78–80, 83, 86, 92, 97, 100–12, 140, 194, 197
Persian Gulf 45, 72, 75, 103–5, 107–12, 118, 120, 136, 142, 144, 156, 158, 172, 178, 222, 227, 231
Persian Corridor 108
Peshawar 78–9, 101

Peter I, the Great, Tsar 22, 42, 45, 83, 96–7, 150, 165
Peterson, N. P. 54
Petrograd 27
Petrogradism 23
Philip of Macedon 24
Philotheus, Monk 25
Podvizhnye granitsy (moving frontiers) 44
Pogodin, M. P. 38–9
Pokrovsky, M. N. 40, 47, 219–20
Poland/Poles 6, 12, 21, 26–7, 32, 44, 62, 78, 87, 140, 170, 246
Polaris Submarines 120
Polevtsov, Lt. Col. A. A. 77
Port Arthur 82, 84, 104–5, 136–7, 227
Potsdam Agreement of 1911 106
Pratap, Raja Mahendra 93
Prokhanov, Alexander/*Prokhanovshtina* 221–5, 240–1, 248–9
Protocols of the Elders of Zion 167, 169
Przewalski, General N. M. 50
Pulkovo Meridian 158
Punjab 79, 94

Quadruple Alliance 175
Queshm 104
Quetta-Nushki Extension Railway 101, 104
Quetta 78, 80, 101
Qom 109

Racial Assimilation 29–34, 43, 56–9, 61–3, 152, 158, 231
Racial Politics as a Weapon of World Revolution (Khomyakov) 23
Radde, G. I. 41
Radek, Karl 169–70, 177, 186, 197, 209
Railways 5, 97–112, 140, 142–5, 156, 226; Baghdad Railway 85, 100–3, 106, 142, 144, 172, 237; Baykal-Amur Mainline (BAM) 116, 144, 156, 233–4; Orenburg-Taskent 71, 87, 90–1, 99–101; Turk-Sib 144, 156; Transcaspian 99–101, 99–101, 109; Trans-Iranian 109, 144; Trans-Mongolian 129,144; Trans-Persian 101–14, 129, 144; Trans-Siberian 13–14, 57, 70–1, 82, 87, 97–8, 105, 107, 109, 114–16, 120, 135, 142–4, 151, 157, 196, 218; Trans-Turkestan 129; in British India 99–101, 119; Xinlan 144; Hitler's Superrailway 178, 189

Ranjit Singh 79
Rapallo Treaty of 1922 174
Rasputin, Valentin 32
Ratzel, Karl 61, 151, 172, 181, 184, 193–4, 208, 222
Rawlinson, Sir Henry 80–1, 92, 112, 118, 125
Raynal, Abbé Guillaume Thomas 75, 124
Reconquista 4, 44, 91–2
Red Sea 120
Reichswehr 170, 197
Revolution: Bolshevik 24–8
Reza Shad 108
Riasanovsky, Nicholas 21
Ribbentrop, Joachim von 7, 107, 175, 178
Richthofen, Ferdinand von 98, 129, 167
Rise and Fall of the Great Powers (Kennedy) 9
Ritter, Karl 42, 167
Rittich, Captain P. A. 104, 109, 130
Romanovs 166
Rome 155
Rosenberg, Alfred V. 166–9, 172, 185
Rothstein, F. A. 149
Roy, M. N. 93, 95
Russia (or Russian Eurasian Empire): Army 51; Center of Gravity 147–64; Demography 59, 152–5; Strategic Diversion and Subversion 79–96; Drive to Warm Waters 96–131; Geography 39, 69–78; Civil War 55; Imperialism 4–6, 97, 112–23; *Mission Civilisatrice* 40–6, 56, 104; Orientalism (*see under Vostokovedenie*) 15; Trade with Asia 44
Russia and China (Martens) 49
Russia and England in Central Asia (Martens) 49
Russia and Europe (Danilevsky) 23
Russia in 1889 (Curzon) 84
Russian Idea 12, 24–37, 51, 150, 219, 248
Russification 29–31, 61–2, 158–9, 231
Russo-Japanese War 4, 51, 60, 71, 82–3, 115, 137
Russo-Turkish War 81

Sadat, President 120
Salang Pass and Tunnel 80, 114, 118, 144
Samara (Kuibyshev) 152
Samizdat 29, 3f

Samotlor 229
Sarakhs 109–10
Sarkisyanz, Emanuel 28, 34–5
Savitsky, P. N. 15, 60–1, 157–8, 160, 163–4, 199–200
Scandinavia 12
Schäfer, Dr. Ernst 81
Scheubner-Richter, Max Erwin von 167–8
Schickedanz, Arno 167
Scholler, Peter 181
Schwartz, L. E. 41
Scythians (Blok) 55, 202
Sea Lane of Communications (SLOC) 108, 120–3
Seeckt, General Hans von 170
Seistan 101–5, 136
Self-determination 26, 193, 201, 207, 246
Semipalatinsk 144
Semirechie 73, 90, 97, 156
Semitic 23
Semyonov, Yuriy 193–5
Semyonov, Yuriy N. 210
Semyonov Tyan-Shansky, Pyotr P. (father) 41, 43, 153, 167
Semyonov Tyan-Shansky, Veniamin P. (son) 153–6, 160, 200, 216
Seton-Watson, Hugh, 4
Shafarevich, Igor 32
Shahrun 109
Shamil, Imam 44
Shevardnadze, Eduard 233, 246
Shteinberg, E. 41
Shur Gaz 112
Siberia 1, 5, 8, 12, 22, 45, 50–2, 70, 73, 89–90, 100, 103, 135, 145, 148, 151, 157, 160, 166, 178, 196, 204–5, 217, 226, 229, 234, 246, 251–2
Sikhs 79
Silk Road 98
Sindh 90
Sinkiang (*see also under* Turkestan) 7, 50, 57, 73, 83, 89, 94, 101, 141, 144–5, 227, 230, 234
Sino-Japanese War 58, 197
Sirjan 109
Skobelev, General Mikhail D. 51, 79, 81, 84–5, 112
Slavophiles 4, 22, 49, 166, 223, 234
Snesarev, General A. E. 75–8, 80–1, 94, 124
Sobornost 22

Sofrerail 110
Sogdiana 73
Solovyov, Sergei M. (father) 39, 54
Solovyov, Vladimir (son) 29, 54, 58, 169, 202, 234
Solzhenitsyn, Alexander I. 32, 74, 234
South Africa 14, 31
Soviet Union (or Soviet Eurasian Empire): Red Army 26–8, 78, 88, 161, 170, 173, 197, 207, 227, 233, 246; Demography 9, 204–6, 231–3, 240, 246–7, 250; Ethnic Friction 231–3, 246–50; Ethnic Policy 28–37; Continuity with Tsarist Russia 6–14 *passim*, 223; Navy 10, 119–23, 198–200, 232, 235, 251; Non-Aggression Pact with Japan 177, 208; Regionalism 251–2; *Sovetskyi narod* or *Sovetskyi Chelovek* (Soviet People or Soviet Man) 29, 204, 233
Spain 9, 155, 221
Spengler, Oswald 23, 169
Spykman, Nicholas 141, 157, 226
St. Petersburg State (*see* Petrogradism) 24, 150, 153, 156
Stalin, J. V. 7, 28, 30, 62, 82, 93, 107, 150, 153, 176–7, 189, 194–7, 204–8, 217, 220, 226–7, 253
Stalin, Svetlana (daughter) 177
Stephan, John J. 164, 169
Stoletov Mission 81
Strausz-Hupé, Robert 141, 174, 181, 184
Struve, P. B. 158
Struve, W. 41
Sudan 72
Suez 103, 120, 151
Surits, Yakov 87
Sweden 21
Syberberg, Hans-Jürgen 190
Sykes, H. R. 105
Syr Darya 74
Syria 72, 75
Szamuely, Tibor 25

Tabriz 101–3, 109
Taiwan 58
Tajikistan 229
Talleyrand, Charles Maurice de 12
Tambov 152
Tannu Tuva 227
Tara 153
Tarakun 110

Tartu (Dorpat) 166
Tarim 140
Tashkent 45, 81, 88, 90, 93, 144
Tatars 11, 40, 44, 91, 166; Crimean 32, 202, 220
Tedzhen 109
Tehran 86, 103, 109
Termez 101, 112, 114, 144
Third International (*see under* Komintern)
Third Rome 15, 28, 46, 150
Tibet 23, 39, 57, 75, 81, 100, 145, 161; SS-Expedition to, 190
Tien-Shan 98
Timur (Temerlan) 73–4, 78, 81
Todt, Dr. Fritz 178
Tolstoy, L. N. 51, 54
Tomsk 152
Tordesillas, Treaty of 178
Toward Understanding of Russia (Mendeleev) 152–6, 209
Toynbee, Arnold 23
Trans-Caspia 53, 88, 97, 114, 194
Trans-Caucasia 27, 88, 97, 114, 116, 194, 232
Transcontinental Bloc 173–5, 177, 180, 182–3, 197, 226, 249
Transoxiana 73
Trans-Siberian Railway (*see under* Railways)
Trotsky, Leon 78, 93–4, 150–1, 207
Trubetskoy, Prince Nikolai S. 60, 65
Tsargrad (*see under* Constantinople) 23
Turanian 23, 43, 51, 58–60, 74, 169
Turkestan 5, 7, 24, 27, 39, 40, 45, 51, 53, 70, 73–6, 79–83, 86–9, 97, 99, 106, 156, 226, 234–5; East Turkestan Republic 227
Turkestan Military District 82, 116
Turkestan Socialist Party (ERK) 99
Turkmenistan 205
Turkish Straits 55, 79, 107, 120, 151, 155, 227
Turkkomissiya 91
Turkey 9, 24, 27, 40, 72, 86, 97, 101, 140, 168
Turukhansk 152–4, 163
TVD (Theater of Military Operations) European 8, 116–17, 222, 246; Far Eastern 8, 10, 82, 116–17, 120–1, 235, 246, 250–2; Southern 116–17, 246, 251
Two-Front-War 71, 82, 87, 116, 121, 195, 208

Tyutchev, F. I. 22, 58

Ukhtomsky, Prince Esper 56–9
Ukraine 26–7, 62, 87, 101, 122, 166, 168, 204, 230, 247, 251
Ulan Bator 144
Ulan Ude 144
Ungern-Sternberg, General Roman F. von 58–9
United States 3, 50, 83, 121–3, 136–7, 151, 161, 203, 226, 228–30, 235, 237; and Manifest Destiny 3, 38, 43, 155; Rapid Deployment Force 72
Ural (river) 21
Urals 5, 8, 9, 11, 12, 21, 43, 73–4, 122, 151, 155–6, 159, 195–6, 204, 218, 230, 234, 246, 250
Urga (Ulan Bator) 59
Urumchi 141
Ussuri 28, 52, 82
Ustryalov, N. V. 31–2, 36, 199–200
Uvarov, Count Sergei 22
Uzbeks 11

Vakhsh 229
Valuev, Count P. A. 45
Vasilev, V. P. 49–51
Vavilov, N. I. 148
Veche (see also under Osipov, V.) 29, 33, 36–7
Velikorusskaya kul'tura (Great Russian Culture – Vernadsky) 61
Venyukov, M. I. 43, 46, 51, 56, 58, 149, 223
Vernadsky, G. V. 61–2, 65
Verne, Jules 98
Versailles Treaty 170, 171, 173, 192
Vienna, Congress of 12
Vinberg, Colonel Fyodor V. 169
Vladivostok 11–14, 71, 81, 103, 120, 169, 178, 196, 249, 250
Voeikov, A. I. 156–7
Volga 4, 12, 17, 21, 39, 58, 74, 140, 156, 195, 218, 222, 231
Volga-Don Canal 199
Vorontsov, Yuli 109
Vorozhdentsy 21

Vostochniki (Easterners) 49–60, 158, 202
Vostokovedenie 15, 59
Wagner, Richard 46, 184
Wakhan Corridor 77
Walker, Martin 12
Walsh, Edmund A. 181
War Office London 95–6, 99–100
Warsaw 27, 207
Warsaw Pact 29
Weigert, Hans 142, 161, 174–6, 181, 194
White Sea and Canal 70, 199
Wilhelm II, German Emperor 42, 106
Witte, S. Y. 56–7, 105
Wittfogel, Karl 200–1, 210, 220
Wolff-Poweska, Anna 210
World War I 60, 77, 83, 101, 106, 153, 159, 170–1, 176, 184, 199–202, 205, 237, 248
World War II 6, 7, 28, 72, 95–6, 107, 141, 144, 161–2, 161, 184, 191, 196, 203–5, 208, 221–2, 245
World Island 2, 139, 143, 161, 173
Wrangel, General P. N. 168
Wrangel, Admiral F. P. 41

Yakub Beg 80
Yakutia 234
Yangtse 197
Yanov, Alexander 248
Yazd 103
Yazov, General Dmitriy 224, 246
Yellow Peril 29, 31, 35–6, 49–54, 58, 139, 150, 172–3, 219, 223, 233–5, 251–2
Yellow Russia 56–9
Yemen 121
Yenisei 140, 153, 155, 160–1, 229
Yeti Su (see also under Semirechie) 73
Yuzhakov, S. N. 52, 149

Zahedan 104, 109–10, 112, 114
Zapadniki (Westerners) 10, 24
Zeitschrift für Geopolitik 174, 182, 209
Zentralasien (Humboldt) 167
Zinoviev, Gregory 92
Zinoviev, I. A. 100